INTERNATIONAL JOBS DIRECTORY

Books and CD-ROMs by Drs. Ron and Caryl Krannich

101 Dynamite Answers to Interview Questions
101 Secrets of Highly Effective Speakers
201 Dynamite Job Search Letters
Best Jobs For the 21st Century
Change Your Job, Change Your Life
The Complete Guide to International Jobs and Careers
The Complete Guide to Public Employment
The Directory of Federal Jobs and Employers
Discover the Best Jobs For You!
Dynamite Cover Letters
Dynamite Networking For Dynamite Jobs
Dynamite Résumés
Dynamite Salary Negotiations
Dynamite Tele-Search
The Educator's Guide to Alternative Jobs and Careers
Find a Federal Job Fast
From Air Force Blue to Corporate Gray
From Army Green to Corporate Gray
From Navy Blue to Corporate Gray
Get a Raise in 7 Days
High Impact Résumés and Letters
International Jobs Directory
Interview For Success
Job-Power Source CD-ROM
Jobs and Careers With Nonprofit Organizations
Jobs For People Who Love Travel
Mayors and Managers
Moving Out of Education
Moving Out of Government
The Politics of Family Planning Policy
Re-Careering in Turbulent Times
Résumés and Job Search Letters For Transitioning Military Personnel
Shopping and Traveling in Exotic Asia
Shopping in Exciting Australia and Papua New Guinea
Shopping in Exotic Places
Shopping the Exotic South Pacific
Treasures and Pleasures of Australia
Treasures and Pleasures of China
Treasures and Pleasures of Hong Kong
Treasures and Pleasures of India
Treasures and Pleasures of Indonesia
Treasures and Pleasures of Italy
Treasures and Pleasures of Paris and the French Riviera
Treasures and Pleasures of Singapore and Malaysia
Treasures and Pleasures of Thailand
Ultimate Job Source CD-ROM

INTERNATIONAL JOBS DIRECTORY

Ronald L. Krannich, Ph.D.
Caryl Rae Krannich, Ph.D.

Third Edition

IMPACT PUBLICATIONS
Manassas Park, VA

INTERNATIONAL JOBS DIRECTORY

Library of Congress Cataloguing-in-Publication Data

Krannich, Ronald L.
International jobs directory: 1001 employers and great tips for success / Ronald L. Krannich, Caryl Rae Krannich. Previous editions (1994, 1991) published as The Almanac of International Jobs and Careers.
    p. cm.
Includes bibliographical references and index.
ISBN 1-57023-086-2
    1. Americans–Employment–Foreign countries–Handbooks, manuals, etc. 2. Employment in foreign countries–Handbooks, manuals, etc.
I. Krannich, Caryl Rae. II. Krannich, Ronald L. Almanac of interna tional jobs and careers. III. Title.
HF5549.5.E45K72   1999
650.14—dc21   98-42736
                                                CIP

Publisher: For information on Impact Publications, including current and forthcoming publications, authors, press kits, online bookstore, and submission requirements, visit Impact's Web site: *www.impactpublications.com*

Publicity/Rights: For information on publicity, author interviews, and subsidiary rights, contact the Public Relations Department: Tel. 703/361-7300.

Sales/Distribution: All bookstore sales are handled through Impact's trade distributor: National Book Network, 15200 NBN Way, Blue Ridge Summit, PA 17214, Tel. 1-800-462-6420. All other sales and distribution inquiries should be directed to the publisher: Sales Department, IMPACT PUBLICATIONS, 9104-N Manassas Drive, Manassas Park, VA 20111-5211, Tel. 703/361-7300, Fax 703/335-9486, or Email: *ij@impactpublications.com*

Contents

CHAPTER 6: Contracting and Consulting Firms 134

- A Re-Invented Public-Private Partnership   134
- New Contracting Frontiers   135
- Strategies   136
- The Organizations   138

CHAPTER 7: Private Voluntary Organizations (PVOs) 167

- Orientation   167
- Strategies   169
- The Organizations   170

CHAPTER 8: Nonprofit Corporations 201

- Orientation   201
- Strategies   202
- The Organizations   202

CHAPTER 9: Colleges and Universities 212

- Major Strengths   212
- Funding Sources   213
- The Beneficiaries   214
- Opportunities   215
- Major Recipients   216

CHAPTER 10: Teaching Abroad—Jobs For People
Who Love to Travel 242

- Opportunities Galore   242
- Teaching English as a Foreign Language   243
- Training Programs to Get You Up and Running   247
- Job Listing Services For Teachers   250
- Other Teaching Opportunities   251
- Key Resources on Teaching   252

User Tips and Expected Changes

W hile we have attempted to provide accurate information in this book, please be advised that names, addresses, phone and fax numbers, and Web addresses do change and that organizations do move, are merged or acquired by other firms, or go out of business altogether. This is especially true for government agencies, associations, and nonprofit organizations located in the New York City and Washington, DC metropolitan areas. Service, program, and product orientations may also change. These are inevitable changes that affect any publication that includes contact information. We regret any inconvenience such changes may cause to your job search.

If you have difficulty contacting a particular organization included in this book, please do one or all of the following:

➤ Check the Internet site for the organization. Most government agencies, associations, nonprofits, and businesses have their own Web sites which include current contact information. While addresses and phone numbers may change, most Web addresses do not change. Best of all, they yield current information on the organization. If you have difficulty locating a Web address, use various Internet search engines or directories to locate the address. We include several gateway sites in Chapter 12 to assist you in locating such addresses.

➤ Consult the latest edition of the **Business Phone Book USA** or call Directory Assistance for current phone numbers. If you dial a phone number and it is no longer in service, call Directory Assistance for the city where the organization was located by dialing "1" followed by the area code and then "555-1212." The Operator will assist you.

➤ Contact the Information section of your local library for online services or directories with the latest contact information.

Inclusion of organizations in this book in no way implies endorsements by the authors or Impact Publications. The recommendations are provided solely for your reference. It is

> **Our addresses should never be used for mass mailing resumes and letters—the most ineffective way to find a job.**

the reader's responsibility to contact, evaluate, and follow-through with employers.

The names, addresses, phone numbers, and services appearing here provide one important component for conducting a successful job search amongst international employers. Placed within the larger context of an effective job search, this component should be carefully linked to your self-assessment, research, networking, and resume writing and distribution activities. Such contact information should never be used for mass mailing resumes and letters—the most ineffective way to find a job. If you succumb to such a temptation, expect numerous rejections as well as a pile of returned mail from the Post Office stamped "Address Unknown" or "Unable to Forward" because the addresses have changed since this book went to press. Whatever you do, please don't waste your time and money on such a fruitless exercise that is destined to disappoint you as well as upset employers with unsolicited resumes and letters from what appear to be thoughtless and unqualified candidates. Use this information—starting with the Web sites—to conduct a well targeted job search aimed at employers who readily seek your skills and experience. Most Web sites will include information on job vacancies and application procedures, including resume databases.

INTERNATIONAL JOBS DIRECTORY

1

Finding an International Job in a World Turned Upside Down!

D o we ever live in interesting, unpredictable, and serendipitous times! This is especially true in the international arena where old ideas and territories seem to regularly get turned into new concepts and countries. While the U.S. economy has undergone fundamental restructuring during the past decade, so too has the international economy. As we enter into the new millennium, we face a newly restructured international community that requires a new breed of international worker who possesses a unique combination of the interests, skills, and abilities to function well in today's rapidly changing international arena. For we see unprecedented opportunities awaiting those who understand the complex of jobs and employers that increasingly define this new and often unpredictable global economy.

The New International Job Disorder

A new international political and economic order—or disorder—that was expected to emerge in the aftermath of the collapse of communism has been anything but quick and easy. Indeed, the journey has been both unpredictable and difficult, a less than stellar situation for many international job seekers who pinned their hopes on breaking into what appeared to be a booming 21st century international business community complete with generous salaries, benefits, and perks.

Take, for example, the case of the newly arrived small enterprise development Peace Corps Volunteer in Almaty, Kazakhstan (former Soviet Union) we reported on five years ago. Her ostensible mission was to promote American-style capitalism in this former communist country. Writing home after a few weeks of in-country training, she tries to put her "new world" experience in perspective:

> Almaty, Kazakhstan is an amazing place to be! I had dinner with some Russian business people who were scientists under the Soviet regime, but now wish to buy American products to sell on the streets of Almaty. This is not so unusual as it is evidently about the only way to make money here because privatization has not gotten a foothold yet, and State owned companies are not paying "competitive" wages. The uniqueness of the meeting is that we were sharing a meal with a man who had been sent to Cuba to spend three years teaching the Cubans about the evils of American capitalism. Now he is requesting assistance from the Peace Corps in finding a U.S. supplier to be his partner in a joint venture....My experiences have been so rich that I cannot begin to paint in words anything but an outline. I miss my good friends and associates, but I would rather have them come to visit me than to return home! (*Peace Corps Today,* Fall 1993)

> **Is this really a good time to be seeking an international job or are you well advised to pursue a more "normal" domestic career?**

One wonders whatever transpired in Almaty, Kazakhstan during the next five years. Did the economy really take off in the direction of 21st century Western capitalism or did it descend into the chaos and economic disintegration that gripped much of once booming Russia and Asia in 1998? Were these the best of times for enterprising international job seekers or did the international job market undergo a major transformation that destroyed more jobs than it created? And what about personal safety in countries where foreign nationals are increasingly targeted by terrorists, gangs, and criminals? Is this really a good time to be seeking an international job or are you well advised to pursue a more "normal" domestic career—one that pays enough money to allow you to regularly travel abroad without incurring the hassles of living and working in an unpredictable and perhaps dangerous international job setting?

A Global Economy Gone South?

The new world order that was expected to emerge in the aftermath of the collapse of communism in the 1990s never really followed the path predicted by optimists. Touting such grand concepts as the "global economy" in which the private sector was supposed to play a major role in developing American-style consumer economies worldwide, what actually evolved was a great deal of "global misery." A combination of naive foreign investors, crony capitalists, and volatile hedge funds operating in unregulated environments lead to major economic melt-downs in countries that appeared to have booming economies. Not surprising, in many parts of the world, the rich got richer and the poor got poorer in what appeared to be a grand global zero-sum game.

The real "global economy" that evolved during the past decade took several unexpected turns. While many American businesses expanded abroad and generated new international job opportunities during much of the 1990s, the house of cards began collapsing in 1997. First came an unexpected economic meltdown in the booming speculative economies of Southeast Asia and East Asia. Russia went next and Brazil stood on the brink of economic collapse. While the U.S. economy continued to boom in the midst of such chaos, its long-term future also was in doubt.

For all intents and purposes, the much touted global economy that was expected to create millions of new jobs for the 21st century was a disaster in the making: it destroyed millions of jobs and ruined many lives. It was essentially a rich man's game—based on a great deal of speculation and corruption in the financial markets. By the end of the 1990s, many people discovered it wasn't such a hot idea to participate in a global economy, an economy that put one country at extreme economic risk in relationship to other countries. A newly despised global economy was largely responsible for increased poverty, social dislocation, and even starvation in countries most affected by the new economic political disorder!

Innocence and Reality Abroad

The signs in 1998 were ominous for many young America's who mistakenly thought they were on new fast track international careers—in hot jobs that seemed to have a bright future in the new booming global economy. You could easily go to Hong Kong or Moscow to find work and perhaps change jobs in these cities within a few months. Many businesses needed young, talented, and adventuresome people—1990's soldiers of fortune—for the tremendous amount of work that had to be done in what appeared to be rapidly expanding economies.

For talented and determined individuals, finding an international job in business during much of the 1990s was not difficult—as long as economies abroad continued to expand at unprecedented rates. From budding entrepreneurs congratulating themselves for having the foresight of being in the right place at the right time to major corporate players who routinely saw their stock prices soar, many of these young international workers were inexperienced in key international economic and work fundamentals: periodic economic downturns, depressions, and job loss; they were unprepared to deal with the new realities and shocks of this international environment. Ironically, many now appeared to have the wrong set of skills for the work that needed to be done abroad.

Moscow was a case in point for understanding the innocence and reality of international jobs in the boom and bust economies of the 1990s. This city revealed the dark side of the international job market that has important implications for many of today's job seekers. The once swinging Bells, Hungry Duck, Rosie O'Grady's, and Papa John's in Moscow frequented by young American professionals fell silent in 1998 as many people lost their jobs and headed for home or looked elsewhere for international jobs—anyone hiring young American entrepreneurs in Paris, London, or Rome? At least in the once booming business community, international jobs became increasingly difficult to find. Not many international headhunters or multinational companies were looking for "Moscow experience"! For many Americans, working in the midst of a major economic meltdown was both a shocking and depressing career experience. While working abroad had been fun for awhile, it lost much of its luster under such dire economic circumstances. Many Americans abroad were ready to "transition" to jobs back home where the economy continued to boom. On the other hand, many international nonprofits were facing new realities attendant with the collapse of economies: greater poverty in economies that had become increasingly

> For talented and determined individuals, finding an international job in business during much of the 1990s was not difficult—as long as economies continued to expand at unprecedented rates.

dependent on the global economy. Nongovernmental organizations (NGOs) and private voluntary groups (PVOs) increasingly found themselves dealing with problems they had helped resolve decades ago: widespread hunger, starvation, and disease. Especially in the case of Indonesia, which experienced near total economic collapse in 1998, NGOs and PVOs moved in to literally save the children and poor people who disproportionately felt the impact of the downturns in the new global economy on their lives. While less financially rewarding than jobs in business, jobs with international nonprofit organizations were on the increase as more and more NGOs and PVOs were called on to "fix" the renewed problems of the world's poor. Business was not a friend.

Opportunities Abound For the Enterprising Few

Today's international arena offers numerous exciting job opportunities for enterprising job seekers, from teaching English in some remote village of Asia to managing a manufacturing plant in Latin America. Opportunities abound for both the inexperienced and the experienced who are sufficiently motivated to seek an international job. Take, for example, new export realities for the U.S. While less than 10 percent of the U.S. economy is dependent upon exports abroad, what the U.S. actually exports is surprising to many people, including international job seekers who wish to work for a U.S. company abroad. The number one export from the United States is American culture. According to the latest figures from the U.S. Department of Commerce, as reported in the *Washington Post* (October 25, 1998), the United States in 1996 exported $60.2 billion in software, entertainment, and publication products:

- Recorded music $9.83 billion
- Movies, television, and video $11.58 billion
- Computer software $34.81 billion
- Newspapers, books, periodicals $3.96 billion

The televisions, VCRs, stereos, personal computers, and satellite dishes may be made in Japan, Hong Kong, Taiwan, or South Korea, but what gets played or transmitted through these mediums is the music, movies, and software produced in the U.S.-dominated media empires centered in Hollywood, New York, the Silicon Valley, and Redmond, Washington. American-style multiplex movie theaters are making major inroads into countries of Europe, Asia, and Latin America. Blockbuster Entertainment now has 2,000 outlets in 26 countries. Tower Records has 70 stores operating in 15 countries. Each day McDonald's opens six new restaurants around the world. *Reader's Digest* is published in 19 different languages and 48 international editions for a total circulation of 48 million (U.S. circulation is 14.7 million). *Cosmopolitan* magazine boasts 4.5 million international circulation from 36 foreign editions (U.S. circulation is 2.7 million). *Playboy* publishes 16 international editions with a circulation of 5 million. And MTV now is available in more households abroad than in the United States. The list of major U.S. international players, from Time Warner, Walt Disney, MGM-UA, and Paramount to Microsoft and the Planet Hollywood restaurant chain goes on and on. A parallel business infrastructure to support these operations—architecture, advertising, accounting, distribution, public relations, marketing, sales, graphic art, and technical support—generates thousands of exciting jobs both at home and abroad. In the end, we may all be going Hollywood!

International job opportunities are being both created and destroyed in response to new economic and political realities. The collapse of communism and the development of independent states in the former Soviet Union and Eastern Europe; the emergence of an economically unified Western Europe; the development of regional trade blocs; continuing poverty in numerous Third and Fourth World countries; the realignment of the Japanese economy; the developing of massive (2.1+ billion people) consumer economies of China and India; the continuing expansion of the U.S. economic activity abroad; and the growth of travel and tourism have created unprecedented opportunities for individuals interested in finding international jobs and pursuing international careers. While the international economy may not appear healthy at present, the long-term outlook should be positive. It's really a question of when it will turn around again and experience major expansion.

Old Habits, New Perspectives and Skills

We live in more than just interesting times. These are rapidly changing times in which the jobs of yesterday may be poor predictors of the jobs of tomorrow. What course of international studies college students pursue today may ill-prepare them for the international job opportunities of tomorrow. In fact, in the 1960s and 1970s, international jobs for

Americans were most likely found with government, educational institutions, nonprofit organizations, and consulting firms specializing in problems of development in Third and Fourth World countries. These institutions and organizations hired large numbers of international specialists with backgrounds in agriculture, economics, anthropology, linguistics, political science, and military intelligence. A government assistance-centered model of development resulted in government-to-government transfer of resources via such popular government organizations as the U.S. Agency for International Development (USAID), the Peace Corps, and the United States Information Agency (USIA) and hundreds of contractors that helped carry out their missions. The U.S. Department of Defense and a multitude of government intelligence agencies—from the Central Intelligence Agency (CIA) to the Defense Intelligence Agency (DIA)—employed thousands of international specialists. Much of this concept of "international development" was rooted in an overall Cold War foreign policy effort to combat the threat of communism.

Whether wrapped in the development theories enunciated by the U.S. Agency for International Development and its army of contractors or in the grassroots efforts of Peace Corps Volunteers, U.S. international development efforts were primarily nonmilitary responses to communism; their ultimate goal was to transfer economic benefits to peoples who might otherwise find an alternative path to development—revolutionary communism. Those who found jobs in these development organizations were most likely motivated by altruism rather than by a political consciousness aimed at combating communism.

How times have changed in the 1990s and as we move into the new millennium! Like it or not, we live in a new, yet ill-defined political and economic order. But a few things are certain. The old government-to-government transfer of resources approach to problems of development has fallen in disfavor with the ending of the Cold War and all its ideological underpinnings. Such an approach resulted in few cases of success; it tended to enhance corruption, strengthen government bureaucracies, and create dependency rather than increase self-sustaining capacity. The Peace Corps has been operating for nearly seven years in Russia, other former Soviet republics, and Eastern Europe where it demonstrates the virtues of small business development and entrepreneurism. The U.S. Information Agency was abolished by Congress in 1998 in a move to absorb its functions within the Department of State. The greatly downsized U.S. Agency for International Development, the ultimate oxymoron—under fire for achieving few measurable results—continues to transform itself into a force for promoting American-style business, entrepreneurism, and consumerism abroad under the reconstituted concept of "sustainable development." In the midst of all these changes, millions of people throughout the world still live in grinding poverty, experience wars and natural disasters, suffer from famine and pestilence, and lack basic sanitation, education, nutrition, and health services. Environmental degradation, accompanied with a failure of governments and businesses to manage natural resources, continues on a massive scale throughout the world. Child care, family planning, social welfare, and vocational services remain in great demand in the developing world.

While the name of the game today is still business—despite recent economic meltdowns in the developing world—the pressing needs of the international community go far beyond business. Never before have we witnessed such a major shift in international jobs from government and development to business and entrepreneurism. The evidence is everywhere. Take a quick survey of international airports or visit major hotels in New York, London, Amsterdam, Paris, Rome, Frankfurt, Prague, Istanbul, Moscow, Cairo, Rabat, Johannesburg, Mumbai, New Delhi, Bangkok, Singapore, Manila, Hanoi, Hong Kong, Beijing, Shanghai, Tokyo, Sydney, and Mexico City and you will quickly discover a new breed of international worker—young business people who are sourcing for new products or seeking new markets and trading partners for their products. Others possess high-tech engineering and communication skills required by businesses abroad. The airport and restaurant conversations are similar—establishing international operations and retaining and/or expanding market shares abroad.

> While the name of the game today is still business—despite recent economic meltdowns in the developing world—the pressing needs of the international community go far beyond business.

These are exciting, creative, and innovative times for those who have the right skills to function in today's new international employment arena. A San Francisco-based architectural firm designs a new condominium and resort complex in Thailand; they must meet with their Thai counterparts in Bangkok to finalize the plans and financial arrangements.

Representatives of a leading fashion house in New York City meet in Manila to discuss their new fall line with their Philippine factory representatives. Lawyers from a Washington, DC law firm meet with their associates in Toyko about a pending court case against a South Korean electronics firm concerning international trademark violations. A computer software company representative based in Boston meets with its field staff in Hong Kong to discuss its failed marketing efforts in China. Representatives of Apple Computer and Mars Candy Company celebrate after opening their new offices in Vladivostok—a city once closed to outsiders. A Houston-based cellular phone company sends its representatives to New Delhi to survey the market potential for its products in South Asia. Meeting planners from Miami meet in Bali with hotel representatives to finalize plans for an upcoming conference in the expansive Nusa Dua hotel and convention complex. A graphic artist in Baltimore emails his design concepts for an advertising brochure to his client in Moscow. A Washington, DC-based contractor specializing in government finance spends three months in Hanoi installing the latest computer software for handling Vietnam's government financial system. They stay at the Metropole Hotel where they have breakfast with representatives of an international hotel chain who are finalizing plans with the Ministry of Finance to build a new 600-room, five-star hotel to accommodate the growing number of business travelers to Saigon. And thousands of other companies regularly communicate with their field operations, partners, and other international players via the Internet, telephone, fax, and video conferencing. The tremendous amount of traffic, conversations, and business transactions indicate that the global economy is well and alive despite its recent illness. Its wellness takes place in airports, hotels, and conference rooms as well as over the Internet.

Sourcing and Selling

Except for those who work for a large complex of international nonprofit organizations, few international workers we encounter today are in the business of transferring resources from one government to another. Rather, they are primarily in the business of international business— manufacturing, entertainment, sourcing, and selling products and services for a profit. New first-class hotels continue to spring up in major cities throughout the world. While some cater to tourists, most are responding to the tremendous growth in business travel that has evolved during the past decade. Eighty percent or more of their hotel clients are business travelers. Despite recent downturns in the international economy, we expect this business trend will continue for at least the next decade.

The best international job opportunities will be with companies of all sizes—large to small—engaged in manufacturing, sourcing, and selling products for international trade. While ten or twenty years ago many large international companies sent managers abroad to oversee their international manufacturing operations, today fewer and fewer companies export their managerial talent. Many countries now have a large pool of local managerial talent from which to staff their field operations. Businesses, in turn, find it is less expensive and more productive to hire local managers. After all, expatriate employees demand much higher compensation packages as well as require numerous perks attendant with an expatriate position. Local talent tends to be less expensive and more competent than expatriates. Indeed, the day of the expatriate landing positions of major responsibility abroad are quickly coming to an end as more and more locals have as much, if not more, international education, training, and experience. As a result, experienced expatriates are finding fewer job opportunities abroad as they must face greater competition from highly skilled and competent locals.

A Developing, Developing World

While business is today's newest and most fashionable international trend and job arena, the development work of hundreds of nonprofit organizations, educational institutions, international organizations, government agencies, and consulting firms continues unabated and on an ever grander scale than in the 1970s and 1980s. The collapse of communism in Eastern Europe and the former Soviet Union, as well as recent international economic turmoil, has opened new frontiers and challenges for these organizations. The work of these organizations, especially in the areas of child care, environmental and natural resource management, disaster relief, agricultural and water resource development, and communication, continues to expand into these newly developing countries. As these and other new nations emerge and undergo complex and chaotic economic, social, and political changes, the services of these international groups will be in even greater demand in the years ahead.

While many of these major international players have focused their field operations on Asia, Africa, Latin America, and the Caribbean during the past 50 years, several of these organizations have recently moved into a new frontier where they apply their development expertise. They have quickly extended their operations into Eastern Europe and the former Soviet republics—today's new developing world: Albania, Armenia, Belarus, Bosnia-Hercegovina, Bulgaria, Croatia, Czech Republic, Estonia, Georgia, Hungary, Kazakhstan, Kyrgystan, Latvia, Lithuania, Moldova, Poland, Romania, Russia, Serbia, Slovak Republic, Tajikistan, Turkmenistan, and the Ukraine. These countries represent a newly evolving, yet still unsettled, political geography that may eventually define a new and more stable international arena.

Changing Employment Settings and Skills

Just a few years ago opportunities looked plentiful in Europe, the Middle East, and many countries in the developing world. Today, opportunities in Europe appear disappointing given employment restrictions and the high costs of doing business in Europe. Despite recent economic setbacks, opportunities will continue to be available in Central and Eastern Europe, Russia, Hong Kong, China, India, Indonesia, and Mexico. Given the emphasis on sourcing and selling, job opportunities in business will tend to be found in countries offering cheap labor and large consumer markets. Consequently, during the next ten years we expect the new and renewed frontiers for international business jobs will be found in China, India, Pakistan, Indonesia, Russia, Mexico,

> **Individuals with high-tech skills in engineering, computers, and information technology will be in great demand throughout the world.**

Vietnam, Burma, Egypt, South Africa, Brazil, Argentina, and much of Africa. The emphasis will continue to be on sourcing and selling in a highly competitive international trade market. Individuals with high-tech skills in engineering, computers, and information technology will be in great demand throughout the world.

False Starts, Bruised Egos, Many Rejections

Many highly motivated job seekers don't know how or where to look for international job opportunities. Lacking both information on and appropriate job search strategies for the international job market, they engage in a random and often frustrating exercise of using the wrong methods and targeting the wrong employers. A typical failed approach, for example, is to engage in mindless mass mailings of resumes and letters to employers with international operations (they even turn this book into their mailing list!) as well as constantly search for classified ads to send equally ineffective resumes and letters. After months of failed expectations, many of these people abandon their dreams of working in the international arena, or they turn to a so-called "international employment expert" usually found through an appealing classified ad who then scams them out of hundreds of dollars in exchange for "feel-good" promises and perhaps a travel video accompanied by a 10-page list of potential international employers. After awhile, many of these job seekers repeat the often-heard lament of the failed job seeker—*"There are no job opportunities available for me."* At best, they find this whole process to be difficult and daunting. It's filled with high expectations, false starts, expensive mailing campaigns, and questionable services which are followed by many rejections. At worst, they lose a lot of time and money engaged in worthless job search activities. In the end, many of them pick up their bruised egos and settle down to a more certain domestic job.

> **A typical failed approach is filled with high expectations, false starts, expensive mailing campaigns, and questionable services which are followed by many rejections.**

What most international job seekers lack is a clear understanding of how to find a job in this often difficult and frustrating employment arena. With the help of this book and other international employment resources, this should not happen to you. You should acquire the necessary knowledge and skills to be effective in this challenging job market.

A Directory of Many Opportunities

The International Jobs Directory is the sequel and critical organization companion volume to our first international jobs and careers book—*The Complete Guide to International Jobs and Careers*. The first book outlined the structure of the international job market, addressed the key issues of individual motivations and skills, and proposed strategies for organizing and implementing an effective job search targeted toward particular organizations and industries. It is the first book anyone interested in international jobs and careers should read before putting this present book to use in attempting to connect with the many organizations that offer the majority of international job opportunities.

Indeed, this present book answers the critical "where" questions of the international job seeker: *"Where are the international jobs?" The Complete Guide to International Jobs and Careers* addressed the critical "what" and "how" questions: *"What are the jobs and how can I best find one?"* Consequently, except for new job search information relating to the Internet in Chapter 12, we say very little about strategies for finding an international job in this volume, because the strategies are outlined in detail—including information on self-assessment, goal setting, research, resume writing, interviews, and salary negotiations—in *The Complete Guide to International Jobs and Careers*. Here we focus solely on identifying organizations that are involved in the international arena and are noted for hiring individuals for international positions.

Our focus on the "where" of finding an international job leads us into ten different sets of organizations that are invariably linked together in the international arena:

- Federal government agencies
- International organizations
- Associations and societies
- Research institutes
- Businesses
- Contracting and consulting firms
- Private voluntary organizations (PVOs)
- Nonprofit corporations
- Foundations
- Colleges and universities

These organizations largely define the "where" of international jobs.

We also include chapters on internships and teaching abroad as well as an annotated bibliography of international employment resources. In addition, you may want to contact foreign chambers of commerce in the U.S. as well as world trade associations or clubs that operate in most major U.S. cities. Names, addresses, and phone numbers for these organizations are easily accessed through the annual *Business Phone*

Book U.S.A., one of the most invaluable resources for international job seekers and one we highly recommend as part of your "essential" resource package for international job hunting. Such contact information is especially important for individuals interested in identifying firms operating in individual countries as well as those interested in starting or expanding their own businesses abroad. The embassy and consulate contact information will assist you in answering any questions concerning work permits in specific countries. Much of this and other useful international job information also is available on the Internet. We identify numerous gateway Web sites as well as URLs of potential employers to assist you in navigating the Internet for international job information.

Our classification of international jobs and careers along these organizational lines should not be interpreted as the only way to organize this information nor should these organizations be viewed in isolation from one another. Indeed, as we observe in *The Complete Guide to International Jobs and Careers* (Chapter 9), there is a tremendous amount of blurring between the public and private sectors in the international arena. You will quickly discover there is a great deal of overlap between categories as well as numerous linkages among organizations which, in turn, provide "opportunity structures" for enterprising international job seekers. Many firms appearing in Chapter 6 (Contracting and Consulting Firms), for example, should also appear in Chapter 5 (Businesses). However, since many of these private firms are primarily oriented toward working in developing countries, we put them into a separate chapter. The same is true for the associations appearing in Chapter 4. Many of the organizations appearing in Chapters 7, 8 and 9 could also be included in Chapter 4. Since the organizations in Chapters 7, 8, and 9 are primarily oriented toward working in developing countries and depend on funding from government, international organizations, and foundations, they are best examined in these separate chapters.

While many of these organizations (government, nonprofits, PVOs) are primarily oriented toward achieving public goals, others pursue their own private agendas (businesses). However, many are linked together by the nature of their activities. International engineering and construction firms, for example, rely heavily on public infrastructure funding; contracting and consulting firms as well as many nonprofits, PVOs, and universities depend on public funding of "development projects" by government, the United Nations, the World Bank, regional financial institutions, and private foundations. In the end, there is a great deal more interaction and cooperation between the public and private-oriented organizations than what you might initially think.

Do First Things First

How you use this book will largely determine whether or not you will be successful in finding an international job with the organizations outlined here. The insatiable quest amongst many job seekers to first know who the employers are and where they are located, leads to the temptation to immediately identify a few "interesting" organizations and then send off resumes and letters or make phone calls in the hope that someone will hire them. Such a random and mindless approach is naive and borders on being "job dumb". It demonstrates little understanding of both how the job market operates and what employers seek in potential employees. Most employers simply don't hire people who approach them in this manner. Such an unsolicited approach will tend to make you a nuisance in the eyes of many employers who don't have time to be pestered by individuals who appear high on motivation but low on job search intelligence. Indeed, some employers have requested that we take their names and addresses out of this book because some of our users are "job dumb" and abusive job seekers. Employers use their networks, job banks, Internet employment sites, and advertising expertise to locate qualified candidates. You especially need to know how to gain access to employers' networks.

> Don't be a "job dumb" and abusive job seeker by pestering potential employers with unsolicited resumes, letters, and phone calls.

You must do first things first. Using this book without first organizing your job search around the critical seven-step job search process outlined in *The Complete Guide to International Jobs and Careers* is a sure way of creating new frustrations and dashing hopes of finding an international job. Doing first things first means using this book only after you have completed a self assessment, set goals, conducted research, and developed a powerful international targeted resume. Then, and only then, should you direct your other job search activities—prospecting, networking, informational interviews, and direct applications—toward the organizations identified in this book or elsewhere.

If you fail to do these first things first, you may quickly join thousands of other wishful thinkers who have yet to learn how to link effective international job search strategies to the specific names, addresses, and telephone numbers outlined in this and other directories of potential international employers. Please don't become one of them! The jobs are out there, but you must approach the market properly.

The World of Work Permits

Work permits are one of the major obstacles to finding employment abroad. While you may be interested in working in Australia, Great Britain, or Norway, restrictive work permit, visa, and immigration policies may quickly dash your hopes of working in these countries. At the very least, they make living and working abroad a big hassle.

Work permits and resident visas go hand in hand. Most countries require foreign employees to acquire a resident visa that includes a work permit. The normal procedure is to require the foreigner to apply for the work permit and resident visa before entering the country, although some countries do allow you to apply after being in country and securing an employment contract. In other words, in most instances, you cannot just arrive in country, look for employment, and then apply for a resident visa. Instead, you must have an employment contract in hand before arriving in country. This procedure achieves what most countries intentionally design—discourage foreigners from seeking employment.

The easiest way to get a work permit is to have an employment contract with a company that routinely takes care of work permit requirements. They, rather than you, must deal with the complexities of the government bureaucracy.

Most countries follow a similar pattern in regards to work permits and resident visas. Except in the cases of the European Union (EU) countries where employment in member countries is relatively open (no work permits required) for EU citizens, most countries protect local labor by placing similar restrictions on foreign workers:

1. **Foreigners are forbidden to acquire jobs that compete with local labor and skills.** When applying for a work permit and resident visa, employers must provide evidence that the job in question cannot be filled by a local worker with similar skills.

2. **Work permits and resident visas are temporary and thus must be renewed periodically** though a Ministry, Department, Bureau, or Office of Labor—every 6, 12, or 24 months. The bureaucracy takes its time in processing such applications. You will witness a great deal of bureaucratic inertia in the process of acting on your application.

3. **Foreigners must pay local taxes and special resident visa fees.** Furthermore, foreigners may be restricted on how much local currency they can take out of the country. Leaving the country even for a short holiday may require tax clearances—including a large cash deposit—and special permissions so you can re-enter without invalidating your work permit and resident visa.

4. **Work permit and resident visa requirements may restrict the number of times foreigners can exit and re-enter a country.** In some countries the work permit and resident visas becomes invalid upon leaving the country. Consequently, the whole application process must be once again initiated upon re-entering the country.

While many of these restrictions seem illogical and the bureaucratic process can be slow, they are designed with one purpose in mind— discourage foreign workers from entering and staying in their countries. Not surprisingly, countries increasingly emphasize "locals only" employment/immigrant policies due to a combination of nationalism and high unemployment rates.

Such restrictions can complicate international jobs considerably and take the excitement out of what was once considered to be the glamorous world of working abroad. While it is difficult to get the work permit in the first place, other restrictions can make life difficult once you get the necessary permissions. Currency, mobility, and re-application restrictions constitute the major headaches in this foreign employment game. Bureaucracies tend to be slow and cumbersome in processing the initial application as well as renewing work permits and resident visas. Indeed, even with an employment contract in hand and having completed all necessary paperwork, you may still have to wait two to six months before getting the proper documentation for entering the country as a foreign worker. You may also have second thoughts about leaving a country that automatically invalidates your hard-to-get-in-the-first-place work permit as well as requires a tax clearance to depart.

Consequently, it is always best to negotiate your employment contract with an international company before arriving in country. Be sure to clarify your understanding of local rules and regulations governing your employment, tax, and mobility status prior to accepting a position. The company will know the local regulations and it should be organized for arranging all work permits and resident visas for you and your family. In other words, it should be the responsibility of the employer to acquire all necessary work permits and resident visas to ensure your employment stability. If you fail to do this, you may be unpleasantly surprised to learn that you are literally "stuck" in a country for the duration of your contract as you are subjected to numerous rules and regulations governing your "foreign worker" status.

Many foreign workers, especially young people engaged in a once-in-a-lifetime work-your-way-around-the-world adventure, successfully avoid work permit and resident visa requirements by working illegally. They arrive in country on a 90-day to 6-month tourist visa, find employment, periodically leave the country in order to renew the visa, and return to their jobs—until the authorities catch them playing this game. This is a risky business and it often results in low-paying and menial jobs. In addition, you may not be eligible for health insurance and other employment benefits that automatically come with "legal" jobs. If you are a student looking for part-time or summer work abroad, you can usually find low-paying jobs in the tourism industry or agriculture without incurring the wrath of the local labor and immigration authorities. But in many countries, such as Denmark and Finland, authorities are even vigilant in enforcing foreign labor laws at this end of the labor spectrum.

It is always best to inquire about the local labor restrictions affecting foreign workers prior to seeking employment in a particular country. You can do this by contacting the foreign embassy or consulate located in your country for information on work permits and resident visas. Again, keep in mind that in most cases it will be the responsibility of the employer to acquire the necessary work permits and visas. And in most cases this means receiving an employment contract prior to entering the country. While you may travel to the country on a tourist visa for a job interview, you may not be able to enter the country on a tourist visa to begin work while waiting for your work permit and resident visa applications to be processed. Since each country differs somewhat in how they structure this situation, check with the embassy or consulate nearest you for clarifying the rules and regulations.

Key Resources

While this book identifies a few hundred of the largest international employers, numerous other organizations operate in the international arena. As you begin narrowing your choices, you may want to supplement this book with a few others that provide access to additional organizations. We strongly recommend consulting the following books which are available in most major libraries; several can be ordered directly from Impact Publications (order form at the end of this book):

➤ *Careers in International Affairs* (Washington, DC: Georgetown University, 1997, $17.95). One of the best international careers books available today. An annotated directory to hundreds of major international employers appropriate for recent college graduates and professionals.

➤ *Work Abroad: The Complete Guide to Finding a Job Overseas* (Amherst, MA: Transitions Abroad, 1997, $15.95). An excellent collection of short work abroad articles published in *Transitions Abroad*. Especially strong on short-term employment, travel related work, teaching English abroad, and volunteer vacations. Popular with students, recent graduates, and others, including retirees, with little international experience but who want to do something "international".

➤ *Business Phone Book U.S.A.* (Detroit: Omnigraphics, 1999, $160.00). An invaluable resource with nearly 1,000 pages packed with names, addresses, and phone numbers of corporations, associations, and universities. Includes a special international section with information on foreign chambers of commerce in the U.S., foreign corporations, and trade contacts and well as a section on the travel industry.

➤ *Kennedy's International Directory of Executive Recruiters* (Fitzwilliam, NH: Kennedy Information, 1998, $149.00). This directory of international executive recruiters identifies 1,087 firms in 59 countries worldwide. Includes 2,508 individual recruiters as well as introductory articles by industry leaders. Each entry comes with full contact information, including e-mail and web addresses; detailed firm descriptions; firm revenues and staff sizes; network affiliates; function and industry specialties; and geographic areas served. Arranged by country and indexed by functions and industries served.

➤ *Encyclopedia of Associations* (Detroit, MI: Gale Research, 1999, $490.00). This essential four-volume reference work is updated annually. It is the single most authoritative resource for identifying nearly 25,000 national and international associations headquartered in the U.S., from trade to public affairs associations. The two-volume companion directory, *Encyclopedia of Associations: International Organizations* ($590.00) identifies nearly 28,800 international associations headquartered abroad.

➤ *Research Centers Directory* (Detroit, MI: Gale Research, 1998, $548.00). Another essential reference work produced by Gale Research Inc. Includes over 14,300 university and nonprofit research organizations in the United States. Many specialize in area studies, international trade, and foreign relations.

➤ *Directory of American Firms Operating in Foreign Countries* (Uniworld, 257 Central Park West, Suite 10A, New York, NY 10024-4110, 1996, $220.00 + $9.50 shipping. *www.uniworld. com*). This three-volume, 2,500+ page directory is invaluable for locating the more than 3,000 U.S. companies operating in 138 countries. Provides information on the products/service lines of each company as well as identifies the countries in which they operate. Includes employment statistics and contact information.

We identify and annotate numerous other useful resources in the final chapter of this book. These include directories, job search books, job listings and subscriptions, Web sites, electronic databases, computer software, audiocassette programs, and CD-ROM. These resources will help you develop the necessary job search skills—from self-assessment to writing resumes and conducting job interviews—and contact potential international employers. Taken together, these resources constitute a rich information base from which you should be able to conduct a successful international job search.

We wish you well as you take this journey into the exciting and sometimes confusing world of international jobs and careers. While this book identifies the key organizations that hire in the international area, other books will take you through the most important stages of the job search. These stages are outlined in our other books: *Discover the Best Jobs For You!, Change Your Job Change Your Life, High Impact Resumes and Letters, Dynamite Resumes, Dynamite Cover Letters, Interview For Success, Dynamite Networking For Dynamite Jobs,* and *Dynamite Salary Negotiations.* We also address particular job and career fields in the following books: *The Complete Guide to Public Employment, Find a Federal Job Fast, The Complete Guide to International Jobs and Careers, The Directory of Federal Jobs and Employers, Jobs and Careers With Nonprofit Organizations, Jobs for People Who Love to Travel,* and *The Educator's Guide to Alternative Jobs and Careers.*

These and many other books are available in your local library and bookstore or they can be ordered directly from Impact Publications by completing the order form at the end of this book. You also may want to request a free copy of Impact's international jobs and careers brochure by sending a self-addressed stamped envelope (#10 business size) to the following address:

IMPACT PUBLICATIONS
ATTN: Free International Brochure
9104-N Manassas Drive
Manassas Park, VA 20111-5211

Impact Publication's comprehensive "Career Superstore" on the World Wide Web includes nearly 2,000 career resources, including many international job and career resources:

www.impactpublications.com

The site contains almost every important career and job finding resource available today, including many titles that are difficult if not impossible to find in bookstores and libraries. You will find everything from self-assessment books to books on resume writing, interviewing, government and international jobs, military, women, minorities, students, entrepreneurs as well as videos and computer software programs. This is an excellent resource for keeping in touch with the major resources that can assist you with every stage of your job search as well as with your future international career development plans.

Impact's Web site also includes new titles, specials, and job search tips for keeping you in touch with the latest in career information and resources. You also can subscribe to Impact's free electronic magazine (*E-zine*) if you wish to receive via email the latest information on career resources. Information on subscribing to this service is found on the front page of Impact's Web site, or you can subscribe by sending your email address to Impact Publications: joinlist@impactpublications.com.

2

The U.S. Federal Government

International positions with the federal government are numerous. They encompass many more agencies than the most popular and visible "big six" federal agencies specializing in international affairs:

- Department of State
- Department of Defense
- U.S. Agency for International Development (USAID)
- United States Information Agency (USIA)
- Peace Corps
- Central Intelligence Agency (CIA)

Thousands of additional international positions are found in the Executive Office of President, within other executive departments and agencies, and throughout congressional agencies, committees, and personal staffs.

International Agencies and Positions

The "big six" agencies offer the largest number of international positions. In addition, these agencies constitute an important international "network" for job seekers. Many former Peace Corps Volunteers, for example, move into positions in the U.S. Agency for International De-

GOVERNMENT OF THE UNITED STATES

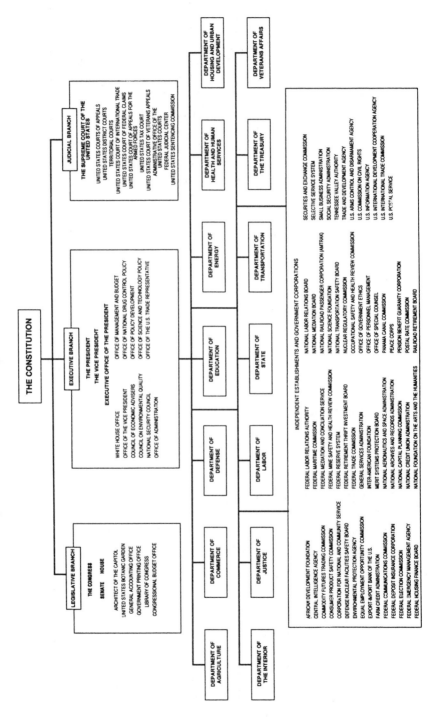

THE CONSTITUTION

LEGISLATIVE BRANCH

THE CONGRESS

SENATE   HOUSE

ARCHITECT OF THE CAPITOL
UNITED STATES BOTANIC GARDEN
GENERAL ACCOUNTING OFFICE
GOVERNMENT PRINTING OFFICE
LIBRARY OF CONGRESS
CONGRESSIONAL BUDGET OFFICE

EXECUTIVE BRANCH

THE PRESIDENT
THE VICE PRESIDENT
EXECUTIVE OFFICE OF THE PRESIDENT

WHITE HOUSE OFFICE
OFFICE OF THE VICE PRESIDENT
COUNCIL OF ECONOMIC ADVISERS
COUNCIL ON ENVIRONMENTAL QUALITY
NATIONAL SECURITY COUNCIL
OFFICE OF ADMINISTRATION

OFFICE OF MANAGEMENT AND BUDGET
OFFICE OF NATIONAL DRUG CONTROL POLICY
OFFICE OF POLICY DEVELOPMENT
OFFICE OF SCIENCE AND TECHNOLOGY POLICY
OFFICE OF THE U.S. TRADE REPRESENTATIVE

JUDICIAL BRANCH

THE SUPREME COURT OF THE UNITED STATES

UNITED STATES COURTS OF APPEALS
UNITED STATES DISTRICT COURTS
TERRITORIAL COURTS
UNITED STATES COURT OF INTERNATIONAL TRADE
UNITED STATES COURT OF FEDERAL CLAIMS
UNITED STATES COURT OF APPEALS FOR THE ARMED FORCES
UNITED STATES TAX COURT
UNITED STATES COURT OF VETERANS APPEALS
ADMINISTRATIVE OFFICE OF THE UNITED STATES COURTS
FEDERAL JUDICIAL CENTER
UNITED STATES SENTENCING COMMISSION

DEPARTMENT OF AGRICULTURE

DEPARTMENT OF THE INTERIOR

DEPARTMENT OF COMMERCE

DEPARTMENT OF JUSTICE

DEPARTMENT OF DEFENSE

DEPARTMENT OF LABOR

DEPARTMENT OF EDUCATION

DEPARTMENT OF STATE

DEPARTMENT OF ENERGY

DEPARTMENT OF TRANSPORTATION

DEPARTMENT OF HEALTH AND HUMAN SERVICES

DEPARTMENT OF THE TREASURY

DEPARTMENT OF HOUSING AND URBAN DEVELOPMENT

DEPARTMENT OF VETERANS AFFAIRS

INDEPENDENT ESTABLISHMENTS AND GOVERNMENT CORPORATIONS

AFRICAN DEVELOPMENT FOUNDATION
CENTRAL INTELLIGENCE AGENCY
COMMODITY FUTURES TRADING COMMISSION
CONSUMER PRODUCT SAFETY COMMISSION
CORPORATION FOR NATIONAL AND COMMUNITY SERVICE
DEFENSE NUCLEAR FACILITIES SAFETY BOARD
ENVIRONMENTAL PROTECTION AGENCY
EQUAL EMPLOYMENT OPPORTUNITY COMMISSION
EXPORT-IMPORT BANK OF THE U.S.
FARM CREDIT ADMINISTRATION
FEDERAL COMMUNICATIONS COMMISSION
FEDERAL DEPOSIT INSURANCE CORPORATION
FEDERAL ELECTION COMMISSION
FEDERAL EMERGENCY MANAGEMENT AGENCY
FEDERAL HOUSING FINANCE BOARD

FEDERAL LABOR RELATIONS AUTHORITY
FEDERAL MARITIME COMMISSION
FEDERAL MEDIATION AND CONCILIATION SERVICE
FEDERAL MINE SAFETY AND HEALTH REVIEW COMMISSION
FEDERAL RESERVE SYSTEM
FEDERAL RETIREMENT THRIFT INVESTMENT BOARD
FEDERAL TRADE COMMISSION
GENERAL SERVICES ADMINISTRATION
INTER-AMERICAN FOUNDATION
MERIT SYSTEMS PROTECTION BOARD
NATIONAL AERONAUTICS AND SPACE ADMINISTRATION
NATIONAL ARCHIVES AND RECORDS ADMINISTRATION
NATIONAL CAPITAL PLANNING COMMISSION
NATIONAL CREDIT UNION ADMINISTRATION
NATIONAL FOUNDATION ON THE ARTS AND THE HUMANITIES

NATIONAL LABOR RELATIONS BOARD
NATIONAL MEDIATION BOARD
NATIONAL RAILROAD PASSENGER CORPORATION (AMTRAK)
NATIONAL SCIENCE FOUNDATION
NATIONAL TRANSPORTATION SAFETY BOARD
NUCLEAR REGULATORY COMMISSION
OCCUPATIONAL SAFETY AND HEALTH REVIEW COMMISSION
OFFICE OF GOVERNMENT ETHICS
OFFICE OF PERSONNEL MANAGEMENT
OFFICE OF SPECIAL COUNSEL
PANAMA CANAL COMMISSION
PEACE CORPS
PENSION BENEFIT GUARANTY CORPORATION
POSTAL RATE COMMISSION
RAILROAD RETIREMENT BOARD

SECURITIES AND EXCHANGE COMMISSION
SELECTIVE SERVICE SYSTEM
SMALL BUSINESS ADMINISTRATION
SOCIAL SECURITY ADMINISTRATION
TENNESSEE VALLEY AUTHORITY
TRADE AND DEVELOPMENT AGENCY
U.S. ARMS CONTROL AND DISARMAMENT AGENCY
U.S. COMMISSION ON CIVIL RIGHTS
U.S. INFORMATION AGENCY
U.S. INTERNATIONAL DEVELOPMENT COOPERATION AGENCY
U.S. INTERNATIONAL TRADE COMMISSION
U.S. POSTAL SERVICE

velopment, Department of State, and the United States Information Agency. Within the intelligence community, individuals who work for the Defense Intelligence Agency (DIA) or Federal Bureau of Investigation also find international job opportunities with the Central Intelligence Agency and the Drug Enforcement Agency (DEA). Many other federal agencies have international interests, offices, and positions. Some of them, such as international agencies within the Department of Agriculture and Department of Commerce, hire a large number of international specialists. Other agencies only have a small number of international positions.

Job Finding Strategies

Finding an international job with the federal government requires carefully observing the formal hiring procedures as well as making personal contacts within targeted agencies. In most cases, hiring takes place at the agency level. Once a vacancy is announced, individuals should submit an application package. In most cases, the requested application package consists of a completed OF-612, Standard Form 171 (SF 171), or federal-style resume—three application options permitted by most federal agencies. You must complete these applications in reference to the qualifications specified in the vacancy announcement. Consequently, the more you know about the agency and position and tailor your application to the position, the better your chances of getting the job.

Some agencies have their own hiring procedures and personnel systems. For example, entry into many positions in the Department of State, U.S. Agency for International Development, and the United States Information Agency is via the Foreign Service. Applicants must pass the Foreign Service Exam which is given each year in early December. For more information on this recruitment procedure, telephone 703/875-7490 write to: United States Department of State, Recruitment Division, Box 9317, Arlington, VA 22209. Other agencies, such as the Central Intelligence Agency, Defense Intelligence Agency, Smithsonian Institution, and the Library of Congress also have their own application procedures and personnel systems.

The following federal agencies and congressional organizations are the major sources for international employment within the federal government. We recommend that you use the Web sites, addresses, and telephone numbers for gathering information on the various agencies.

When vacancies occur, they will be announced through the agency personnel office in the form of a position vacancy announcement. The position may also be listed through the Office of Personnel Management's Web site (*www.usajobs.opm.gov*), the agency's Web site, or published in such printed job listings as *Federal Career Opportunities* and *Federal Jobs Digest* (see the end of this chapter for order information). However, coverage of vacancies is not always complete nor timely through published sources.

It is always best to keep in close contact with the hiring agency in order to learn about impending vacancies. Start by going directly to the agency's Web site. Most federal agencies now have their own Web sites which include vacancy announcements and information on the agency's operations. Four good starting places for accessing information via the Web on agencies are these key gateway Web sites:

www.whitehouse.gov
www.fedgate.org
www.fedworld.gov
www.usajobs.opm.gov

You also may wish to call the agency personnel office for information on current vacancies. Better still, make contact with the hiring officials within the agency to learn if and when a vacancy will become available.

Executive Office of the President

You can easily access information on the Executive Office of the President by going directly to the White House's Web site:

www.whitehouse.gov

Start by clicking on to "Interactive Citizens' Handbook" and then "Search the White House Web Sites" and "Contents of This Web Site." Next, use the "Title" section of the search engine to locate a particular office within the Executive Office of the President. For example, if you are interested in learning more about the National Security Council (NSC), just type in "National Security Council." You'll go to a section that includes the NSC's Web site:

www.whitehouse.gov/WH/EOP/NSC/html/nschome2.html

Do the same type of search for other offices in the Executive Office of the President. You will quickly discover the White House's Web site (*www.whitehouse.com*) is one of the most useful gateway sites for accessing information, including vacancy announcements, on agencies within all three branches of the federal government.

COUNCIL OF ECONOMIC ADVISORS
Old Executive Office Building
Washington, DC 20502
Tel. 202/395-5084

Analyzes the economy and makes policy recommendations to the President for economic growth and stability.

NATIONAL SECURITY COUNCIL (NSC)
Old Executive Office Building
Washington, DC 20506
Tel. 202/456-1414

Advises the President on all policy matters (domestic, foreign, and military) relating to national security. Includes area (Asia, Africa, Europe, Russia, the former Soviet republics, Near East, and South Asia) and policy (arms control, intelligence, economic affairs, and legislative affairs) divisions.

OFFICE OF MANAGEMENT AND BUDGET (OMB)
Executive Office Building
Washington, DC 20503
Tel. 202/395-3080

Assists the President in preparing and formulating the federal budget as well as controlling the administration of the budget. Informs the President on the progress of government agencies. Includes a **National Security and International Affairs** office (Tel. 202/395-4657)

OFFICE OF NATIONAL DRUG CONTROL POLICY
Executive Office of the President
Washington, DC 20500
Tel. 202/395-6700

Coordinates federal, state, and local efforts to control illegal drug abuse as well as devises national strategies relating to anti-drug activities.

OFFICE OF SCIENCE AND TECHNOLOGY POLICY
New Executive Office Building
Washington, DC 20506
Tel. 202/395-7347

Advises the President on all matters relating to science, engineering, and technology relevant to the economy, national security, health, foreign relations, and the environment.

OFFICE OF THE UNITED STATES TRADE REPRESENTATIVE
600 - 17th Street, NW
Washington, DC 20506
Tel. 202/395-3230

Responsible for formulating and coordinating all trade policy for the United States. Functions as the country's chief trade representative and negotiator for all multinational (GATT, UN) and bilateral trade matters. Many former employees who worked in this office as U.S. trade negotiators are noted for playing the "revolving door" game by becoming high paid consultants to foreign governments on U.S. trade matters after working in this office.

WHITE HOUSE OFFICE
1600 Pennsylvania Avenue, NW
Washington, DC 20500
Tel. 202/456-1414

Provides the President with staff assistance necessary for the orderly day-to-day administration of the Office of President. Includes such divisions as Chief of Staff, Counsel to the President, Press Secretary, Presidential Personnel, Communications, Presidential Advance, Presidential Scheduling, Legislative Affairs, Economic and Domestic Policy, Public Liaison, Administration, National Service, Military, Office of the First Lady, Cabinet Affairs, Domestic Policy Council, Economic Policy Council, and Agriculture, Trade, Food Assistance.

The Departments

DEPARTMENT OF AGRICULTURE
14th Street and Independence Avenue, SW
Washington, DC 20250
Tel. 202/720-2791
Web site: *www.usda.gov*

The Department of Agriculture is one of the largest employers of international specialists who are involved with foreign agricultural issues affecting U.S.

agricultural and trade policies. The **Foreign Agricultural Service**, for example, posts nearly 100 agricultural specialists in more than 60 American embassies and consulates worldwide. It monitors foreign agriculture policies and commercial trade relations and promotes U.S. agricultural products. Other offices and divisions within the department deal with specific policy matters (conservation, forestry, inspection, transportation) or provide policy support services (research, marketing, information). The major international-related agencies within the department include:

- **Foreign Agricultural Service:** Tel. 202/720-3935. *www.usda.gov/fas*
- **Office of International Cooperation and Development:** Tel. 202/690-0776
- **International Trade Policy:** Tel. 202/720-6887
- **Economic Research Service:** 1301 New York Ave., NW, Washington, DC 20005-4788, Tel. 202/219-0300. *www.econ.ag.gov*
- **Agricultural Marketing Service:** Tel. 202/720-5115. *http://usda.gov/ams.titlepage.htm*
- **Agricultural Research Service:** Tel. 202/720-3656. *www.ars.usda.gov*
- **Animal and Plant Health Inspection Service:** 6505 Belcrest Road, Hyattsville, MD 20782, Tel. 301/436-7550
- **Food Safety and Inspection Service:** International Programs, Tel. 202/720-7025. *www.usda.gov/agency/fsis/homepage.html*
- **Forest Service:** International Forestry Staff, 202/205-1661. *www.fs.fed.us*
- **World Agricultural Outlook Board:** Tel. 202/720-6030. *www.usda.gov/agency/oce/waob/waob.htm*

DEPARTMENT OF COMMERCE
14th and Constitution Avenue, NW
Washington, DC 20230
Tel. 202/482-2000
Web site: *www.doc.gov*

The mission of this department is to promote the Nation's international trade, economic growth, and technological advancement. Its international interests and activities are extensive, from promoting competitive foreign trade, standardization, and telecommunications and protecting trademarks and copyrights to encouraging foreign travel to the U.S. The major international employers within the Department of Commerce include:

- **International Trade Administration:** Tel. 202/482-2867. *www.ita.doc/gov*
- **United States and Foreign Commercial Service:** Tel. 202/482-5777
- **Bureau of Census:** Tel. 301/457-2135. *www.census.gov*
- **Market Access and Compliance:** Tel. 202/482-3022
- **International Economics:** Tel. 202/606-9604
- **Import Administration:** Tel. 202/482-1780
- **Export Administration:** Tel. 202/482-1455. *www.doc.gov/resources/BXA_info.html*

- **Trade Development:** Tel. 202/482-1461
- **National Oceanic and Atmospheric Administration:** Tel. 202/482-3436. *www.noaa.gov*
- **Bureau of Economic Analysis:** International Economics, Tel. 202/606-9600. *www.bea.doc.gov*
- **National Institute of Standards and Technology:** Tel. 301/975-3000. *www.nist.gov*
- **National Technical Information Service:** Tel. 703/487-4636.
- **National Telecommunications and Information Administration:** Tel. 202/482-1804. *www.ntia.doc.gov*
- **Oceanic and Atmospheric Research:** Tel. 301/713-2458
- **United States Patent and Trademark Office:** Tel. 703/305-8600. *www.uspto.gov*

DEPARTMENT OF DEFENSE AND RELATED AGENCIES
The Pentagon
Washington, DC 20310
Tel. 703/545-6700
Web site: *www.dtic.mil*

The Department of Defense is by definition extensively involved in international affairs. Its activities involve everything from defense and security matters to educating the children of U.S. military personnel assigned abroad. International-related jobs in this department range from high-level policy, information, and security positions based in Washington, DC to blue-collar positions at U.S. military bases abroad. The major offices that hire international specialists include:

- **Deputy Undersecretary for Security Policy:** Tel. 703/697-0286
- **Defense Security Assistance Agency:** Tel. 703/695-3291
- **Advanced Research Projects Agency (ARPA):** 3701 North Fairfax Drive, Arlington, VA 22203-1714, Tel. 703/694-3077
- **Defense Intelligence Agency:** Tel. 703/695-7353
- **International Security Policy:** Tel. 703/695-0942
- **Department of Defense Dependents Schools:** 4040 North Fairfax Drive, Arlington, VA 22203, Tel. 703/696-4413
- **National Security Agency:** Tel. 301/688-7111

Many civilian government positions are available with U.S. military bases in Europe, Asia, and the Pacific. For information on the Departments of Army, Navy, and Air Force, please visit their relevant Web sites:

Department of Army	*www.army.mil*
Department of Navy	*www.nctsnavy.mil*
Department of Air Force	*www.af.mil*

DEPARTMENT OF EDUCATION
600 Independence Avenue, SW
Washington, DC 20202
Tel. 202/708-5366
Web site: *www.ed.gov*

The Department of Education is involved in providing training and research services related to international education through its **Center for International Education**.

DEPARTMENT OF ENERGY
1000 Independence Avenue, SW
Washington, DC 20585
Tel. 202/586-5000
Web site: *www.doe.gov*

The Department of Energy is responsible for developing a comprehensive national energy plan, promoting energy technology, marketing federal power, conserving energy, operating the nuclear weapons program, and collecting and analyzing data on energy. This is a unique department in which over 80 percent of its personnel are private contractors. Since energy policy has important international dimensions, the department has important international interests. The major agencies and offices within the department hiring international specialists include:

- **Office of International Affairs:** Tel. 202/586-5493
- **Policy and International Affairs:** Tel. 202/586-5800
- **Coal, Nuclear, Electric & Alternative Fuels:** Tel. 202/426-1200
- **Nuclear Energy, Science and Technology:** Tel. 202/586-6450
- **Intelligence:** Foreign Intelligence Division, Tel. 202/586-5174
- **Energy Information Administration:** Energy Markets and End Use, International and Contingency Information Division, Tel. 202/586-1617
- **Office of Energy Research:** Fusion Energy, International Programs Staff, 19901 Germantown Rd., Germantown, MD 20874, Tel. 301/903-3068

DEPARTMENT OF HEALTH AND HUMAN SERVICES
200 Independence Avenue, SW
Washington, DC 20201
Tel. 202/619-0257
Web site: *www.os.dhhs.gov*

The Department of Health and Human Services is responsible for promoting the Nation's health and welfare. Extensively involved in international health matters, its international activities primarily center on conducting research and promoting international health policy. The major agencies and offices within the department with international interests and which tend to hire international specialists include:

- **International Health Program:** Tel. 770/488-1085
- **International Emergency and Refugee Act:** Tel. 770/488-1094
- **National Institutes of Health:** Tel. 301/496-2433. *www.nih.gov*
- **National Center for Health Statistics:** International Statistics Office, Tel. 301/436-7016
- **National Institute of Mental Health:** Tel. 301/443-3673. *www.nimh.nih.gov*
- **Centers for Disease Control and Prevention:** International Health Associate Director, Tel. 770/488-1080. *www.cdc.gov*
- **National Cancer Institute:** Tel. 301/496-5615. *www.nci.nih.gov*
- **International and Refugee Health:** Tel. 301/443-1774
- **National Institute of Environmental Health Sciences:** Tel. 919/541-3201. *www.niehs.nih.gov*

DEPARTMENT OF HOUSING AND URBAN DEVELOPMENT
451 Seventh Street, SW
Washington, DC 20410
Tel. 202/708-1422
Web site: *www.hud.gov*

While the Department of Housing and Urban Development is primarily responsible for administering federal housing programs and for improving and developing communities within the United States, it also has some international interests. While in 1989 the department abolished the Office of International Affairs—which used to be the center for international housing and urban development specialists—it still pursues international interests. However, it remains unclear where these interests are centered. The best bet for now is the Office of Policy Development and Research (Tel. 202/708-1600).

DEPARTMENT OF INTERIOR
1849 C Street, NW
Washington, DC 20240
Tel. 202/208-3171
Web site: *www.doi.gov*

The Department of Interior is responsible for protecting and managing federally owned lands and natural resources. It is also responsible for American Indian reservation communities and for the peoples populating island territories under U.S. jurisdiction. The major agencies and offices within the department with international interests include:

- **Office of Territorial and International Affairs:** Tel. 202/208-4822
- **National Park Service:** International Affairs, 1100 L Street, NW, Washington, DC 20013-7127, Tel. 202/565-1293
- **U.S. Geological Survey:** Tel.703/648-7442. *www.usgs.gov/doil/usgs.html*
- **Bureau of Land Management:** Tel. 202/208-3801. *www.blm.gov*

- **Bureau of Reclamation:** External Affairs, Tel. 202/208-4157. *www. usbr.gov*
- **Fish, Wildlife, and Parks:** External Affairs, International Affairs, Tel. 703/358-1754

DEPARTMENT OF JUSTICE AND RELATED AGENCIES
Constitution Avenue and 10th Street, NW
Washington, DC 20530
Tel. 202/514-2000
Web site: *www.usdoj.gov*

One of the fastest growing federal departments, the Department of Justice is responsible for enforcing federal laws. Its thousands of lawyers, investigators, and agents are involved in protecting citizens from criminals and subversion, ensuring business competition, safeguarding consumers, and enforcing drug, immigration, and naturalization laws. Its international interests are especially pronounced in the areas of drug enforcement and immigration matters. The major offices and agencies within the **Department of Justice** with international interests include:

- **Antitrust Division:** Foreign Commerce Section, Tel. 202/514-2464. *www.usdoj.gov/atr/atr.html*
- **Civil Division:** International Trade Field Office, Tel. 212/264-9232. *www.usdoj.gov/civil/civil.html*
- **Criminal Division:** International Affairs Office, Tel. 202/514-0000. *www.usdoj.gov/criminal/criminal-home.html*
- **Drug Enforcement Administration:** International Operations Programs Office, Tel. 703/307-4233. *www.usdoj.gov/dea/deahome.html*
- **U.S. Marshals Service:** International Operations, Tel. 703/307-9120. *www.usdoj.gov/marshals*
- **Interpol-U.S. National Central Bureau:** Tel. 202/616-9000.
- **Foreign Claims Settlement Commission of the United States:** Tel. 202/616-6985. *www.usdoj.gov/offices/foreign.html*

Other Department of Justice related agencies with international interests include:

- **Federal Bureau of Investigation:** Tel. 202/324-3515. *www.fbi.gov*
- **Immigration and Naturalization Service:** International Affairs Office. Tel. 202/305-2798. *www.usdoj.gov/ins*

DEPARTMENT OF LABOR
200 Constitution Avenue, NW
Washington, DC 20210
Tel. 202/219-5000
Web site: *www.dol.gov*

The Department of Labor is responsible for the welfare of wage earners in the U.S. It administers federal labor laws relating to the safety, welfare, and compensation of workers, including unemployment insurance and workers' compensation. The major agencies and offices with international interests include:

- **International Labor Affairs:** International Organizations Office. Tel. 202/219-7682. *http://gatekeeper.dol.gov/dol/ilab*
- **Prices and Living Conditions:** Prices Division, Tel. 202/606-7100
- **Solicitor:** International Affairs Counsel, Tel. 202/219-8627. *www.dol. gov/dol/sol*

DEPARTMENT OF STATE
2201 C Street, NW
Washington, DC 20520
Tel. 202/647-4000
Web site: *www.state.gov*

The Department of State is responsible for advising the President on foreign policy matters and for implementing U.S. foreign policy. It represents the U.S. abroad through its network of embassies and consulates and participates in the United Nations and over 50 major international organizations. It is the federal government's major employer of international specialists with a total personnel level of over 25,000. Entry into many positions within this department involves taking the Foreign Service examination (Recruitment Division, Department of State, Box 9317, Arlington, Virginia 22209 or Tel. 703/875-7490) which used to be given each year in December; however, since this examination situation keeps changing, be sure to check on the status of the examination and dates. The examination also is used for several Foreign Service Officer (FSO) positions with the Agency for International Development (USAID), the U.S. Information Agency (USIA), and the U.S. Department of Commerce. The Foreign Service constitutes a separate personnel system within the federal government with its own rules, regulations, and procedures. Other positions within the Department of State fall under the personnel system administered by the Office of Personnel Management (OPM) and its General System (GS) salary schedule. Some of the most interesting agencies and offices in this department include:

- **Economic and Business Affairs Bureau**
- **International Energy Policy Office:** Tel. 202/647-2875
- **International Communication & Information Policy Deputy Assistant Secretary:** Tel. 202/647-5212
- **Bilateral & Regional Affairs Office:** Tel. 202/647-6842
- **Bilateral Trade Affairs Office:** Tel. 202/647-4017
- **Multilateral Trade Affairs Office:** Tel. 202/647-8958
- **Global Affairs:** Tel. 202/647-6240
- **Population, Refugees, and Migration:** Tel. 202/647-7360
- **Foreign Service Institute:** Tel. 703/302-6703
- **International Communication and Information Policy Bureau**
- **International Security Affairs**
- **African Affairs Bureau:** Tel. 202/647-4440
- **East Asian and Pacific Affairs Bureau:** Tel. 202/647-9596

- **European and Canadian Affairs Bureau:** Tel. 202/647-9626
- **Intelligence and Research Bureau:** Tel. 202/647-9176
- **Inter-American Affairs Bureau:** Tel. 202/647-5780
- **International Organization Affairs Bureau:** Tel. 202/647-9600
- **International Narcotics and Law Enforcement Affairs:** Tel. 202/647-8464
- **Near Eastern Affairs Bureau:** Tel. 202/647-7206
- **South Asian Affairs:** Tel. 202/736-4325
- **Oceans and International Environmental and Scientific Affairs Bureau**
- **Bureau of Politico Military Affairs**
- **Bureau of Refugee Programs**
- **Bureau of Consular Affairs**

DEPARTMENT OF TRANSPORTATION
400 Seventh Street, SW
Washington, DC 20590
Tel. 202/366-4000
Web site: *www.dot.gov*

The Department of Transportation is responsible for the Nation's overall transportation policy in the areas of highways, mass transit, railways, aviation, waterways, and ports. It is also responsible for the safety of oil and gas pipelines. Its international transportation interests center on aviation, maritime, and trade issues. These are centered in the following agencies and offices:

- **Policy: International Cooperation Division:** Tel. 202/366-9632. *http://cti1.volpe.dot.gov/fhwa/aaphome.html*
- **Policy and International Trade:** International Activities Office, Tel. 202/366-5773
- **Policy, Planning, and International Aviation:** Tel. 202/267-3033
- **Maritime Administration:** Congressional and Public Affairs Office, Tel. 202/ 366-1707. *http://marad.dot.gov*
- **National Highway Safety Administration:** International Harmonization Director, Tel. 202/366-2114
- **Saint Lawrence Seaway Development Corporation:** Tel. 202/ 366-0118. *www.dot.gov/dotinfo/slsdc*
- **United States Coast Guard:** Tel. 202/267-2390
- **Aviation and International Affairs:** Tel. 202/366-8822. *www.dot.gov/aviation*
- **International Aviation:** Tel. 202/366-2423
- **Aviation and International Economic:** Tel. 202/366-1053
- **International Transportation and Trade:** Tel. 202/366-4368

DEPARTMENT OF TREASURY
1500 Pennsylvania Avenue, NW
Washington, DC 20220
Tel. 202/622-2000
Web site: *www.ustres.gov*

The Department of Treasury is responsible for formulating and recommending economic, financial, tax, and fiscal policies. It is the federal government's chief financial agent enforcing tax laws and manufacturing coins and currency. Its international interests focus on international tax and revenue, monetary, finance, trade, investment, and banking issues as well as the U.S. Custom Service. The major offices and agencies involved with international issues include:

- **Under Secretary for International Affairs:** Tel. 202/622-0060. International Development, Debt, and Environment Policy Office: Tel. 202/622-0153; Trade and Investment Policy: Tel. 202/622-0168; International Monetary and Financial Policy: Tel. 202/622-0656; International Development, Debt, and Environment Policy: Tel. 202/622-0153; Asia, The Americas, and Africa: Tel. 202/622-7222; Eurasia and The Middle East: Tel. 202/622-0770; Trade and Investment Policy, International Monetary and Financial Affairs, Eastern Europe and the former Soviet Union, and Middle East and Energy Policy located at 1500 Pennsylvania Avenue, NW, Washington, DC 20005.
- **United States Customs Service:** Tel. 202/927-1000. *www.customs. ustreas.gov*
- **Assistant Secretary for Tax Policy:** 15th & Pennsylvania Ave., NW, Washington, DC 20220, Tel. 202/622-0050—International Tax Counsel; International Taxation Division
- **Bureau of Alcohol, Tobacco, and Firearms**: Tel. 202/927-8700. *www. atf.gov*
- **Internal Revenue Service:** Tel. 202/622-4155. *www.irs.ustreas.gov*
- **Office of the Comptroller of the Currency:** Tel. 202/847-4900
- **United States Secret Service:** 1800 G Street, NW, Washington, DC 20223, Tel. 202/435-5708

Independent Agencies and Government Corporations

The following independent agencies and government corporations offer numerous international job opportunities. Inquiries and applications should be addressed directly to each organization. Start by visiting the Web site of each organization. In most cases, the Web site will provide information on vacancies as well as application procedures. Some sites, such as the Central Intelligence Agency (*www.cia.gov*), will provide linkages to other related agencies.

AFRICAN DEVELOPMENT FOUNDATION
1400 Eye Street, NW, 10th Floor
Washington, DC 20005
Tel. 202/673-3916
Web site: *www.adj.gov*

This nonprofit, government corporation supports self-help efforts of grassroots organizations in Africa to solve development problems. It provides grants, loans, and loan guarantees to private African groups, associations, and other organizations engaged in such self-help activities.

CENTRAL INTELLIGENCE AGENCY (CIA)
Washington, DC 20505
Tel. 703/482-1100
Web site: *www.cia.gov* or *www.odci.gov/cia*

The Central Intelligence Agency is one of three major federal intelligence agencies involved in collecting, evaluating, and disseminating information on political, military, economic, and scientific developments relevant to national security. Employing over 30,000 individuals, it hires numerous international specialists with area and foreign language skills who become intelligence officers and analysts.

CONSUMER PRODUCT SAFETY COMMISSION
East-West Towers
4330 East West Highway
Bethesda, MD 20814
Tel. 301/504-0580
Web site: *www.cpsc.gov*

The Consumer Product Safety Commission is responsible for maintaining the safety of consumer products. It does this by setting uniform product safety standards and by conducting research and investigating the causes and prevention of product-related deaths, illnesses, and injuries. Its international activities are centered in the Office of International Affairs (Tel. 301/492-6554).

ENVIRONMENTAL PROTECTION AGENCY
401 M Street, SW
Washington, DC 20460
Tel. 202/260-2090
Web site: *www.epa.gov*

The Environmental Protection Agency is responsible for controlling and abating pollution in the areas of air, water, solid waste, pesticides, radiation, and toxic substances. While most of its activities center on coordinating federal, state, and local government efforts, it has become increasingly involved in international environmental issues. Its international interests are centered in the **Office of International Activities** (Tel. 202/260-4870).

EXPORT-IMPORT BANK OF THE UNITED STATES
811 Vermont Avenue, NW
Washington, DC 20571
Tel. 1-800-565-EXIM
Web site: *www.exim.gov*

The Export-Import Bank is responsible for promoting the export of U.S. products. It does this by assisting private firms with commercial export financing involving loans, guarantees, and insurance. Most offices and positions within this organization involve international activities. For example, the **Export Finance Group** is organized by regions (Asia, Europe, Latin America, Africa, and Middle East) with loan officers attached to each region.

FEDERAL COMMUNICATIONS COMMISSION
1919 M Street, NW
Washington, DC 20554
Tel. 202/418-0200 or 888/225-5322
Web site: *www.fcc.gov*

The Federal Communications Commission is responsible for regulating interstate and foreign communications (radio, television, wire, satellite, and cable) as well as developing and operating broadcast services and providing for rapid, efficient nationwide and worldwide telephone and telegraph services at reasonable rates. Its international interests are centered in:

- **Mass Media:** Policy and Rules Division, International Branch, Tel. 202/254-3394
- **Common Carrier Bureau:** The International Facilities Division, Tel. 202/632-7834
- **Federal Operations Bureau:** Tel. 202/632-7592
- **Private Radio Bureau:** Tel. 202/632-7197

FEDERAL EMERGENCY MANAGEMENT AGENCY (FEMA)
500 C Street, SW
Washington, DC 20472
Tel. 202/646-4600
Web site: *www.fema.gov*

The Federal Emergency Management Agency is responsible for coordinating the nation's emergency preparedness, mitigation, and response activities. Its international interests center on the **International Affairs Office** (Tel. 202/646-4200).

FEDERAL MARITIME COMMISSION
800 N. Capitol Street, NW
Washington, DC 20573-0001
Tel. 202/523-5707
Web site: *www.fmc.gov*

The Federal Maritime Commission is responsible for regulating waterborne foreign and domestic offshore commerce of the U.S. It ensures that waterborne commercial activities are conducted on a fair and equitable basis. Works with the Department of State in eliminating discriminatory practices against U.S.-flag shipping.

FEDERAL RESERVE SYSTEM
20th Street and Constitution Avenue, NW
Washington, DC 20551
Tel. 202/452-3000
Web site: *www.bog.frb.fed.us*

As the central bank of the United States, the Federal Reserve System is responsible for administering and making policy for the nation's credit and monetary affairs. It is responsible for promoting a sound banking system that is responsive to both domestic and international needs of the nation. Its international interests are centered on the **International Finance Staff** (Tel. 202/452-3614).

GENERAL SERVICES ADMINISTRATION
18th and F Streets, NW
Washington, DC 20405
Tel. 202/708-5082
Web site: *www.gsa.gov*

The General Services Administration establishes policy for and provides economical and efficient management of government property and records, including construction and operation of buildings, procurement and distribution of supplies, utilization and disposal of property; transportation, traffic, and communications management; and management of the government-wide automatic data processing resources program.

GOVERNMENT NATIONAL MORTGAGE ASSOCIATION
3900 Wisconsin Avenue, NW
Washington, DC 20016
Tel. 202/708-0926

The Federal National Mortgage Association is responsible for promoting the health of the mortgage insurance industry. Its international interests are centered in the office of **International Housing Finance** (Tel. 202/752-6661).

INTER-AMERICAN FOUNDATION
901 North Stuart, 10th Floor
Arlington, VA 22203-1821
Tel 703/841-3800
Web site: *www.iaf.gov*

This independent government corporation is responsible for supporting social and economic activities in Latin American and the Caribbean by providing grants to private, indigenous organizations that operate self-help projects benefiting poor people.

NATIONAL AERONAUTICS AND SPACE ADMINISTRATION
300 E Street, SW
Washington, DC 20546
Tel. 202/348-1000
Web site: *www.nasa.gov*

The National Aeronautics and Space Administration (NASA) conducts research and operates programs relating to flight within and outside the Earth's atmosphere, including the Nation's major space programs and centers. Its international interests center on the office of **Policy, Coordination and International Relations** (International Relations Division, Tel. 202/358-0900, International Programs Policy, Tel. 202/358-1651, and International Planning and Programs, Tel. 202/358-1665).

NATIONAL SCIENCE FOUNDATION
4201 Wilson Blvd.
Arlington, VA 22230
Tel. 703/306-1234
Web site: *www.nsf.gov*

The National Science Foundation is responsible for promoting research and education programs in science and engineering. It does this through grants, contracts, and cooperative agreements with universities, university consortia, and nonprofit and other research organizations. Its international interests center on several offices and divisions within the office of **Science and Technology Infrastructure** (Tel. 202/357-9808).

NUCLEAR REGULATORY COMMISSION
Washington, DC 20555-0001
Tel. 301/415-7000
Web site: *www.nrc.gov*

The Nuclear Regulatory Commission is responsible for licensing and regulating civilian use of nuclear energy to protect public health and safety and the environment. Makes rules, sets standards, and inspects those licensed to build and operate nuclear reactors and other facilities as well as to own and use nuclear materials. Its international interests center on the **International Programs Office**, Tel. 301/492-0347).

PANAMA CANAL COMMISSION
1825 I Street, NW, Suite 1050
Washington, DC 20006
Tel. 202/634-6441

The Panama Canal Commission operates the Panama Canal to ensure efficient, safe, and economical transit service for the benefit of world commerce.

PEACE CORPS
1111 20th Street, NW
Washington, DC 20526
Tel. 202/606-3386
Tel. 1-800/424-8580 (on becoming a Peace Corps Volunteer)
Tel. 202/606-3950 (Employment)
Tel. 202/606-3214 (Job Hotline)
Web site: *www.peacecorps.gov*

The Peace Corps promotes world peace, friendship, and understanding by providing over 6,500 volunteers to work in nearly 100 developing countries for periods of two to three years. Volunteers work in a variety of programs, from teaching English to community development, health care, and small enterprise development. For many individuals interested in international jobs and careers, the Peace Corps offers excellent "entry-level" opportunities to get international experience that will become invaluable for later finding jobs with the U.S. State Department, U.S. Agency for International Development, private contractors and consultants, nonprofit organizations, and PVOs. All positions within the Peace Corps, either Volunteer or Staff, should be considered "international" positions because they involve international operations. Major Congressional budgetary initiatives in October 1998 should result in the Peace Corps undergoing a major expansion that should bring the total number of volunteers up to 10,000 by the year 2002.

SECURITIES AND EXCHANGE COMMISSION
450 5th Street, NW
Washington, DC 20549
Tel. 202/272-3100
Web site: *www.sec.gov*

The Securities and Exchange Commission is responsible for administering federal securities laws that protect investors and ensure that the securities markets are operated fairly and honestly. Its international interests center on the following offices and divisions:

- **Corporation Finance:** International Corporate Finance Office, Tel. 202/272-3246
- **General Counsel:** International Litigation and Administrative Practices, Tel. 202/272-2454
- **Enforcement:** International Affairs, Tel. 202/272-2306

SMITHSONIAN INSTITUTION
1000 Jefferson Drive, SW
Washington, DC 20560
Tel. 202/357-1300
Web site: *www. si.edu*

The Smithsonian Institution is responsible for promoting historical, technological, scientific, and artistic knowledge of the Nation. It does this by presenting exhibits, conducting research, publishing studies, and participating in cooperative international programs of scholarly exchange. Its international-related activities are found in numerous positions throughout the organization, including the museums and galleries. However, the largest concentration of international specialists are found in:

- **International Center:** Tel. 202/357-4795
- **Woodrow Wilson International Center for Scholars:** Tel. 202/357-2429

U.S. INFORMATION AGENCY (USIA)
301 Fourth Street, SW
Washington, DC 20547
Tel. 202/619-4700
Web site: *www.usia.gov*

USIA, known abroad as the United States Information Service or USIS, is responsible for U.S. overseas information and cultural programs, including the Voice of America. It is involved in a wide range of overseas communication activities—from academic and cultural exchanges to press, radio, television, film, seminar, library, and cultural centered programs. It maintains a full-time staff abroad which is primarily recruited and promoted through the Foreign Service. In October 1998, Congress decided to merge this independent agency into the U.S. Department of State.

U.S. INSTITUTE OF PEACE
1200 17th Street, NW
Suite 2000
Washington, DC 200036-3006
Tel. 202/429-6063
Web site: *www.usip.org*

Created in 1984, the U.S. Institute of Peace, an independent, nonpartisan federal institution created and funded by Congress, is responsible for strengthening the Nation's ability to promote international peace and the peaceful resolution of conflicts throughout the world. It does this by providing grants and fellowships to individual scholars, conducting in-house research, and sponsoring educational activities.

U.S. INTERNATIONAL DEVELOPMENT COOPERATION AGENCY
Ronald Reagan Building
Washington, DC 20523-0016
Tel. 202/647-1850

This is the Nation's major international development organization which consists of three organizations: U.S. Agency for International Development (USAID), U.S. Trade and Development Program, and the Overseas Private Investment Corporation. It's also one of the more controversial government agencies given its changing international missions following the collapse of the Soviet Union and the ending of the Cold War. Major cutbacks and reorganizations during the past decade have had a negative impact on morale throughout the agency. A recent ambitious yet disastrous attempt to install a state-of-the-art computer system to integrate USAID worldwide has thrown this sometimes arrogant agency into amazing disarray.

U.S. AGENCY FOR INTERNATIONAL DEVELOPMENT (USAID)
Ronald Reagan Building
Washington, DC 20523-0016
Tel. 202/712-4810
Web site: *www.info.usaid.gov*

The Agency for International Development is responsible for developing and implementing U.S. economic assistance programs aimed at developing countries. This is the single most important U.S. government agency involved in the developing world which encompasses nearly 75 percent of the world's population. It defines the focus and provides the funding for a great deal of public and private sector development efforts in Third and Fourth World countries. AID missions abroad are staffed with project officers and specialists in agriculture, rural development, health, nutrition, population planning, education, human resource development, private sector development, environment, and energy. It provides billions of dollars in funds for projects that are implemented by the many private contractors, nonprofit organizations, and PVOs outlined in subsequent chapters. Although not a part of the Department of State, entry into most AID positions is via the Foreign Service. AID is primarily organized by both area (Africa Bureau; Asia, Near East, and Europe Bureau; Latin America and the Caribbean Bureau) and program offices (Trade and Development Programs; Private Enterprise Bureau; U.S. Foreign Disaster Assistance; Food for Peace and Voluntary Assistance Bureau; and Program and Policy Coordination Bureau).

U.S. TRADE AND DEVELOPMENT PROGRAM
Room 309
State Annex 16
Washington, DC 20523-1602
Tel. 703/875-4357
Web site: *www.tda.gov*

Established in 1988 as an independent agency within the International Development Cooperation Agency, the Trade and Development Program promotes economic development in Third World and middle-income development countries through the export of U.S. goods and services. It sponsors feasibility studies conducted by U.S. firms for high-priority development projects to be funded by the World Bank, other international lending institutions, or through host country resources.

OVERSEAS PRIVATE INVESTMENT CORPORATION
1100 New York Avenue, NW
Washington, DC 20527
Tel. 202/336-8799
Fax 202/336-8700

The Overseas Private Investment Corporation assists U.S. companies in making profitable investments in over 100 developing countries. While helping companies minimize investment risks abroad, the Corporation also encourages investment projects that will assist countries with social and economic development. It provides U.S. investors with assistance in finding investment opportunities, insurance to protect investments, and loans and loan guaranties to help finance their projects.

U.S. INTERNATIONAL TRADE COMMISSION
500 E Street, SW
Washington, DC 20436
Tel. 202/205-2000

The International Trade Commission is responsible for providing the President, Congress, and other government agencies with studies, reports, and recommendations relating to international trade and tariffs. Its major activities involve conducting investigations, public hearings, and research projects concerning the international policies of the U.S. as well as the trade and tariff policies of other countries that affect U.S. trade and trade negotiations. For example, the Commission's work plays an important role in selecting items included in the Generalized System of Preferences (GSP), identifying unfair import practices, and interference with U.S. agricultural programs. Since much of its work involves laws, rules, and regulations, this organization is heavily staffed with lawyers.

U.S. POSTAL SERVICE
475 L'Enfant Plaza West, SW
Washington, DC 20260-0010
Tel. 202/268-2000
Web site: *www.usps.gov*

The U.S. Postal Service is responsible for the orderly processing and delivery of mail. Since its work involves international mail—individuals, businesses, and military—the U.S. Postal Service is increasingly involved in international matters. Its major international interests are centered in the **International and Military Mail Operations Division** (Tel. 202/268-4365). The U.S. Postal Service operates its own personnel system separate from other government agencies.

U.S. Congress

The U.S. Congress is very much involved in the international arena. International job opportunities are found on "Capitol Hill" (Senate and House personal and committee staffs) as well as amongst congressional agencies. While not as numerous as executive departments and agencies, nonetheless, many international positions are available in this branch of government. These positions often become "stepping stones" to other international positions in the executive departments and with private firms.

Finding a job with a congressional agency is similar to finding a job with an executive agency—contact the agency directly for information on vacancies and application procedures. It's best to start with the agency's Web site for vacancy and application information.

Agencies

Congressional agencies are the bureaucratic equivalent to executive agencies. They are responsible to and under the control of Congress rather than the Executive branch. Reflecting the international interests and work of Congress, these agencies offer several international opportunities for enterprising job seekers. Congressional agencies with the largest number of international activities include the Library of Congress, Congressional Budget Office, and the General Accounting Office.

THE LIBRARY OF CONGRESS
101 Independence Avenue, SE
Washington, DC 20540
Tel. 202/707-5000
Web site: *http//:lcweb.loc.gov*

The Library of Congress is the national library. It maintains an extensive collection of documents, provides important publishing and library services, and serves as a critical information base for Congress. Its international activities are found in several offices but especially in the **Congressional Research Service** which provides congressional committees and members of Congress with information on questions relating to their day-to-day work, including foreign policy matters. Other offices involved in international matters include:

- **Collections Services:** Acquisitions Office, Overseas Operations, Tel. 202/707-5273
- **Constituent Services:** Public Service and Collection Management— African-Middle Eastern Division (Tel. 202/707-7937) and Asian Division (Tel. 202/707-5420), both located at 2nd and Independence Ave., SE, Washington, DC 20540; European Division (Tel. 202/707-5414) and Hispanic Division (Tel. 202/707-5400)

CONGRESSIONAL BUDGET OFFICE
Ford House Office Building
2nd and D Streets, SW
Washington, DC 20515
Tel. 202/226-2621
Web site: *www.cbo.gov*

The Congressional Budget Office is Congress' counterpart to the Executive's Office of Management and Budget. It provides Congress with basic budget data as well as analyzes alternative fiscal, budgetary, and programmatic policy issues. Its international activities are centered in the **International Affairs Unit** of the office of Fiscal Analysis (Tel. 202/226-2761).

GENERAL ACCOUNTING OFFICE (GAO)
441 G Street, NW
Washington, DC 20548
Tel. 202/512-3000
Web site: *www.gao.gov*

The General Accounting Office is the investigative arm of Congress which is responsible for examining all matters relating to the receipt and disbursement of public funds. As such, it closely monitors and audits all executive agencies involved in international matters, especially the Department of State, Department of Defense, and the U.S. Agency for International Development. Its major international activities are centered in the office of **National Security and International**

Affairs. However, other offices within GAO also have international responsibilities (General Counsel, Tel. 202/275-5205, Accounting and Financial Management, Tel. 202/275-9459).

Congress

International positions within Congress are found in two different areas:

- on personal staffs of members of the House and Senate
- on committee staffs within both the House and Senate

Both the House and Senate have their own administrative staffs, but these have little to do with international matters other than foreign travel.

Senate

International jobs opportunities in the Senate center on the staffs of the following committees and subcommittees:

- **Appropriations:** Foreign Operations, Tel. 202/224-7284
- **Banking, House, and Urban Affairs:** International Finance and Monetary Policy, Tel. 202/224-7391
- **Budget:** Tel. 202/224-0642
- **Commerce, Science, and Transportation:** Foreign Commerce and Tourism, Tel. 202/224-9325.
- **Finance:** International Trade; International Debt; Tel. 202/224-4515
- **Foreign Relations:** Tel. 202/224-4651
- **Judiciary:** Immigration and Refugee Affairs, Tel. 202/224-7878
- **Intelligence Select Committee:** Tel. 202/224-1700

Senators who chair or are members of these committees and subcommittees also hire staff members who are responsible for international-related issues. Each Senator hires one to four Legislative Assistants and other staffers who are responsible for foreign affairs, foreign relations, foreign trade, military, arms control, intelligence, human rights, immigration, refugee, and international drug and terrorism issues.

House of Representatives

International positions in the House of Representatives follow the same pattern as in the Senate—committee and subcommittee staffs and personal staffs. House committees and subcommittees with international specialists include the following:

- **Agriculture:** Department of Operations and Nutrition, Research, and Foreign Agriculture and Hunger, Tel. 202/225-1867
- **Appropriations:** Defense, Tel. 202/225-2847; Foreign Operations, Export Financing, and Related Programs, Tel. 202/225-2041
- **Armed Services:** Tel. 202/225-4151
- **Banking, Finance, and Urban Affairs:** International Development, Finance, Trade, and Monetary Policy, Tel. 202/226-7515
- **Budget:** 202/226-7234
- **Foreign Affairs:** 202/225-5021
- **Judiciary:** Immigration, Refugees, and International Law, Tel. 202/225-5727
- **Science, Space, and Technology:** International Advisor, Tel. 202/226-6375
- **Ways and Means:** Trade, Tel. 202/225-3625
- **Intelligence Select Committee:** Tel. 202/225-4121

Several members of the House of Representatives also designate one to three Legislative Assistants or other staff members to handle international-related issues. Like their Senate counterparts, these individuals are also responsible for other policy areas which may or may not be related to international concerns.

Key Resources

If you are interested in pursuing international jobs with the federal government, we recommend the following books and computer software programs:

➤ *How to Find an Overseas Job With the U.S. Government,* Will Cantrell and Francine Modderno (Oakton, VA: WorldWise Books, 1992, $28.95). The only book to focus exclusively on international positions within the federal government. Includes an extensive section on the State Department and profiles many other agencies. Describes agencies, qualifications required, and application procedures. Currently out of print. May be difficult to find.

➤ *Find a Federal Job Fast: How to Cut the Red Tape and Get Hired,* Ron and Caryl Krannich (Manassas Park, VA: Impact Publications, 1999, $15.95). A basic primer on how to find a federal job. Dispels myths and covers everything from application procedures to networking and interviewing.

➤ *Federal Applications That Get Results: From SF-171s to Federal-Style Resumes,* Russ Smith (Manassas Park, VA: Impact Publications, 1996, $23.95). The definitive guide to completing the all-important federal applications—Standard Form 171, OF-612, and federal-style resumes. Outlines what federal employers look for on these applications, major writing principles, and the best language to use. Includes examples.

➤ *Quick and Easy Federal Jobs Kit* (Harrisburg, PA: DataTech, 1998). This easy-to-use computerized program produces SF 171s, OF-612s, and federal-style resumes on blank paper. Uses most printers on the market. Direct support provided for over 50 dot matrix printers, the DeskJet 500, and laser printers that are compatible with the Hewlett Packard LaserJet II. Prints the form which is approved by OPM. Available in 4 versions: Personal (single user only, $49.95); Family (2 users only, $59.95); Office (8 users only, $129.95); and Professional/ Organization (unlimited users, $399.95).

➤ *Federal Career Opportunities* (Vienna, VA: Federal Research Service). This comprehensive listing of current federal job vacancies includes 3,400 positions from grades GS5 thru SES in each issue. Organized by GS series within each agency. Published biweekly as a 64-90 page directory. Subscriptions: 6 issues, $39; 26 issues (1 year), $175. APO/FPO subscribers should add $1 per issue for first-class shipping.

➤ *Federal Jobs Digest* (Ossining, NY: Breakthrough Publications). Largest source of current job openings listing over 15,000 immediate civil service vacancies in the US and overseas in each issue. Published biweekly: 6 issues, $29; 25 issues (1 year), $110.

All of these resources are available directly through the individual publishers or they can be purchased through Impact Publications (see the order form at the end of this book).

3

International Organizations

International organizations provide numerous job opportunities for global specialists who are interested in a variety of issues relating to international economic and social development as well as regional security. The largest employer of international specialists is the United Nations (UN) bureaucracy and its complex of affiliated organizations. While the UN is headquartered in New York City, its many specialized agencies are spread throughout the world. A majority of these offices are headquartered in Geneva, Brussels, Vienna, Rome, Montreal, and Washington, DC.

Many other international organizations employ international specialists. The World Bank, for example, offers excellent job opportunities for individuals with expertise in international economics and finance. Like many other jobs in the UN system, positions with the World Bank tend to be well paid and come with numerous benefits. Compensation, benefits, and perks with these organizations are much better than with the U.S. government.

Job Outlook

Many international organizations, such as the United Nations and the World Bank, have been undergoing major cutbacks in personnel during the past five years. The World Bank, for example, receives nearly 30,000

applications each year for 200 professional positions it actually fills—
and the World Bank expects the number of vacancies to decrease during
the next three years! Many U.N. agencies remain under hiring freezes or
are downsizing their personnel due to budgetary shortfalls and political
pressure from the United States to overhaul what appears to be an
extremely bloated bureaucracy. Consequently, competition is very keen
for what few positions become available. You'll need to put together a
terrific application and hopefully have some "inside connections" to help
you through these highly competitive international employment arenas.

Hiring Practices and the Internet

Each international organization has its own hiring procedures. Indeed,
even within the United Nations, much of the hiring is decentralized to the
individual agencies. Therefore, it's important to understand the structure
and function of each organization in order to properly approach it. Many
of these organizations purposefully discriminate by only hiring individuals from member states. Fortunately,
most international organizations now
have their own Web sites, which include
a great deal of information on the organization as well as job vacancy announcements and application procedures, including online application forms that can
be downloaded and printed. Some agencies accept emailed resumes or those
transmitted in ASCII format. Since a
great deal of this international hiring is
wired via the Internet, it is to your advantage to conduct much of your job
search on the Internet.

> Most international organiza-
> tions now have their own Web
> sites which include informa-
> tion on the organization as
> well as job announcements
> and application procedures,
> including application forms.

If you are not using the Internet in your international job search, you
will simply be at a distinct disadvantage since much of the hiring process
with international organizations has moved online. Internet savvy job
seekers can now quickly access employment information on the United
Nations and its agencies, the World Bank, the Asian Development Bank,
or the Organization of American States by visiting these organizations'
Web sites. Writing, calling, or faxing their personnel or human resources
departments for job information will be a great waste of your time and

their time. Indeed, if you call these organizations for information, you will most likely be told *"all the information about our organization and employment opportunities is on our Web site."* As a potential employer, I would not be impressed by someone who doesn't use the Internet—an indication they lack proper skills for the 21st century! Do everyone a favor and follow our rule for finding an international job: *"You got to get wired if you want to get hired!"*

In this chapter we include several Internet sites to assist you in your research. Since international organizations and their employment needs are constantly changing, you are well advised to *first* visit their Web sites for the latest information on employment needs and opportunities. The sites will answer many of your questions. Only after reviewing the content of a site should you phone, fax, or write for information. Do not send a resume to any of our addresses until you understand the application procedures. In many cases, you must complete an agency application form as well as submit a lengthy curriculum vita, which is not the same as a pithy one- or two-page American resume.

> **International organizations tend to hire professionals with a great deal of international experience and higher educational degrees.**

International organizations tend to hire professionals with a great deal of international experience and higher educational degrees. Many positions within the United Nations and the World Bank, for example, involve research, writing, consulting, and meeting skills as well as procurement—obligating funds for projects. Indeed, if you are interested in getting involved in the nitty-gritty of development—working with people at the local level on development projects—becoming employed by one of these international organizations may frustrate you. Few of these organizations are involved in implementing projects. At best, they fund the implementation activities of government agencies, contractors, and nonprofit organizations and host frequent meetings where they function as forums for "exchanging ideas". The United Nations, for example, is well noted for its culture of meetings, reports, and consultation. However, it does get involved in many "field operations" through the United Nations Development Program (UNDP) and various Peacekeeping operations. If you are interested in working for one of these organizations, you may quickly discover that you are competing with many other individuals who have lengthy resumes that demonstrate their extensive international-relevant education, research, writing, consulting, and meeting skills.

The international organizations outlined in this chapter represent the major ones employing U.S. citizens. Numerous other international organizations also provide job opportunities for enterprising job seekers. If you are interested in exploring additional international organizations, we recommend consulting the following directories:

- *Encyclopedia of Associations: International Organizations*
- *Europa World Year Book*
- *The World Factbook* (CIA)
- *Yearbook of International Organizations*

Current volumes of these directories are available in most major libraries. But if you are using the Internet, you can easily access the CIA's useful *World Factbook* online by going to the agency's Web site:

www.odci.gov/cia/publications/factbook

While most of this book is devoted to country profiles, Appendix C ("International Organizations and Groups") includes basic information on the UN and other major international organizations *(www.odci.gov/ cia/publications/factbook/app-frame.html)*

United Nations and Its Specialized Agencies

The United Nations offers numerous international job opportunities within the Secretariat and specialized agencies. It is the largest employer of international specialists with a bureaucracy of nearly 65,000 individuals working in over 600 duty stations throughout the world. Fewer than 10 percent of the UN civil servants are U.S. citizens.

The Organization

A mammoth organization, the United Nations consists of six major organizational units and numerous specialized and autonomous agencies, standing committees, commissions, and other subsidiary bodies. Given the decentralized nature of the United Nations, all specialized agencies and related organizations recruit their own personnel. The six principal

United Nations organs are:

- General Assembly
- Security Council
- Economic and Social Council
- Trusteeship Council
- International Court of Justice
- Secretariat

While job opportunities are available with all of these organs, the most numerous jobs are found with the Economic and Social Council and the UN Secretariat.

The **Economic and Social Council** is under the General Assembly. It coordinates the economic and social work of the United Nations and numerous specialized agencies, standing committees, commissions, and related organizations. The work of the Council involves international development, world trade, industrialization, natural resources, human rights, status of women, population, social welfare, science and technology, crime prevention, and other social and economic issues. Its overall goal is to promote world cooperation on economic, social, cultural, and humanitarian problems.

The Economic and Social Council is divided into a headquarters staff in New York City and five regional economic commissions:

- Economic Commission for Africa (Addis Ababa)
- Economic and Social Commission for Asia and the Pacific (Bangkok)
- Economic Commission for Europe (Geneva)
- Economic Commission for Latin America and the Caribbean (Santiago)
- Economic Commission for Western Asia (Beirut)

Each Commission maintains a large staff of specialists. Furthermore, they promote the work of several standing committees and commissions which also have their own staffs.

Specialized or intergovernmental agencies are autonomous organizations linked to the United Nations by special intergovernmental agreements. In addition, they have their own membership, budgets, personnel systems, legislative and executive bodies, and secretariats. The Food and

Agriculture Organization (FAO), for example, consists of a staff drawn from 184 member nations. It is administered by a professional staff of nearly 3,200 which is headquartered in Rome; some employees work in FAO regional offices located in Ghana, Thailand, Chile, New York City, and Washington, DC. Each year the FAO hires nearly 500 staff members; 60 to 65 of these new hirees are U.S. citizens.

The Economic and Social Council coordinates the work of these organizations with the United Nations as well as with each other. Altogether, there are 12 specialized agencies:

- Food and Agriculture Organization (FAO)
- International Civil Aviation Organization (ICAO)
- International Fund for Agricultural Development (IFAD)
- International Labour Organization (ILO)
- International Maritime Organization (IMO)
- International Monetary Fund (IMF)
- International Telecommunication Union (ITU)
- United Nations Educational, Scientific, and Cultural Organization (UNESCO)
- United Nations Industrial Development Organization (UNIDO)
- Universal Postal Union (UPU)
- World Health Organization (WHO)
- World Intellectual Property Organization (WIPO)
- World Meteorological Organization (WMO)

Several other major organizations also are attached to the Economic and Social Council as well as the Secretariat. These consist of:

- International Seabed Authority (ISA)
- International Atomic Energy Agency (IAEA)
- International Bank for Reconstruction and Development (IBRD or World Bank)
- Office of the United Nations Disaster Relief Co-ordinator (UNDRO)
- United Nations Centre for Human Settlements (HABITAT)
- United Nations Children's Fund (UNICEF)
- United Nations Conference on Trade and Development (UNCTAD)
- United Nations Development Programme (UNDP)
- United Nations Environment Programme (UNEP)

- United Nations Fund for Population Activities (UNFPA)
- United Nations High Commission for Refugees (UNHCR)
- United Nations Industrial Development Organization (UNIDO)
- United Nations Institute for Training and Research (UNITAR)
- United Nations International Drug Control Programme (UNDCP)
- United Nations Observer Mission and Peacekeeping Forces in the Middle East
- United Nations Relief and Works Agency for Palestine Refugees in the Near East (UNRWA)
- World Food Council (WFC)
- World Food Programme (WFP)
- World Trade Organization (WTO)

The UN Secretariat employs nearly 14,000 international civil servants from 160 countries. Most are stationed at the United Nations headquarters in New York City. The Secretariat is the central "bureaucracy" in charge of carrying out the day-to-day work of the United Nations.

The largest UN agencies—those employing at least 1,500 individuals—consist of the following:

- Food and Agriculture Organization
- International Labor Organization
- International Monetary Fund
- UNESCO
- UNICEF
- United Nations Development Programme
- World Bank
- World Health Organization

The United States is especially involved in the following United Nations organizations which are headquartered in various cities throughout the world:

- Food and Agricultural Organization (Rome)
- International Atomic Energy Agency (Vienna)
- International Bank For Reconstruction and Development, or popularly known as the World Bank (Washington, DC)
- International Civil Aviation Organization (Montreal)

- International Finance Corporation (Washington, DC)
- International Monetary Fund (Washington, DC)
- International Telecommunication Union (Geneva)
- Universal Postal Union (Bern, Switzerland)
- World Health Organization (Geneva)

Consequently, U.S. citizens may have a much higher probability of landing jobs with these UN agencies than with other agencies that tend to favor hiring nationals from other member countries.

Hiring Process

Since the hiring process is largely decentralized within the United Nations and among the specialized agencies and related organizations, you should directly contact each agency for job vacancy information. The good news is that the UN personnel system is highly wired via the Internet. You can easily access information on agencies and job vacancies by visiting several Web sites. One of the first places to start is the U.S. Department of State's gateway Web site to the UN hiring system:

www.state.gov/www/issues/un_contacts.html

From here you can link to the UN Secretariat's Office of Human Resource Management and the personnel offices of various regional economic commissions and agencies. The UN Secretariat's Office of Human Resource Management includes a great deal of information on application procedures and vacancies. Go to their Web site first. Most other UN human resources offices have Web sites, although a few still must be contacted by fax or mail. These contacts will get you started:

➤ **United Nations Secretariat**
Office of Human Resource Management
Room, S-2500
United Nations
New York, NY 10017
Fax 212/963-3134
Web site: *www.un.org/Depts/OHRM*

➤ **Economic Commission For Africa (ECA)**
P.O. Box 3001
Addis Ababa, Ethiopia
Fax 251-1-514-416

➤ **Economic Commission For Europe (ECE)**
Palais des Nations
CH-1211 Geneva 10, Switzerland
Fax 41-22-917-0123

➤ **Economic Commission For Latin America (ECLAC)**
Casilla, 179-D
Santiago, Chile
Fax 562-2080252

➤ **Economic and Social Commission For Asian and the Pacific (ESCAP)**
UN Building, Rajdamnern Avenue
Bangkok 10200, Thailand
Fax 66-2-281-4508 or 282-9602

➤ **Food and Agriculture Organization of the United Nations (FAO)**
Viale delle Caracalla
00100 Rome, Italy
Fax 39-6-5705-4329/6910/5131
Web site: *www.fao.org/va/employ.htm*

  FAO Liaison Office for North America
  1001 22nd St., NW, Suite 300
  Washington, DC 20437
  Fax 202/653-5760

➤ **International Atomic Energy Agency (IAEA)**
Wagramerstrasse 5, P.O. Box 100
A-1400 Vienna, Austria
Fax 43-1-20607
Web site: *www.iaea.or.at/worldatom/vacancies*

➤ **International Civil Aviation Organization (ICAO)**
1000 Sherbrooke Street West, Suite 400
Montreal, Quebec H3A2R2, Canada
Fax 514/288-4772
Web site: *www.icao.int/cgi/goto.pl?icao/en/vacancy.htm*

➤ **International Fund For Agricultural Development (IFAD)**
Via del Serafico 107
00142 Rome, Italy
Fax 39-6-504-3463
Web site: *www.unicc.org/ifad/vac395en.html*

➤ **International Labor Organization (ILO)**
4, route des Morillons
CH 1211 Geneva 22, Switzerland
Fax 41-22-798-86-85

    Washington Branch Office
    1828 L Street, NW, Suite 801
    Washington, DC 20036
    Fax 202/653-7687

➤ **International Maritime Organization (IMO)**
4 Albert Embankment
London, SE17SR, England
Fax 171-587-3210

➤ **International Telecommunications Union (ITU)**
Palais des Nations
CH-1211 Geneva 20, Switzerland
Fax 41-22-733-72-56
Web site: *www.itu.int.itudoc/GS/vacancy/1998.html*

➤ **International Trade Center (ITC)**
Palais des Nations
CH-1211 Geneva 10, Switzerland
Fax 41-22-730-06-03

➤ **Pan American Health Organization (PAHO)**
525 23rd Street., NW
Washington, DC 20037
Fax 202/861-3379
Web site: *www.paho.org/english/apl/aplvacan.htm*

➤ **United Nations Center For Human Settlements (HABITAT)**
P.O. Box 30030
Nairobi, Kenya
Fax 25-42-226473

➤ **United Nations Children's Fund (UNICEF)**
3 UN Plaza (H-5F)
New York, NY 10017
Fax 212/326-7536

➤ **United Nations Conference On Trade and Development
   (UNCTAD)**
Palais des Nations
CH 1211 Geneva 10, Switzerland
Fax 41-22-917-0123

➤ **United Nations Development Program (UNDP)**
One United Nations Plaza
New York, NY 10017
Fax 212/906-5282
Web site: *www.undp.org*

➤ **United Nations Educational, Scientific, and Cultural
   Organization (UNESCO)**
7 Place de Fontenoy
75700 Paris, France
Fax 3-1-45-67-16-90
Web site: *www.unesco.org/general/eng/about/recrut.html*

➤ **United Nations Environment Program (UNEP)**
P.O. Box 67578
Nairobi, Kenya
Fax 25-42-217-839/622-615

Washington Office
1775 K Street, NW
Washington, DC 20006
Fax 202/331-9333

➤ **United Nations Fund For Population Activities (UNFPA)**
220 East 42nd Street
New York, NY 10017
Fax 212/297-4908
Web site: *www.unfpa.org/ABOUT/EMPLOYM.HTM*

➤ **United Nations High Commissioner For Refugees (UNHCR)**
Palais des Nations
CH 1211 Geneva, Switzerland
Fax 41-22-739-8475

Washington Office
1775 K Street, NW
Washington, DC 20006
Fax 202/296-5660

➤ **United Nations Industrial Development Organization (UNIDO)**
Recruitment Section, VIC, Room E0544
P.O. Box 300
A-1400 Vienna, Austria
Fax 43-1-232-156/230-7004
Web site: *unido.org/start/services/vacancies/navigator.htmls*

➤ **United Nations Institute For Training and Research (UNITAR)**
Palais des Nations
CH-1211 Geneva 10, Switzerland
Fax 41-22-733-13-83

➤ **United Nations International Drug Control Program (UNDCP)**
UNOV, Room E-1045, VIC
P.O. Box 500
A-1400 Vienna, Austria
Fax 43-1-237-496
Web site: *www.undcp.org/vacancy/index.htm*

➤ **United Nations Office/Geneva**
Palais des Nations
CH-1211 Geneva 10, Switzerland
Fax 41-22-917-0123

➤ **United Nations Office/VIENNA**
Room D0439, VIC, P.O. Box 500
A-1400 Vienna, Austria
Fax 43-1-237-496
Web site: *www.un.or.at/Vacancy-Announcements/index.html*

➤ **United Nations Relief and Works Agency For Palestine**
  Refugees in the Near East (UNRWA)
Chief, Recruitment Division
P.O. Box 371
Gaza City, Israel
Fax 00972-7-822-552

➤ **United Nations University**
53-70 Jingumae, 5-ChomeShibuya-ku
Tokyo 150, Japan
Fax 81-3-3499-2828

➤ **United Nations Volunteers**
(ATTN: HRU-E1) Palais des Nations
CH-1211 Geneva 10, Switzerland
Fax 41-22-788-5854
Web site: *www.unv.org/unvols/index.htm*

  Or, contact Peace Corps
  1111 20th Street, NW
  Washington, DC 20526
  Web site: *www.peacecorps.gov*

➤ **Universal Postal Union (UPU)**
Weltpoststrasse 4
Bern, Switzerland
Fax 41-31-43-22-10

➤ **World Food Programme (WFP)**
HHR, Via Cristoforo Colombo 426
00145 Rome, Italy
Fax 39-6-596-02348/02111
Web site: *www.wfp.org/vacancies/index.html*

➤ **World Health Organization (WHO)**
20 Avenue Appia
CH-1211 Geneva 27, Switzerland
Fax 41-22-791-0746
Web site: *www.who.int/per.vacancies/index.htm*

Washington Office
1775 K Street, NW
Washington, DC 20006
Fax 202-331-9097

➤ **World Intellectual Property Organization (WIPO)**
34 Chemin des Colombettes
CH-1211 Geneva 2, Switzerland
Fax 41-22-734-2326
Web site: *www.wipo.int/eng/vacancy/index.htm*

➤ **World Meteorological Organization (WMO)**
Case Postale No. 2300
CH-1211 Geneva 2, Switzerland
Fax 41-22-734-23-26
Web site: *www.wmo.ch/web/gcos/vacancy.htm*

➤ **World Trade Organization (WTO)**
Centre William Rappard
Rue de Lausanne 154
CH-1211 Geneva 21, Switzerland
Fax 41-22-739-57-72

The U.S. Department of State assists U.S. citizens in finding employment with the United Nations, its specialized agencies, and other international organizations. Its UN Employment Information and Assistance Unit is responsible for improving American participation in UN programs by providing employment information through its "Fact Sheet" and by maintaining electronic linkages with various UN agencies. A good starting place for conducting a job search with various UN agencies is this helpful U.S. State Department office:

> Staffing Management Officer
> UN Employment Information and Assistance Unit
> Bureau of International Organization Affairs
> IO/S/EA—Room 4808
> Department of State
> Washington, DC 20520
> Tel. 202/647-3396

Before contacting this office by mail or phone, please visit its informative Web site which will probably answer most of your questions about UN employment:

www.state.gov/www/issues/ioemployment.html

This site takes you to the Unit's "Fact Sheet: Employment Opportunities" which provides a wealth of information on employment with the United Nations, including a listing of International Vacancy Announcements which is updated biweekly. The "Fact Sheet" provides information on employment opportunities and requirements; professional and senior positions; short term emergency relief and peacekeeping positions; translator and interpreter positions; secretary positions; other positions; grade structure, salaries, and related allowances; U.S. government assistance; and a list of U.S. government agencies involved in recruiting for UN positions. For example, you'll learn that the UN's typical employee has the following characteristics:

> A 40-year-old economist, with a minimum of a masters degree, some international field experience, who has fluency in at least one of the official languages of the organization (Arabic, Chinese, English, French, Russian, Spanish) and a strong working knowledge of at least one other.

You'll also learn there are very few UN openings available for Junior Applicants—students, recent college graduates, or persons lacking pertinent experience or language skills. The UN regularly recruits for the following professional positions: administrative, agriculture/forestry, demography, development, economics, engineering, information systems, legal, political/international affairs, public health, public information, social welfare, statistics, teaching, and telecommunications. The UN also recruits for short-term (usually one-year) relief and peacekeeping positions relating to election monitoring, emergency relief, transportation, and logistics. The UN Department of Peacekeeping Operations (Staffing Unit, Rm. S-2280A, New York, NY 10017) has recently recruited for the following positions:

➤ Air Operations and Safety Officers
➤ Assets Managers (Supply and Inventory Control)
➤ Building and Facilities Managers (Engineers)
➤ Local Transport Managers
➤ Finance Officers and Managers (with computer background)
➤ Satellite Communications Technicians
➤ Procurement Officers
➤ Contract Officers
➤ Legal Affairs Officers

The UN also operates a few special employment programs: UN Guides, Intern Programs (for graduate students), and UN Volunteers. You'll need to arrange personnel interviews for these positions which usually take place in the fall. Contact UN headquarters in New York for information on these opportunities: United Nations Central Employment Service, Room DC-200, New York, NY 10017, Tel. 212/754-8841).

Several federal government agencies recruit and refer candidates to UN technical and specialized agencies. The following federal agencies recruit for the UN and other international organizations:

U.S. counterpart agency	UN agency
U.S. Agency for International Development (USAID) Washington, DC	FAO, WFP, UNDP
Department of Agriculture 14th & Independence Ave. Washington, DC 20250	FAO, WFC, IFAD, OECD, IICA
Department of Commerce Washington, DC 20230	UN, GATT, OECD, ILO, WIPO, Econ. Comm's.

Department of Energy	IAEA, UNEP
Office of International Affairs	
Washington, DC 20545	
Department. of Health and Human Services (HHS)	WHO, PAHO
Office of International Health	
Public Health Services	
5600 Fishers Lane	
Rockville, MD 20852	
Environmental Protection Agency	UNEP
Washington, DC	
Federal Aviation Administration	ICAO
Office of International Organization Aviation Affairs	
Department of Transportation	
Washington, DC 20553	
National Oceanic and Atmospheric Administration (NOAA)	WMO, FAO
Office of International Affairs	
Washington Science Center	
Building 5	
Rockville, MD 20852	
U.S. Postal Service	UPU
International Postal Affairs	
Washington, DC 20260	
U.S. Department of Justice	UNDCP
Drug Enforcement Administration	
600 Army-Navy Drive	
Arlington, VA 22202	

Secretariat and Special Programs

UNITED NATIONS HIGH COMMISSIONER FOR REFUGEES
Office of Recruitment, Career Development and Placement
94, rue Ruppard, Momtbrillant
CH-1202 Geneva, Switzerland
Tel. 41-22-7398111 or Fax 41-22-7397377

Responsible for protecting refugees throughout the world. Coordinates international relief efforts for refugees. Maintains a professional staff of 2,500 in 80 countries. Its New York and Washington offices have 10 staff members. For

U.S.-based positions, contact: Washington Liaison Office, UNHCR, 1718 Connecticut Avenue, NW, Suite 200, Washington, DC 20009.

UNITED NATIONS CHILDRENS' FUND (UNICEF)
Chief, Recruitment and Staff Development Section
3 United Nations Plaza
New York, NY 10017
Tel. 212/326-7000 or Fax 212/888-7465

Conducts programs to protect children and enhance their development. Involved in maternal health, child nutrition, sanitation, and training programs. Helps equip health centers, schools, and day-care and community centers. Has a professional staff of nearly 1,700 (150 U.S. citizens) operating from 100 field offices. Main offices are located in New York, Tokyo, Geneva, and Copenhagen. The New York office alone employs nearly 300. Total staff nearly 7,000.

UNITED NATIONS DEVELOPMENT PROGRAMME
Chief, Recruitment Section, Division of Personnel
1 United Nations Plaza
New York, NY 10017
Tel. 212/906-5315 or Fax 212/906-5364
Web site: *www.undp.org*

The official development agency of the United Nations, UNDP provides financial and technical assistance to developing countries in numerous fields, from agriculture to education and housing. Has a professional staff of nearly 1000 operating through a network of 115 field offices. Also supports nearly 20,000 technical experts and consultants who work on projects funded and monitored by UNDP but implemented by the specialized UN agencies.

UNITED NATIONS ENVIRONMENT PROGRAM (UNEP)
Chief, Recruitment Union, P.O. Box 30552
Nairobi, Kenya
Tel. 254-2-621234 or Fax 254-2-622624
Web site: *www.unep.org*

A small coordinating body that monitors environmental issues and initiatives for the UN. Employs nearly 300 professionals who are stationed in 15 countries.

UNITED NATIONS POPULATION FUND
220 East 42nd St.
New York, NY 10017-5880
Tel. 212/297-5020
Web site: *www.unfpa.org*

Supports population and family planning by coordinating information and providing financial and technical assistance to both developing and developed countries. Functions as the focal point for strengthening government population and family planning programs.

UNITED NATIONS INDUSTRIAL DEVELOPMENT ORGANIZATION (UNIDO)
Vienna International Centre
P.O. Box 300
A-1400 Vienna, Austria
Tel. 43-1-21130
Fax 43-1-232156

Promotes industrial development in developing countries by providing information and financial assistance for industrial projects. Has a staff of nearly 1,400. Operates offices in New York and Washington, DC. Hires nearly 2,000 experts and consultants for special projects. The U.S. withdrew from UNIDO in 1996, which affects the future employment of U.S. citizens.

UNITED NATIONS INSTITUTE FOR TRAINING AND RESEARCH (UNITAR)
Chief, Program Support Service
801 United Nations Plaza
New York, NY 10017
Tel. 212/370-1122

Conducts research on problems facing the international community as well as provides training for UN officials and officials of members' governments. Has a professional staff of 50 based in Geneva, Rome, Nairobi, and New York.

UNITED NATIONS RELIEF AND WORKS AGENCY FOR PALESTINE REFUGEES IN THE NEAR EAST (UNRWA)
Chief, Personnel Services Division
P.O. Box 371
Gaza City, Israel
Tel. 7-861196 or Fax 7-822552

Provides refugee relief services in the areas of health, education, and welfare for Palestinian refugees living in Lebanon, Syria, East Jordan, and the West Bank. Operates nearly 600 schools staffed with more than 8,000 Palestinian teachers. Has a staff of 150 based in Vienna, Lebanon, Syria, Jordan, and Israel.

UNITED NATIONS UNIVERSITY
53-70 Jingumae
5-ChomeShibuya-ku
Tokyo 150, Japan
Fax 81-3-3499-2828

Offers educational programs focusing on the problems of developing countries, such as hunger, water resources, human rights, international trade, and law.

UNITED NATIONS VOLUNTEERS
Palais des Nations
CH-1211 Geneva 10, Switzerland
Tel. 41-22-7882455
Fax 41-22-7882501

Similar in concept and operation to the U.S. Peace Corps, United Nations Volunteers provide technical assistance in the fields of health, education, engineering, and community development at the local level. Has a professional staff of 200 in Geneva and 400 support staff for volunteers in other countries throughout the world. U.S. citizens interested in applying for Volunteer positions must do so through the U.S. Peace Corps: UN Volunteers, 1111 20th Street, NW, Washington, DC 20526, Tel. 800/424-8580, ext. 2243.

Specialized Agencies

FOOD AND AGRICULTURAL ORGANIZATION (FAO)
Via delle Terme di Caracalla
I-00100 Rome, Italy
Tel. 39-6-57051
Fax 39-6-57053152
Web site: *www.fao.org*

U.S. Liaison Office: 1001 22nd Street, NW
Washington, DC 20437
Tel. 202/653-2498

Promotes better nutrition and the improved production and distribution of food and agricultural products amongst rural populations by collecting and disseminating information on food production and providing technical assistance to governments. Has a professional staff of 3,200 operating from Rome, Ghana, Thailand, Chile, and New York.

INTERNATIONAL ATOMIC ENERGY AGENCY
Wagramerstrasse 5
P.O. Box 100
A-1400 Vienna, Austria
Tel. 43-1-20600 or Fax 43-1-20607
Web site: *www.iaea.or.at*

U.S. address:　　1 United Nations Plaza, Suite DC1-1155
New York, NY 10017
Tel. 212/963-6011

Monitors compliance to the 1970 Non-Proliferation Treaty, promotes the peaceful uses of atomic energy, coordinates research, and promotes scientific exchanges relevant to atomic energy.

INTERNATIONAL CIVIL AVIATION ORGANIZATION
999 University Street
Montreal, PQ, Canada H3C 5H7
Tel. 514/954-8219 or Fax 514/954-6077
Web site: *www.ca.org/ICAO*

Promotes international cooperation in air transportation. Establishes international aviation standards relevant to licensing personnel, safety, aeronautical charts, rules of the air, and the development of adequate ground facilities. Has a professional staff of nearly 100 operating from Montreal, Bangkok, Cairo, Dakar, Lima, Mexico City, Nairobi, and Paris.

INTERNATIONAL FUND FOR AGRICULTURAL DEVELOPMENT
Via del Serafico 107
I-00142 Rome, Italy
Tel. 396-54591 or Fax 396-5043463

Promotes increased agricultural production in developing countries by promoting low-cost loans and providing technical assistance.

INTERNATIONAL LABOR ORGANIZATION (ILO)
Personnel Development Branch
4, route des Morillons
CH-1211 Geneva 22, Switzerland
Tel. 41-22-7996111 or Fax 41-227988685
Web site: *www.ilo.org*

Formulates international policies and programs for improving labor conditions, promoting employment opportunities, and creating international labor standards.

Provides technical assistance as well as conducts training and research. Has a professional staff of 900 stationed in 41 countries.

INTERNATIONAL MARITIME ORGANIZATION (IMO)
4 Albert Embankment
London, SE1 7SR
United Kingdom
Tel. 44-171-7357611 or Fax 44-171-5873210
Web site: *www.imo.org*

Promotes the safety of international shipping and serves as a mechanism for cooperation in establishing international standards for ship building, navigation, pollution control, and maritime trade.

INTERNATIONAL TELECOMMUNICATIONS UNION
Palacis des Nations
CH 1211 Geneva 20, Switzerland
Tel. 41-22-7305111 or Fax 41-22-7305785

Promotes the international cooperation among its 157 members in the field of telecommunications. Provides technical assistance to member countries for developing and improving their telecommunications systems.

INTERNATIONAL TRADE CENTER (ITC)
Palais des Nations
CH-1211 Geneva 20, Switzerland
Tel. 41-22-7300603

Promotes trade among member nations by developing national trade promotion strategies, training government trade officials and businesspeople in export marketing, and providing information and advice on marketing opportunities for export products.

UNITED NATIONS EDUCATIONAL, SCIENTIFIC, AND CULTURAL ORGANIZATION (UNESCO)
2 UN Plaza, Rm. 900
New York, NY 10017
Tel. 212/963-5995
Web site: *www.unesco.org*

Promotes cooperation among member states in the fields of education, science, and culture. Conducts research, provides training services, and hosts international conferences.

UNIVERSAL POSTAL UNION (UPU)
Case Postale
CH-3000 Bern 15, Switzerland
Tel. 41-31-3503111
Fax 41-31-3503110
Web site: *http://ibis.ib.upu.org*

Promotes improving the organization and efficiency of the international postal system through education, training, and technical assistance.

WORLD FOOD PROGRAMME (WFP)
Via Cristoforo Columbio 426
00145 Rome, Italy
Tel. 6-522-821
Web site: *www.wfp.org*

Functions as the UN's food aid organization. Provides relief assistance to victims of natural and man-made disasters.

WORLD HEALTH ORGANIZATION (WHO)
Head, Manpower Resources, Personnel Division
20 Avenue Appia
CH-1211 Geneva 27, Switzerland
Tel. 41-22-7912111 or Fax 41-22-7910746

Serves as a coordinating body for international health work. Supports national health programs in developing countries, gathers and disseminates information on diseases, and establishes standards for drugs and vaccines. Its staff of 1,500 operates from Geneva (600) and numerous regional and field offices (900).

WORLD INTELLECTUAL PROPERTY ORGANIZATION (WIPO)
Personnel Recruitment Section
34, chemin des Colombettes
CH-1211 Geneva 20, Switzerland
Tel. 41-22-73091111 or Fax 41-22-7335428
Web site: *www.wipo.int*

Promotes the protection of intellectual property by encouraging member states to cooperate in matters concerning patent and trademark laws. Conducts studies and publishes newsletters, reports, and books. Has a staff of 125 stationed primarily in Geneva and Vienna.

WORLD METEOROLOGICAL ORGANIZATION
Case Postale 2300
CH-1211 Geneva 20, Switzerland
Tel. 41-22-7308111
Fax 41-22-7342326
Web site: *www.wmo.ch*

Promotes the coordination, standardization, and improvement of meteorological activities throughout the world. Provides technical assistance for strengthening member states' meteorological and hydrological services.

International Financial Institutions

AFRICA DEVELOPMENT BANK
B.P. No. 1387
Abidjan, Ivory Coast (Côte d'Ivoire)
Tel. 20-44-44 or Fax 20-49-09

Promotes the economic and social development of its 53 regional members by providing loans for high priority development projects. Also includes 24 non-African members.

ASIAN DEVELOPMENT BANK
P.O. Box 789
1099 Manila, Philippines
Fax 63-2-6362444
Web site: *www.asiandevbank.org*

Promotes regional economic growth by providing financial assistance for development projects in Asia and the South Pacific. Provides low-cost loans for high priority projects.

INTER-AMERICAN DEVELOPMENT BANK
1300 New York Avenue, NW
Washington, DC 20577
Tel. 202/623-1000
Fax 202/623-3096
Web site: *www.iadb.org*

Promotes regional economic and social development by providing financial assistance for development projects in Latin America and the Caribbean. Helps mobilize private capital from the international financial markets.

INTERNATIONAL MONETARY FUND
Recruitment Division, Room 6-525
700 19th Street, NW
Washington, DC 20431
Tel. 202/623-7000
Fax 202/623-7201
Web site: *www.imf.org*

Promotes international monetary cooperation, balanced international trade, and exchange stability. It does this by monitoring the economic problems of countries and providing financial assistance when necessary for improving the balance-of-payments problems of member nations. Has a Washington-based professional staff of 2,000 and an overseas staff of 40.

THE WORLD BANK GROUP

The following financial institutions make up the United Nation's World Bank Group. The two largest and most visible institutions are the World Bank and the International Monetary Fund (IMF):

INTERNATIONAL BANK FOR RECONSTRUCTION AND DEVELOPMENT (THE WORLD BANK)
1818 H Street, NW
Washington, DC 20433
Tel. 202/458-2001
Fax 202/477-1305
Web site: *www.worldbank.org*

The largest international lending institution primarily concerned with promoting economic development in the developing countries of Asia, Africa, and Latin America. Provides direct loans, technical assistance, and policy advice. Has a professional staff of 3,500.

INTERNATIONAL DEVELOPMENT ASSOCIATION (IDA)

Operated by the World Bank staff, IDA operates a special loan program that provides funds for the very poorest countries on concessionary terms, i.e., receive special interest rates and payment terms not allowable in loan programs designed for most other countries..

MULTI-LATERAL INVESTMENT GUARANTEE AGENCY (MIGA)

Encourages the flow of foreign direct investment to, and among, developing member countries, through the mitigation of political risk in the form of investment insurance.

INTERNATIONAL FINANCE CORPORATION (IMF)
1850 Eye Street, NW
Washington, DC 20433
Tel. 202/477-1234
Fax 202/477-6391
Web site: *www.ifc.org*

Provides loans to and makes equity investments in private growth enterprises of developing countries. In contrast to the IBRD and IDA loans, IFC loans are not backed by government guarantees.

Regional Organizations

Some of the major regional international organizations provide a variety of employment opportunities in various cities as well as in island nations worldwide:

INTER-AMERICAN DEFENSE BOARD
2600 16th Street, NW
Washington, DC 20441
Tel. 202/939-6600
Fax 202/939-6620

Studies and recommends to the governments of the American Republics measures necessary for close military collaboration in preparation for the collective self-defense of the American continents.

INTER-AMERICAN INSTITUTE FOR COOPERATION ON AGRICULTURE
Apartado 55, 2200 Coronado
San Jose, Costa Rica
Tel. 506/229-4741
Fax 506/229-4741
Web site: *www.iica.ac.cr*

U.S. address: 1889 F Street, NW
                  Suite 840
                  Washington, DC 20006
                  Tel. 202/458-3767

Promotes the agricultural development efforts of member states of the Organization of American States (OAS). Conducts research and provides technical assistance.

INTERNATIONAL ORGANIZATION FOR MIGRATION
17 Route des Morillons, P.O. Box 71
CH-1211 Geneva 19, Switzerland
Tel. 41-227179111 or Fax 41-227986150
Web site: *www.iom.int*

U.S. office: 1750 K Street, NW, Suite 1110
                      Washington, DC 20006
                      Tel. 202/862-1826

Formerly known as the Intergovernmental Committee for Migration as will as the Intergovernmental Committee for European Migration, this organization promotes the resettlement of refugees and the orderly migration of peoples to other countries for employment and educational purposes.

NORTH AMERICAN TREATY ORGANIZATION (NATO)
B-1110 Brussels, Belgium
Tel. 32-2-7074111 or Fax 32-2-7074579
Web site: *www.NATO.INT*

An intergovernmental defense alliance with 15-member nations of Europe and the North Atlantic. Promotes the peace and stability of the North Atlantic region through collective defense mechanisms and actions.

ORGANIZATION OF AMERICAN STATES (OAS)
17th Street and Constitution Ave., NW
Washington, DC 20006
Tel. 202/458-3000 or Fax 202/458-6421
Web site: *www.oas.org*

Promotes the political, social, economic, and cultural cooperation of member states. Functions as a forum for resolving political disputes, enhancing regional security, and promoting trade, investment, and the transfer of technology.

ORGANIZATION FOR ECONOMIC COOPERATION AND DEVELOPMENT (OECD)
2, rue Andre-Pascal
F-75775 Paris Cedex 16, France
Tel. 331-45257200 or Fax 33-1-45248500
Web site: *www.oecd.org*

Promotes economic growth, employment, and stability among member European countries.

PAN AMERICAN HEALTH ORGANIZATION
Chief, Manpower Planning and Staffing Unit
Department of Personnel
525 23rd St., NW
Washington, DC 20037
Tel. 202/974-3000 or Fax 202/974-3663
Web site: *www.paho.org*

Promotes and coordinates the efforts of the countries of the Western Hemisphere to combat disease, lengthen life, and promote the physical and mental health of the people.

PACIFIC COMMUNITY
BP D-5
Noumea Cedex 98848, New Caldeonia
Tel. 687-262000
Fax 687-263818
Web site: *www.spc.org.nc*

Advises participating governments and administrations on matters affecting the economic and social development of the territories within SPC's area for the welfare and advancement of their people: American Samoa, Australia, the Cook Islands, the Federated States of Micronesia, Fiji, France, French Polynesia, Guam, Kiribati, the Marshall Islands, Nauru, New Caledonia, New Zealand, Niue, the Northern Mariana Islands, Palau, Papua New Guinea, Pitcairn Island, the Solomon Islands, Tokelau, Tonga, Tuvalu, the United Kingdom the United States, Vanuatu, Wallis and Futuna, and Western Samoa.

The international community includes more than 1,000 additional international organizations. Some of the largest and most important ones include:

➤ Andean Community of Nations (Lima, Peru)
➤ Association of South East Asian Nations (Jakarta, Indonesia)
    Web site: *www.aseansec.org*
➤ Asian-Pacific Economic Co-Operation (Singapore)
    Web site: *www.apec.sec.org.sg*
➤ Central American Common Market (Guatemala City, Guatemala)
➤ Common Market For Eastern and South Africa (Lusaka, Zambia)
➤ The Commonwealth (London)
    Web site: *www.commonwealth.org*
➤ The Commonwealth of Independent States (Minsk, Kirava, Belarus)

- ➤ Council of Europe (Strasbourg Cedex, France)
  Web site: *www.coe.fr*
- ➤ European Bank For Reconstruction and Development (London)
  Web site: *www.esa.int*
- ➤ European Space Agency (Paris Cedex, France)
  Web site: *www.opec.org*
- ➤ European Union
  Web site: *www.europa.eu.int* and *www.eurunion.org*
- ➤ International Chamber of Commerce (Paris)
  Web site: *www.iccwbo.org*
- ➤ International Confederation of Free Trade Unions (Brussels, Belgium)
  Web site: *www.icftu.org*
- ➤ International Olympic Committee (Lausanne, Switzerland)
- ➤ International Committee of the Red Cross (Geneva, Switzerland)
  Web site: *www.icrc.org*
- ➤ Nordic Council (Copenhagen, Denmark)
  Web site: *www.norden.org*
- ➤ North American Free Trade Agreement (Washington, DC)
  Web site: *www.nafta.net*
- ➤ Organization For Security and Co-Operation in Europe (Vienna)
  Web site: *www.osceprag.cz*
- ➤ Organization of Arab Petroleum Exporting Countries (OAPEC)
  Web site: *www.kuwait.net/~oapect*
- ➤ Organization of Petroleum Exporting Countries (OPEC)
  Web site: *www.opec.org*
- ➤ South Pacific Forum Secretariat (Suva, Fiji)
  Web site: *www.forumsec.org.fj*
- ➤ Western European Union (Brussels, Belgium)
  Web site: *www.weu.int*

The Commonwealth and the new European Union are two of the largest regional groups. When seeking employment with these regional international organizations, keep in mind that most of them only hire individuals who are citizens of their member states. However, there are exceptions to this hiring rule, especially if you have special skills that are not available through their own regional talent pools. Most of these organizations list job vacancies, with qualifications, on their Web sites.

4

Associations, Societies, and Research Institutes

The United States is truly an organizational society. Every industry and interest appears to be represented by some type of organization. The organizations engage in many different types of activities: education, training, research, publishing, lobbying, and extending insurance and travel benefits to their members. While many organizations are very small and loosely structured, others are very large and are operated by full-time staffs. The largest association, the American Automobile Association (AAA—*www.aaa.com*), has 40 million members and is operated by a full-time staff of nearly 2,000. These organizations are disproportionately headquartered in three metropolitan areas: Washington, DC, New York City, and Chicago.

Strategies

Unknown to many job seekers, associations, societies, and research institutes offer numerous international job opportunities. Some of these organizations, such as Amnesty International and the Center for Strategic and International Studies, focus solely on the international arena. Others, such as the Chamber of Commerce of the United States and American Bar Association, have international sections within what is primarily a

U.S.-oriented organization. Many of these organizations also maintain placement services or provide job assistance to their members.

If you are interested in exploring employment opportunities with associations, societies, and research institutes, you should begin examining three directories which are available in most libraries:

> ➤ *Encyclopedia of Associations* (4 volumes)
> ➤ *National Trade and Professional Associations in the U.S.*
> ➤ *Research Center Directory*

These directories also can be ordered directly from Impact Publications (see order form at the end of this book).

While all of the organizations included in this chapter are based in the United States, several thousands of similar organizations are headquartered in other countries. If you are interested in identifying these organizations, we recommend consulting the following directories:

> ➤ *Encyclopedia of Associations: International Organizations* (2 volumes)
> ➤ *Europa World Year Book*
> ➤ *Yearbook of International Organizations*

These directories also are available in major libraries.

If you plan to investigate employment opportunities with these organizations in depth, we recommend contacting three organizations that maintain extensive libraries on associations as well as operate either referral or placement services for job seekers:

> ➤ **American Society of Association Executives**
> 1575 Eye Street, NW
> Washington, DC 20005
> Tel. 202/626-2723
> Web site: *www.asaenet.org*

> ➤ **Greater Washington Society of Association Executives**
> 1426 21st Street, NW, Suite 200
> Washington, DC 20036-5901
> Tel. 202/429-9370
> Web site: *www.gwsae.org*

➢ **U.S. Chamber of Commerce**
1615 H Street, NW
Washington, DC 20062
Tel. 202/659-6000
Web site: *www.uschamber.org*

The Organizations

The following associations, societies, and research institutes have international interests as well as offer international job opportunities. Several additional associations and research institutes are identified in Chapters 6, 7, 8, and 9 as major recipients of government and foundation funding; they provide technical assistance to developing countries while also performing functions normally associated with associations and research institutes. Therefore, you may want to include those organizations with the ones found in this chapter when you examine international job opportunities with associations and research institutes.

AEROSPACE INDUSTRIES ASSOCIATION OF AMERICA
1250 Eye Street, NW
Suite 1100
Washington, DC 20005-3924
Tel. 202/371-8400
Fax 202/371-8470
Web site: *www.aia-aerospace.org*

This 54-member association represents the interests of manufacturers of aerospace products—aircraft, spacecraft, guided missiles, navigation and guidance systems, parts, accessories, and materials.

AGRIBUSINESS COUNCIL
1312 18th Street, NW
Suite 300
Washington, DC 20036
Tel. 202/296-4563
Fax 202/887-0238

The 50 members of this organization represent businesses, universities, foundations, and others interested in promoting agribusiness for solving world food problems. Operated by a staff of 5.

AIR LINE PILOTS ASSOCIATION, INTERNATIONAL, PAC
1625 Massachusetts Ave., NW
Washington, DC 20036-2283
Tel. 202/797-4033 or Fax 703/689-4370
Web site: *www.alpa.org*

This 42,000-member association is operated by a staff of 360. It serves as the collective bargaining agent for airline pilots.

AMERICAN BAR ASSOCIATION (ABA)
750 N. Lake Shore Drive
Chicago, IL 60611-4497
Tel. 312/988-5000 or Fax 312/988-5528
Web site: *www.abanet.org*

This 378,000-member association is operated by a staff of 650. Considered one of the most powerful and active interest groups in the United States. Promotes the interests of attorneys through research, education, and lobbying activities at the national, state, and local levels. Publishes the quarterly *International Lawyer* as well as operates a membership International Law and Practice Section within the association.

AMERICAN CHEMICAL SOCIETY (ACS)
1155 16th Street, NW
Washington, DC 20036-4899
Tel. 202/872-4600 or Fax 202/872-4615
Web site: *www.acs.org*

One of the oldest (since 1876) and largest scientific and educational societies with a membership of nearly 145,000 and a staff of over 2,100. Conducts studies, provides special programs, monitors legislation, offers courses, publishes newsletters and journals, and offers employment assistance.

AMERICAN CONCRETE INSTITUTE (ACI)
P.O. Box 9094
Farmington Hills, MI 48333-9094
Tel. 248/848-3700 or Fax 248/848-3701
Web site: *www.aci-int.org*

A 20,000-member technical society of engineers, architects, contractors, and educators operated by a staff of 50. Promotes improved techniques of design construction and maintenance relating to concrete products and structures. Publishes the monthly magazine *Concrete International*.

AMERICAN ENTERPRISE INSTITUTE (AEI)
1150 17th Street, NW
Washington, DC 20036
Tel. 202/862-5800
Fax 202/862-7178
Web site: *www.aei.org*

A conservative public policy research institute operated by a staff of 125. Conducts research on economics, government, and foreign and defense policy. Oriented toward an open economy and limited government.

AMERICAN FOREST AND PAPER ASSOCIATION
1111 19th Street, NW
Washington, DC 20009
Tel. 202/463-2700
Fax 202/463-2785
Web site: *www.afandpa.org*

This 166 member organization is operated by a staff of 140. It represents the interests of U.S. manufacturers of pulp, paper, and paperboard. Includes an International Department which focuses on the international aspects of the American paper industry.

AMERICAN GEOPHYSICAL UNION (AGU)
2000 Florida Avenue, NW
Washington, DC 20009-1275
Tel. 202/462-6900
Fax 202/328-0566
Web site: *www.agu.org*

This 30,000-member organization is operated by a staff of 110. It promotes the study of geophysics through research, education, and publication programs. Involved with many international activities including publications on Russia and the Antarctic.

AMERICAN INSTITUTE FOR FOREIGN STUDY (AIFS)
102 Greenwich Avenue
Greenwich, CT 06830-5577
Tel. 203/869-9090 or Fax 203/869-9615
Web site: *www.aifs.com*

Has 650,000 participants and a staff of 495. Sponsors international courses, home-stays, and cultural exchanges for students and teachers at all levels.

AMERICAN INSTITUTE OF CHEMICAL ENGINEERS
3 Park Avenue
New York, NY 10016
Tel. 212/591-7338
Fax 212/752-3294
Web site: *www.aiche.org*

This 56,000-member professional society of chemical engineers is operated by a staff of 90. Promotes the interests of members through educational programs. Maintains a career guidance and job placement service.

AMERICAN INSTITUTE OF PHYSICS (AIP)
One Physics Ellipse
College Park, MD 20740
Tel. 301/209-3100
Fax 301/209-0843
Web site: *www.aip.org*

This corporation of 10 national societies representing 110,000 members has a staff of 476. Promotes the development and application of physics through research, education, and publications programs. Translates and publishes several Soviet journals.

AMERICAN INSURANCE ASSOCIATION (AIA)
1130 Connecticut Avenue, NW, Suite 1000
Washington, DC 20036
Tel. 202/828-7100
Fax 202/293-1219
Web site: *www.aiadc.org*

This association of 195 members with a staff of 150 represents the interests of companies offering property and liability insurance and suretyship.

AMERICAN INTERNATIONAL AUTOMOBILE DEALERS ASSOCIATION (AIADA)
99 Canal Center Plaza, Suite 500
Alexandria, VA 22314
Tel. 703/519-7800 or Fax 703/519-7810
Web site: *www.aiada.org*

Represents the interests of 9,200 members who are import automobile dealers. Conducts research and issues reports on the import automobile industry.

AMERICAN MANAGEMENT ASSOCIATION INTERNATIONAL
1601 Broadway
New York, NY 10019-7420
Tel. 212/586-8100
Fax 212/903-8168
Web site: *www.amanet.org*

Includes a membership of 10,000 and a staff of 149. This is the international division of the 75,000 member American Management Association. Represents the professional interests of managers in industry, commerce, and government as well as educators and administrators abroad. Conducts training programs.

AMERICAN PETROLEUM INSTITUTE (API)
1220 L Street, NW
Washington, DC 20005-4070
Tel. 202/682-8000
Fax 202/682-8029
Web site: *www.api.org*

This association is comprised of 300 members with a staff of over 400. It represents the interests of petroleum industries, including producers, marketers, and transporters of crude oil, gasoline, natural gas, lubricating oil, and oil refiners.

AMERICAN SOCIETY OF INTERNATIONAL LAW (ASIL)
2223 Massachusetts Avenue, NW
Washington, DC 20008-2864
Tel. 202/939-6000
Fax 202/797-7133
Web site: *www.asil.org*

A 4,200-member study group with a staff of 16. Focuses on the study and application of international law relevant to maintaining an orderly system of international relations. Members consist of lawyers, educators, government officials, students, businessmen, clergy, and others.

AMNESTY INTERNATIONAL OF THE USA
322 Eighth Avenue
New York, NY 10001-4808
Tel. 212/807-8400 or Fax 212/627-1451
Web site: *www.amnesty-usa.org*

A 300,000-member organization operated by a staff of 60. A human rights organization dedicated to freeing political detainees throughout the world.

APA: THE ENGINEERED WOOD ASSOCIATION
P.O. Box 11700
Tacoma, WA 98411-0700
Tel. 253/565-6600 or Fax 253/565-7265
Web site: *www.apawood.org*

A 136-member association operated by a staff of 180. Represents the interests of plywood manufacturers. Includes an International Markets committee.

AUTOMOTIVE PARTS AND ACCESSORIES ASSOCIATION
4600 East-West Highway, Suite 300
Bethesda, MD 20814-3415
Tel. 301/654-6664
Fax 301/654-3299
Web site: *www.apaa.org*

Includes a membership of over 2,000 and a staff of 30. Furthers the interests of automotive parts and accessories manufacturers, retailers, and distributors. Includes an International Trade division, a *Foreign Buyers Directory,* and a bimonthly *International Report.*

BANK ADMINISTRATION INSTITUTE (BAI)
1 North Franklin, Suite 1000
Chicago, IL 60606
Tel. 312/553-4600
Fax 312/683-2426
Web site: *www.bai.org*

This 8,000-member group is operated by a staff of 160. Organized as a resource for the banking industry—conducts studies, provides information, and publishes reports. International interests center around the bimonthly international banking journal, *World of Banking: The International Magazine of Bank Management.*

BREAD FOR THE WORLD
1100 Wayne Avenue, Suite 1000
Silver Spring, MD 20910
Tel. 301/608-2400 or Fax 301/608-2401
Web site: *www.bread.org*

A 45,000-member organization with a staff of 70. A Christian organization dedicated to fighting world hunger and poverty. Lobbies members of Congress and conducts the Bread for the World program. Has other offices in Minneapolis, Chicago and Los Angeles.

BROOKINGS INSTITUTION
1775 Massachusetts Avenue, NW
Washington, DC 20036
Tel. 202/797-6000
Fax 202/797-6004
Web site: *www.brook.edu*

A public policy research organization and think tank operated by a staff of 250. Conducts economic, government, and foreign policy studies as well as sponsors conferences and publishes journals, reports, and books.

CATO INSTITUTE
1000 Massachusetts Avenue, NW
Washington, DC 20001-5403
Tel. 202/842-0200
Fax 202/842-3490
Web site: *www.cato.org*

A conservative public policy research institute and think tank operated by a staff of 70. Conducts research on numerous domestic and international related issues. Noted for its unique conservative/libertarian orientation to public policy issues.

CEC INTERNATIONAL PARTNERS
12 W. 31st Street, 4th Floor
New York, NY 10001
Tel. 212/643-1985 or Fax 212/643-1996
Web site: *www.cecip.org*

Previously known as the Citizen Exchange Council. This 750-member organization is operated by a staff of 12. Promotes mutual learning, understanding, and cooperation between Americans and citizens of the USSR by sponsoring intercultural programs involving citizens of both countries. Organizes travel groups to the USSR and coordinates conferences.

CENTER FOR APPLIED LINGUISTICS (CAL)
4646 40th Street, NW
Washington, DC 20016-1859
Tel. 202/362-0700 or Fax 202/362-3740
Web site: *www.cal.org*

Operates with a staff of 65. Conducts research, provides technical assistance, and serves as a clearinghouse for applied linguistics. Emphasizes adult language education, literacy testing, and cross-cultural communications. Does not have overseas positions.

CENTER FOR GLOBAL EDUCATION

Augsburg College
2211 Riverside Ave.
Minneapolis, MN 55454
Tel. 612/330-1159
Fax 612/330-1695
Web site: *augsburg.edu/global*

Operated by a staff of 34. Promotes experiential education on international development. Conducts international education programs and travel seminars.

CENTER FOR INTERNATIONAL PRIVATE ENTERPRISE

1155 15th Street, NW, Suite 700
Washington, DC 20005
Tel. 202/721-9200 or Fax 202/721-7250
Web site: *www.cipe.org*

Promotes the development of voluntary business organizations and private enterprise abroad. Conducts training programs, promotes exchange programs with local U.S. Chambers of Commerce, and serves as a clearinghouse for research on international businesses.

CENTER FOR STRATEGIC AND INTERNATIONAL STUDIES

1800 K Street, NW, Suite 400
Washington, DC 20006-0000
Tel. 202/887-0200 or Fax 202/775-3199
Web site: *www.csis.org*

Operated with a staff of over 150, this public policy research institute and think tank conducts studies on numerous international issues. Affiliated with Georgetown University. Publishes monographs and books.

CHAMBER OF COMMERCE OF THE UNITED STATES

1615 H Street NW
Washington, DC 20062
Tel. 202/659-6000
Fax 202/463-5836
Web site: *www.uschamber.org*

This nationwide network (219,200 members) of business organizations maintains important linkages to affiliated Chambers of Commerce abroad. Represents the interests of businesses. Conducts research, publishes newsletters and magazines, operates own television and radio programs, lobbies Congress, and has its own placement program for professionals. Operated by a staff of 1,200.

CHICAGO MERCANTILE EXCHANGE (CME)
30 S. Wacker Drive
Chicago, IL 60606-7499
Tel. 312/930-1000
Fax 312/648-3625
Web site: *www.cme.com*

This 2,724-member commodity futures exchange organization is operated by a staff of 880. Deals with live hogs, cattle, lumber, gold, foreign currencies, government securities, and options on equity futures.

COUNCIL FOR INTERNATIONAL EXCHANGE OF SCHOLARS (CIES)
3007 Tilden Street, NW, Suite 5L
Washington, DC 20008-3009
Tel. 202/686-4000 or Fax 202/362-3442
Web site: *www.cies.org*

Operated by a staff of 75. Works with the U.S. Information Agency and the Board of Foreign Scholarships in administering the Fulbright-Hays program. Arranges for visiting scholars and awards grants and scholarships.

COUNCIL OF THE AMERICAS
680 Park Avenue
New York, NY 10021
Tel. 212/628-3200 or Fax 212/517/6247
Web site: *www.counciloftheamericas.org*

An association of 200 members operated by a staff of 20. Represents the interests of U.S. corporations operating in Latin America. Aims to promote understanding and cooperation between U.S. corporations and the peoples and countries doing business with each other.

COUNCIL ON FOREIGN RELATIONS
58 E. 68th Street
New York, NY 10021-5984
Tel. 212/734-0400 or Fax 212/861-1789
Web site: *www.foreignrelations.org*

This organization of 2,500 members is operated by a staff of 95. Conducts research on international affairs. Awards grants to international specialists and publishes the popular *Foreign Affairs* journal.

COUNCIL ON INTERNATIONAL
EDUCATIONAL EXCHANGE (CIEE)
205 E. 42nd Street
New York, NY 10017-5776
Tel. 212/822-2600 or Fax 212/822-2699
Web site: *www.ciee.org*

Operated by a staff of 350. Promotes international education exchanges among member institutions. Administers many study programs abroad, sponsors international work camps and educational exchange programs, hosts international conferences, arranges inexpensive travel programs, issues international student identification cards, and assists U.S. students in finding summer employment abroad. Publishes several useful international education, travel, and work guides for students.

EARTHWATCH INSTITUTE
680 Mt. Auburn Street, Box 9104
Watertown, MA 02272-9104
Tel. 617/926-8200 or Fax 617/926-8532
Web site: *www.earthwatch.org*

A 40,000-member research and education organization operated with a staff of 44. Places individuals who are interested in the sciences and humanities on two to three-week field research projects. Many archaeology, marine, and earth science projects are conducted abroad.

ELECTRONIC INDUSTRIES ASSOCIATION (EIA)
2500 Wilson Blvd.
Arlington, VA 22201
Tel. 703/907-7500 or Fax 703/907-7501
Web site: *www.eia.org*

This trade association of 1,200 members is operated by a staff of 150. It represents the interests of manufacturers of electronics. Includes a placement service and an international business council.

ETHICS AND PUBLIC POLICY CENTER
1015 15th Street, NW, Suite 900
Washington, DC 20005
Tel. 202/682-1200 or Fax 202/408-0632
Web site: *www.eppc.org*

Operated by a staff of 165. Conducts research, publishes, and sponsors conferences on major domestic and foreign policy issues.

FASHION GROUP INTERNATIONAL
597 Fifth Avenue, 8th Floor
New York, NY 10017
Tel. 212/593-1715 or Fax 212/593-1925
Web site: *www.fgi.org*

Formerly known as the International Fashion Group. This 6,400-member organization is operated by a staff of 10. Includes 29 state groups and 10 international groups. Members are women executives in fashion and allied fields who meet on numerous topics relevant to the American and European fashion industry.

FOREIGN AFFAIRS RECREATION ASSOCIATION
Department of State Building, Rm. 2928
320 21st Street, NW
Washington, DC 20520
Tel. 202/530-5752
Fax 202/530-5657
Web site: *www.fararec.org*

This 24,000-member organization is operated by a staff of 34. Includes employees of Action, the Agency for International Development, the Arms Control and Disarmament Agency, the United States Information Agency, the State Department, and the Peace Corps. Sponsors cultural, social, and athletic activities as well as clubs, shopping services, seminars, and housing programs.

FOREIGN CREDIT INSURANCE ASSOCIATION (FCIA)
40 Rector Street, 11th Floor
New York, NY 10006-1778
Tel. 212/306-5000 or Fax 212/513-4704

Cooperates with the Export-Import Bank in insuring U.S. exporters against nonpayment by foreign buyers. Helps promote the export of U.S. products.

FOREIGN POLICY ASSOCIATION
470 Park Avenue S., 2nd Floor N.
New York, NY 10016
Tel. 212/481-8100 or Fax 212/481-9275
Web site: *www.fpa.org*

Operated by staff of 31. An educational organization for promoting greater understanding of international relations. Promotes world affairs programs in schools, colleges, and communities. Sponsors the "Great Decisions" series on public television and radio stations and publishes journals, books, and reports.

FREEDOM HOUSE
120 Wall Street, 26th Floor
New York, NY 10005
Tel. 212/515-8040 or Fax 212/514-8050
Web site: *www.freedomhouse.org*

A 2,000-member organization operated by a staff of 22. A conservative research
and documentation center stressing the development and strengthening of free
institutions at home and abroad. Champions causes of dissenters-in-exile.

THE FRIENDSHIP FORCE
57 Forsyth Street, NW, Suite 900
Atlanta, GA 30303
Tel. 404/522-9490 or Fax 404/688-6148
Web site: *www.friendship-force.org*

The 12,000-member organization is operated by a staff of 18. Promotes international understanding by establishing personal friendships through exchange visits
of individuals, couples, and families. Organizes travel groups for short-term exchange visits.

HERITAGE FOUNDATION
214 Massachusetts Ave., NE
Washington, DC 20002
Tel. 202/546-4400
Fax 202/546-8328
Web site: *www.heritage.org*

A conservative think tank that conducts public policy studies and sponsors conferences on important domestic and foreign policy issues.

HOOVER INSTITUTION ON WAR, REVOLUTION, AND PEACE
Stanford University
Stanford, CA 94305-6010
Tel. 415/723-0603
Fax 415/723-1687
Web site: *www.hoover.org*

Also known as the Hoover Institution. Operates with a staff of nearly 320. A
conservative think tank and research organization that focuses on numerous
international and domestic policy issues—international relations, national security,
and domestic issues. Publishes monographs and books.

HUDSON INSTITUTE
Herman Kahn Center
5395 Emerson Way
Indianapolis, IN 46226
Tel. 317/545-1000 or Fax 317/545-9639
Web site: *www.hudson.org*

A 175-member organization operated by a staff of 70. Conducts public policy studies on numerous domestic and international issues relating to national security, international and domestic economics, education and employment, energy and technology, and the future. A noted public policy "think tank".

HUMAN RIGHTS WATCH
350 5th Avenue, 34th Floor
New York, NY 10118-3299
Tel. 212/290-4700
Fax 212/736-1300
Web site: *www.hrw.org*

A 2,000 member organization operated by a staff of 30. Monitors and promotes human rights practices of governments throughout the world in accordance with the United Nations Declaration of Human Rights and the Helsinki Accords.

INSTITUTE FOR DEFENSE ANALYSES (IDA)
1801 N. Beauregard
Alexandria, VA 22311
Tel. 703/845-2174 or Fax 703/578-0726
Web site: *www.ida.org*

Operated by a staff of 700, this research institute works closely with the Office of the Secretary of Defense and the Joint Chiefs of Staff in providing studies and advice on critical national defense issues.

INSTITUTE FOR THE INTERNATIONAL EDUCATION OF STUDENTS
223 W. Ohio Street
Chicago, IL 60610-4196
Tel. 312/944-1750 or Fax 312/944-1448
Web site: *www.iesabroad.org*

Formerly known as the Institute of European and Asian Studies. Has a staff of 36. Operates undergraduate study programs for U.S. students who attend European and Asian universities.

INTERNATIONAL ASSOCIATION OF DRILLING CONTRACTORS (IADC)
P.O. Box 4287
Houston, TX 77210-4287
Tel. 281/578-7171 or Fax 281/578-0589
Web site: *www.iadc.org*

This 2,170 member organization is operated by a staff of 30. It represents the interests of oil well contract drilling firms. Conducts research and education and training programs.

INTERNATIONAL ASSOCIATION OF FIRE CHIEFS
4025 Fair Ridge Drive
Fairfax, VA 22033
Tel. 703/273-0911
Fax 703/273-9363
Web site: *www.iafc.org*

This 9,000-member association is operated by a staff of 25. Promotes the interests of fire chiefs in government, industry, and the military through research and education. Publishes the bimonthly *International Connections.*

THE INTERNATIONAL CENTER
731 Eighth Street, SE
Washington, DC 20003
Tel. 202/547-3800
Fax 202/546-4780
Web site: *www.internationalcenter.com*

Operated by a staff of 23. Focuses on analyzing U.S. foreign policy in developing countries of Asia, Africa, and Latin America. A public interest group that develops policy options.

INTERNATIONAL COMMUNICATIONS INDUSTRIES ASSOCIATION
11242 Waples Mill Road, Suite 200
Fairfax, VA 22030-6079
Tel. 703/273-7200 or Fax 703/278-8082
Web site: *www.infocom.org*

A 1,500 member association managed by a staff of 15. Members are manufacturers, suppliers, and dealers of audiovisual, video, and microcomputer products. Includes international members and an international trade council.

INTERNATIONAL FEDERATION OF ACCOUNTANTS
535 5th Avenue, 26th Floor
New York, NY 10017
Tel. 212/286-9344
Fax 212/286-9570
Web site: *www.ifac.org*

This 100-member international organization with a staff of 5 represents accounting firms in 75 countries with over 1 million members. Promotes international standards for accountants.

INTERNATIONAL FOOD POLICY RESEARCH INSTITUTE
1200 17th Street, NW
Washington, DC 20036-3006
Tel. 202/862-5600
Fax 202/467-4439
Web site: *www.cgiar.org*

Operated by a staff of 100, this research center analyzes and develops alternative public policy strategies for solving world hunger and malnutrition.

INTERNATIONAL FOUNDATION OF EMPLOYEE BENEFIT PLANS
18700 W. Bluemound Road
P.O. Box 69
Brookfield, WI 53008
Tel. 414/786-6700
Fax 414/786-6647
Web site: *www.ifebp.org*

This 31,000-member organization is operated by a staff of 110. Promotes employee benefit plans in the United States and Canada through consultation, educational programs, research, and publications.

INTERNATIONAL LAW INSTITUTE
1615 New Hampshire Ave., NW
Washington, DC 20009
Tel. 202/483-3036
Fax 202/483-3029
Web site: *www.ili.org*

Operated by a staff of 15, the institute conducts research and training relating to the legal aspects of international business and trade. Sponsors an international exchange program and conferences.

INTERNATIONAL NARCOTIC ENFORCEMENT OFFICERS
112 State Street, Suite 1200
Albany, NY 12207
Tel. 518/463-6232
Fax 518/432-3378
Web site: *www.ineoa.org*

This 7,500-member association is operated by a staff of 8. Promotes the interests of narcotic enforcement officers through education and training programs and lobbies for the improvement of international, national, state, and local laws and law enforcement pertaining to drugs. Publishes the monthly *International Drug Report.*

INTERNATIONAL RESEARCH AND EXCHANGES BOARD
1616 H Street, NW
Washington, DC 20006
Tel. 202/628-8188 or Fax 202/628-8189
Web site: *www.irex.org*

Sponsored by the American Council of Learned Societies and the Social Science Research council and operated with a staff of 29. Responsible for the academic exchange programs with the USSR, Bulgaria, Czechoslovakia, Germany, Hungary, Poland, Romania, and Yugoslavia.

INTERNATIONAL ROAD FEDERATION
2600 Virginia Avenue, NW, Suite 208
Washington, DC 20024
Tel. 202/338-4641 or Fax 202/338-8104

Operated by a staff of 7, this 500-member organization promotes the development of highways and highway transportation throughout the world. Members are drawn from over 70 countries.

INTERNATIONAL SCHOOLS SERVICES
15 Roszel Road
P.O. Box 5910
Princeton, NJ 08543
Tel. 609/452-0990 or Fax 609/452-2690
Web site: *www.iss.edu*

Has a staff of 275. Serves as the key organization in providing educational services —personnel, procurement, facility planning, curriculum and administrative guidance—for American and international schools. Operates some schools for U.S. industry abroad. Conducts research and publishes newsletters and reports.

INTERNATIONAL TRADE COUNCIL
3114 Circle Hill Road
Alexandria, VA 22305
Tel. 703/548-1234
Fax 703/548-6216

Consists of 850 members and a staff of 35. Promotes the free trade interests of importers and exporters in over 300 major industries. Conducts research, sponsors educational programs, and publishes reports.

MERIDIAN INTERNATIONAL CENTER
1630 Crescent Place, NW
Washington, DC 20009-4099
Tel. 202/667-6800
Fax 202/667-1475
Web site: *www.meridian.org*

Formerly known as Meridian House International. Operated by a staff of 100, Meridian House International promotes international understanding through intercultural exchange programs. Provides visitor service program for international visitors and diplomats as well as sponsors meetings and exhibits.

NAFSA/ASSOCIATION OF INTERNATIONAL EDUCATORS
1875 Connecticut, NW, Suite 1000
Washington, DC 20009-5737
Tel. 202/462-4811
Fax 202/667-3419
Web Site: *www.nafsa.org*

A 6,200-member organization operated by a staff of 35. Promotes international education by working with foreign student advisers, teachers of English as a second language, U.S. students abroad, overseas education advisors, and embassy personnel involved with educational matters.

NATIONAL ASSOCIATION OF BROADCASTERS
1771 N Street, NW
Washington, DC 20036
Tel. 202/429-5300 or Fax 202/429-5406
Web site: *www.nab.org*

This 7,500-member association is managed by a staff of 165. It represents the interests of radio and television stations and networks. Includes an International committee.

NATIONAL ASSOCIATION OF CREDIT MANAGEMENT
8815 Centre Park Drive
Suite 2000
Columbia, MD 21045
Tel. 410/740-5560
Fax 410/740-5574
Web site: *www.nacm.org*

The 1000 members of this organization are managed by a staff of 12. Promotes the interests of exporters through international credit workshops and studies.

NATIONAL ASSOCIATION OF MANUFACTURERS (NAM)
1331 Pennsylvania Avenue, NW, Suite 1500-N
Washington, DC 20004
Tel. 202/637-3000 or Fax 202/637-3182
Web site: *www.nam.org*

This 14,000-member association is operated by a staff of 180. Represents the interests of major U.S. manufacturers relating to national and international problems. Lobbies government, maintains public relations program, and publishes information on issues and activities. Includes an International Economic Affairs policy group.

NATIONAL ASSOCIATION OF WHEAT GROWERS
415 Second Street, NE, Suite 300
Washington, DC 20002-4900
Tel. 202/547-7800
Fax 202/546-2638
Web site: *www.wheatworld.org*

This 60,000-member association has a staff of 15. Promotes the interests of American wheat growers through education and research. Includes an International Market Development committee.

NATIONAL FOREIGN TRADE COUNCIL
1270 Avenue of the Americas, Suite 206
New York, NY 10020-0000
Tel. 212/399-7128
Fax 212/399-7144

Includes 550 members and a staff of 15. Promotes the foreign trade and investment interests of its members which include manufacturers, insurance companies, law firms, exporters, importers, and foreign investors.

NATIONAL GEOGRAPHIC SOCIETY
1145 17th Street, NW
Washington, DC 20036-4688
Tel. 202/857-7588
Fax 202/775-6141
Web site: *www.nationalgeographic.com*

This 10.5 million member organization is operated by a staff of 2,400. Promotes knowledge on geography, natural history, archaeology, astronomy, ethnology, and oceanography through research and study programs. Operates exhibits, education programs, and a large library as well as produces radio and television shows.

NATIONAL INSTITUTE FOR PUBLIC POLICY
3031 Javier, Suite 300
Fairfax, VA 22031-4662
Tel. 703/698-0563
Fax 703/698-0566

Operated by a staff of 20. Conducts public policy studies relating to national and international security. Sponsors seminars and publishes research findings.

NEAR EAST FOUNDATION
342 Madison Avenue
Suite 1030
New York, NY 10173-0020
Tel. 212/867-0064
Fax 212/867-0169
Web site: *www.neareast.org*

Operated by a staff of 25, the foundation promotes food production and rural and community development in the Middle East and Africa by funding start-up projects and assigning specialists to provide technical assistance abroad.

NEW ORLEANS BOARD OF TRADE
316 Board of Trade Place
New Orleans, LA 70130
Tel. 504/525-3271
Fax 504/525-9039

A 250-member organization consisting of representatives from banking, insurance, transportation, export-import, warehouse, and commodity industries and operated by a staff of 8. Promotes trade and commerce interests in New Orleans. Operates the Mayor's Council on International Trade and Economic Development.

NEW YORK MERCANTILE EXCHANGE
1 North End Avenue
World Financial Center
New York, NY 10282-1101
Tel. 212/299-2000
Fax 212/301/4700
Web site: *www.nymex.com*

This 816-member commodity trade organization is operated by a staff of 227. Deals in commodity futures and trade options.

OVERSEAS DEVELOPMENT COUNCIL (ODC)
1875 Connecticut Avenue, NW, Suite 1012
Washington, DC 20009
Tel. 202/234-8701 or Fax 202/745-0067
Web site: *www.odc.org*

Operates with a staff of 30. Conducts research, sponsors conferences, and publishes information for better understanding the economic and social problems facing developing countries.

PHARMACEUTICAL RESEARCH AND MANUFACTURERS OF AMERICA
1100 15th Street, NW, Suite 900
Washington, DC 20005-1797
Tel. 202/835-3400
Fax 202/835-3429
Web site: *www.phrma.org*

Formerly known as the Pharmaceutical Manufacturers Association. This association consists of 105 members and a staff of 90. It represents the interests of pharmaceutical manufacturers through research, information, and public relations activities. Includes an international section.

PROFESSIONAL SECRETARIES INTERNATIONAL
P.O. Box 20404
Kansas City, MO 64195-0404
Tel. 816/891-6600
Fax 816/891-9118
Web site: *www.gvi.net/psi*

This 45,000 member organization of professional secretaries is operated by a staff of 30. It certifies secretaries (Certified Professional Secretary), sponsors programs, and provides insurance and retirement benefits for members.

RAND CORPORATION
1700 Main Street
Santa Monica, CA 90407-2138
Tel. 310/451-6913
Web site: *www.rand.org*

Operates with a staff of over 1000. Conducts public policy research on numerous domestic and foreign policy issues. Noted for its involvement in classified national security research. Publishes a newsletter, reports, and books.

RODALE INSTITUTE
611 Siegfriedale Road
Kutztown, PA 19530-9749
Tel. 610/683-1400
Fax 610/824-3850
Web site: *www.envirolink.org/seel/rodale*

This 50,000 member association is operated by a staff of 30. The Rodale Institute promotes the use of regenerative agricultural techniques in preserving farms, soil, and food quality.

SIERRA CLUB
85 2nd Street, 2nd Floor
San Francisco, CA 94105-3459
Tel. 415/977-5500 or Fax 415/977-5799
Web site: *www.sierraclub.org*

This 420,000-member organization of environmentalists is operated by a staff of 294. Seeks to stop the abuse of wilderness lands, save endangered species, and protect the global environment through grassroots conservation efforts and an extensive publication and information dissemination program. Operates programs in education, environment and natural resource management, and public policy and advocacy. Operates with a $43 million annual budget.

TRILATERAL COMMISSION
345 E. 46th Street, Suite 711
New York, NY 10017
Tel. 212/661-1180
Fax 212/949-7268
Web site: *www.trilateral.org*

Operated by a staff of 16, the 300 international members of the commission are drawn from business, labor, higher education, and the media in North America, Western Europe, and Japan. Promotes cooperation among the three industrialized regions of the world through research and publications.

US-CHINA BUSINESS COUNCIL
1818 N Street, NW, Suite 200
Washington, DC 20036
Tel. 202/429-0340
Fax 202/775-2476
Web site: *www.uschina.org*

Includes 325 members with a staff of 30. Represents the trading interests of American companies doing business in the People's Republic of China. Provides information, assistance, and business advisory services as well as sponsors conferences and briefings on trade with China.

UNITED STATES CHAMBER OF SHIPPING
900 19th Street, NW, Suite 850
Washington, DC 20006
Tel. 202/775 4399 or Fax 202/659-3795

Formerly known as the American Institute of Merchant Shipping. A 23-member institute operated by a staff of 6. Promotes the interests of the U.S. Merchant Marine industry (owners and operators of ocean-going vessels) through research, publication, and lobbying activities.

UNITED STATES COUNCIL FOR INTERNATIONAL BUSINESS
1212 Avenue of the Americas
New York, NY 10036
Tel. 212/354-4480 or Fax 212/575-0327
Web site: *www.uscib.org*

Consisting of 300 members and operated by a staff of 27, this council is part of the International Chamber of Commerce. Represents the interests of multinational enterprises to governments and maintains communication among members through publications and meetings.

UNITED STATES OLYMPIC COMMITTEE
1 Olympic Plaza
Colorado Springs, CO 80909-5760
Tel. 719/632-5551 or Fax 719/578-4677
Web site: *www.olympic.usa.org*

This 58-member organization is operated by a staff of 60. Consisting of a federation of amateur sports governing bodies, it is responsible for supporting the U.S. Olympic Team. Operates three Olympic Training Centers.

WORLD FUTURE SOCIETY
7910 Woodmont Avenue, Suite 450
Bethesda, MD 20814-0000
Tel. 301/656-8274 or Fax 301/951-0394
Web site: *www.wfs.org/wfs*

This 30,000-member association is operated by a staff of 13. It promotes the study of the future through research, education, and publication programs.

WORLD LEARNING
Kipling Road
Brattleboro, VT 05302-0676
Tel. 1-800-336-1616 or 802/257-7751
Fax 802/258-3500
Web site: *www.worldlearning.org*

Operates with a staff of 250. Previously known as the Experiment in International Living School for International Training, World Learning provides extensive international educational, training, travel, and development services. Conducts language classes, sponsors homestay and travel programs, and offers a four-year college degree program in world studies.

WORLD NEIGHBORS
4127 NW 122nd Street
Oklahoma City, OK 73120-9933
Tel. 405/752-9900
Fax 405/752-9393
Web site: *www.wn.org*

A 10,000-member organization operated by a staff of 28. Promotes world understanding by sponsoring community development and self-help efforts in 17 countries of Asia, Africa, and Latin America.

WORLD TRADE CENTER OF NEW ORLEANS
2 Canal Street, Suite 2900
New Orleans, LA 70130
Tel. 504/529-1601
Fax 504/529-1691
Web site: *www.wtc-no.org*

This 3,300 member organization is operated by a staff of 140. Organized to promote international trade, friendship, and understanding by sponsoring visits of foreign VIPs and sending U.S. business and civic leaders abroad. Sponsors language programs and produces television programs on international affairs.

YOUTH FOR UNDERSTANDING
INTERNATIONAL EXCHANGE
3501 Newark Street, NW
Washington, DC 20016-3167
Tel. 202/966-6800
Fax 202/895-1104
Web site: *www.yfu.org*

Operates with a staff of 250. Sponsors international student exchange programs for teenagers as well as administers scholarship programs.

5

Businesses With International Interests and Operations

Businesses employ the largest number of individuals in the international arena. Indeed, as the global economy continues to expand and nations become more interdependent, international business operations, from manufacturing to consulting services, should expand accordingly.

While businesses may employ many people internationally, don't expect to find many entry-level international business positions except in sales. In contrast to other types of organizations which may hire individuals for entry-level international positions, many businesses promote employees to positions that involve international operations only *after* several years of progressive experience within the organization. However, this is not always the case. Some businesses may assign young, inexperienced, but well trained employees to overseas posts, especially if their jobs involve specialty consulting, sourcing, sales, and technical operations.

Key Resources and Cross-Listings

The businesses identified in this chapter represent only a few, albeit some of the largest firms, with international operations. For a more complete listing, including U.S. firms operating in specific countries, consult the following directories which are available at most major libraries:

- ➢ *World Business Directory*
- ➢ *Directory of American Firms Operating in Foreign Countries*
- ➢ *Directory of Foreign Firms Operating in the U.S.*
- ➢ *The International Corporate 1,000*
- ➢ *The Multinational Marketing and Employment Directory*
- ➢ *American Register of Exporters and Importers*
- ➢ *Dun and Bradstreet Exporter's Encyclopedia*
- ➢ *Hoover's Handbook of World Business*
- ➢ *Jane's Major Companies of Europe*
- ➢ *Principal International Business*
- ➢ *Directory of U.S. Firms Operating in Latin America*
- ➢ *Major Companies of Europe*

If you use the Internet, you'll have a wealth of information on international businesses at your fingertips 24-hours a day. By using the major search engines on the Web, you should be able to locate many businesses with international operations. For example, AltaVista has a very good search feature for finding businesses on the Web:

www.altavista.digital.com

Once you enter this site, just click on to "Business and Finance" and then go to "International Business." AltaVista will bring up numerous resources that link to hundreds of international businesses. For example, you can go into a useful Boise State University international business resource site that links to numerous resources that identify businesses with overseas operations: *www.idbsu.edu/carol/busintl.htm*.

The national Yellow Pages directory also has a good search engine for locating businesses:

www1.bigyellow.com

Two other online "yellow pages" also are worth checking out for locating particular businesses:

BigBook   *www.bigbook.com*
GTE Superpages   *www.superpages.gte.net*

We particularly recommend Hoover's online service for researching many corporations:

www.hoovers.com

A unique feature of the Hoover site is its links to a company's competition. Other sites worth checking out include:

BizWeb Business Guide to the Web   *www.bizweb.com*
Business Wire's Corporate Profiles   *www.businesswire.com/cnn.shtml*
EDGAR Database of Corporate Info   *www.sec.gov/edgarhp.htm*
Companies Online   *www.companiesonline.com*
The Inc. 500   *www.inc.com/500*
JobVault   *www.jobvalut.com*
The Web 100   *www.100.com*

In addition, many of the contracting and consulting firms identified in Chapter 6 could be incorporated with those found in this chapter. Large firms, such as the M. W. Kellogg Company, Ralph M. Parson Company, Metcalf & Eddy International, and Lummus Crest, operate throughout the world in developing and implementing major engineering and construction projects, especially roads, bridges, dams, airports, tunnels, sewerage systems, nuclear power facilities, petrochemical factories, and pharmaceutical plants. Chapter 6 also includes numerous businesses involved in providing financial and technical assistance services to developing countries in the areas of accounting, agricultural development, health care, education, and energy. Major firms such as Ernst & Young and PricewaterhouseCoopers are identified there too. You may also want to get a copy of the current annual edition of *The Business Phone Book USA* which includes the names, addresses, phone and fax numbers, and Web sites of thousands of businesses involved in the international arena.

The following listing of businesses with international interests and operations represents some of the largest U.S.-based firms. For more detailed information, including job listings, go directly to each company's homepage. By so doing, you should be able to access a wealth of information on each company by reviewing their Web site. If a Web site is not listed, use one of the search engines to see if the company now has a Web site. Some sites were not available as we went to press.

MAJOR CORPORATIONS

Airborne Express
air freight services
3101 Western Avenue
Seattle, WA 98111
Tel. 206/285-4600
Fax 206/281-3890
www.airborne-express.com

Allen-Bradley Co.
motor starters, relays
P.O. Box 2086
Milwaukee, WI 53201
Tel. 414/671-2000
Fax 414/382-4444
www.ab.com

Allied Signal Inc.
aerospace, chemical, oil, gas
101 Columbia Road
Morristown, NJ 07962-4658
Tel. 973/455-2000
Fax 973/455-4807
www.alliedsignal.com

Amerada Hess—*petroleum
exploration and production*
1185 Avenue of the Americas
New York, NY 10036-2665
Tel. 212/997-8500
Tel. 212/536-8390
www.hess.com

American Greetings Corp.
greeting cards
1 American Road
Cleveland, OH 44144
Tel. 216/252-7300
Fax 216/252-6778
www.americangreetings.com

American Home Products
*prescription drugs and
home products*
5 Giralda Farms
Madison, NJ 07940
Tel. 973/660-5000
Fax 973/660-5771
http://ahpc.com

American International Group
insurance
70 Pine Street
New York, NY 10270-0002
Tel. 212/770-7000
Fax 212/943-1125
www.aig.com

American Standard, Inc.
plumbing, heating, brakes
P.O. Box 6820
Piscataway, NJ 08855
Tel. 732/980-6000
Fax 732/980-6122
www.americanstandard.com

AMP, Inc.—*conductors,
electronic components*
441 Friendship Road
Harrisburg, PA 17111
Tel. 717/564-0100
Fax 717/780-7019
www.amp.com

Ansell Corp.
protective gloves and clothing
1300 Walnut Street
Coshocton, OH 43812
Tel. 614/622-4311
Fax 614623-3512

AT&T Worldnet
communications
32 Avenue of the Americas
New York, NY 10013
Tel. 212/387-5400
Fax 212/387-5965
www.att.com

Avon Products, Inc.
cosmetics
1345 Avenue of the Americas
New York, NY 10105
Tel. 212/282-5000
Fax 212/282-6514
www.avon.com

AVX Corporation
ceramic capacitors
P.O. Box 867
Myrtle Beach, NC 29578-0867
Tel. 843/448-9411
Fax 843/448-7139
www.avxcorp.com

Bausch & Lomb, Inc.
*optical products, health care
equipment, pharmaceuticals*
P.O. Box 54
Rochester, NY 14601
Tel. 716/338-6000
Fax 716/338-6007
www.bausch.com

Bell Helicopter Texton
aircraft and defense products
P.O. Box 482
Fort Worth, TX 76101
Tel. 817/280-2011
Fax 817/280-2321
www.bellhelicopter.textron.com

Bell & Howell Co.
business equipment
5215 Old Orchard Road
Skokie, IL 60077
Tel. 847/470-7100
Fax 847/470-9825
www.bellhowell.com

BellSouth Corporation
communications
1155 W. Peachtree Street, NE
Atlanta, GA 30367-6000

Tel. 404/249-2000
Fax 404/249-5599
www.bellsouth.com

Black & Decker—*electrical
tools and machines*
701 East Joppa Road
Towson, MD 21286
Tel. 410/716-3900
Fax 410/716-2610
www.blackanddecker.com

Block Drug Co., Inc.
pharmaceuticals
257 Cornelison Avenue
Jersey City, NJ 07302-9988
Tel. 201/434-3000
Fax 201/451-8424

Boeing Company—*aircraft
and aerospace manufacturer*
P.O. Box 3707
Seattle, WA 98124-2207
Tel. 206/655-2121
Fax 206/655-3987
www.boeing.com

Borden Inc.—*food
and industrial products*
180 E. Broad Street
Columbus, OH 43215
Tel. 614/225-4000
Fax 614/225-7408

Borg-Warner Automotive, Inc.
automotive parts, chemicals
200 S. Michigan
Chicago, IL 60604-2488
Tel. 312/322-8500

Bose Corporation
audio and video equipment
110 The Mountain Road
Framingham, MA 01701

Tel. 508/879-7330
Fax 508/872-6541
www.bose.com

Bristol-Meyers Squibb—*healthcare and pharmaceutical products*
345 Park Avenue, 3rd Floor
New York, NY 10154
Tel. 212/546-3751
Fax 212/546-9707
www.bms.com

Calgon Corp.
industrial chemicals, personal hygiene items
P.O. Box 1346
Pittsburgh, PA 15230
Tel. 412/777-8000
Fax 412/777-8104
www.calgon.com

Cabot Corporation
chemicals and natural gas
75 State Street
Boston, MA 02116
Tel. 617/345-0100
Fax 617/342-6103
www:cabot-corp.com

Caterpillar Tractor Company
earthmoving equipment
100 N.E. Adams Street
Peoria, IL 61629-0001
Tel. 309/675-1000
Fax 309/675-4332
www.cat.com

Cendant Corporation
personnel and consumer goods
707 Summer Street
Stamford, CT 06901
Tel. 203/324-9261
Fax 203/324-3468
www.cendant.com

Chevron USA, Inc.—*oil*
575 Market Street
San Francisco, CA 94103-2894
Tel. 415/894-7700
Fax 415/894-2248
www.chevron.com

Chubb Corporation—*insurance*
15 Mountain View Road
Warren, NJ 07059
Tel. 908/903-2000
Fax 908/903-2027
www.chubb.com

Cigna Corporation
finance and insurance
1 Liberty Place
Philadelphia, PA 19192
Tel. 215/761-1000
Fax 215/761-5008
www.cigna.com

Clorox Co.—*cleaning products*
1221 Broadway
Oakland, CA 94612
Tel. 510-271-4900
Fax 510/271-7883
www.clorox.com

The Coca-Cola Company
beverage manufacturer
P.O. Box 1734
Atlanta, GA 30301-1734
Tel. 404/676-3478
Fax 404/515-2560
www.cocacola.com

Colgate-Palmolive Co.
cosmetics, hygiene products
300 Park Avenue
New York, NY 10022
Tel. 212/310-2000
Fax 212/310-3284
www.colgate.com

Commercial Intertech Corp.
fluid purification and
hydraulic equipment
1775 Logan Avenue
Youngstown, OH 44501
Tel. 330/746-8011
Fax 330/746-1148

Compaq Computers Corps.
computer hardware
P.O. Box 69200
Houston, TX 77269-2000
Tel. 281/370-0670
Fax 281/370-1740
www.compaq.com

Computer Associates Intl.
computer software
One Computer Associates Plaza
Islandia, NY 1788-7000
Tel. 516/342-5224
Fax 516/342-5329
www.cal.com

Continental General Tire, Inc.
tires, inner tubes
1800 Continental Blvd.
Charlotte, NC 28273
Tel. 704/588-5895
Fax 704/583-8540
www.contigentire.com

Core Laboratories
petroleum testing
5295 Hollister Road
Houston, TX 77040
Tel. 713/460-9600
Fax 713/460-4389
www.corelab.com

Corning Inc.
kitchenware, optical equipment
1 Riverfront Plaza
Corning, NY 14831
Tel. 607/974-9000

Fax 607/974-8688
www.corning.com

CPC International
food manufacturer
International Plaza
700 Sylvan Avenue
Englewood Cliffs, NJ 07632
Tel. 201/894-4000
Fax 201/894-2186
www.cpcinternational.com

Cuna Mutual Insurance Group
insurance
5910 Mineral Point Road
Madison, WI 53705
Tel. 608/238-5851
Fax 608/238-0830
www.cunamutal.com

DDB Needham Worldwide
advertising
437 Madison Avenue
New York, NY 10022
Tel. 212/415-2000
Fax 212/415-3562
www.ddbn.com

Del Monte Corporation
food products
One Market Plaza
Stuart Street Towers
San Francisco, CA 94119
Tel. 415/247-3000
Fax 415/247-3565
www.delmonte.com

Dell Computer Corp.
computer hardware
1 Dell Way
Round Rock, TX 78682
Tel. 512/338-4400
Fax 512/728-3653
www.dell.com

DH Technology Inc.
high-speed printers
15070 Avenue of Science
San Diego, CA 92128
Tel. 619/451-3485
Fax 619/451-3573
www.dhtech.com

Digital Equipment Corp.
computers
146 Main Street
Maynard, MA 01754-2571
Tel. 508/493-5111
Fax 508/493-9490
www.dec.com

Domino's Pizza, Inc.
retail food products
30 Frank Lloyd Wright Drive
Ann Arbor, MI 48106-0997
Tel. 313/930-3030
Fax 313/668-4614
www.dominos.com

Dow Jones & Co.
finance and business products
200 Liberty Street
New York, NY 10281
Tel. 212/416-2000
Fax 212/416-2655
http://bis.dowjones.com

Dow Chemical Company
chemical manufacturer
Willard H. Dow Center, Suite 2030
Midland, MI 48674-0001
Tel. 517/636-1463
Fax 517/636-0922
www.dow.com

Dresser Industries, Inc.
industrial equipment
2001 Ross Avenue
Dallas, TX 75221

Tel. 972/740-6000
Fax 972/740-6715
www.dresser.com

**Du Pont El de Nemours
& Co., Inc.**—*chemicals*
1007 Market Street
Wilmington, DE 19898
Tel. 302/774-1000
Fax 301/774-7321
www.dupont.com

Eastman Kodak—*photographic
supplies and equipment*
343 State Street
Rochester, NY 14650-0001
Tel. 716/724-4000
Fax 716/724-0633
www.kodak.com

Ecology and Environment, Inc.
hazardous waste disposal
368 Pleasantview Drive
Lancaster, NY 14086
Tel. 716/684-8060
Fax 716/684-0844
www.ecolen.com

Eli Lilly & Co.
pharmaceutics and cosmetics
Lilly Corporate Center
Indianapolis, IN 46285-0001
Tel. 317/276-2000
Fax 317/277-9721
www.lilly.com

Emerson Electric Company
electronics manufacturer
8000 West Florissant Avenue
St. Louis, MO 63136-1415
Tel. 314/553-2000
Fax 314/553-3527
www.emersonelectric.com

Emery Worldwide—*air freight*
1 Logoon Drive, Suite 400
Redwood, CA 94065
Tel. 650/596-9600
Fax 650/596-7904
www.emergyworld.com

Exxon Corporation—*oil*
5959 Las Colinas Blvd.
Irving, TX 75039
Tel. 972/444-1000
Fax 972/444-1348
www.exxon.com

Falk Corporation
transmissions, gears
3001 W. Canal Street
Milwaukee, WI 53208
Tel. 414/342-3131
Fax 414/937-4359
www.falk.com

Firestone Tire & Rubber Co.
tire producer
25375 Cabot #210
Hayward, CA 94545
Tel. 415/786-0420
www.firesyn.com

Ford Motor Company
auto manufacturer
The American Road
Dearborn, MI 48121-0000
Tel. 313/322-3000
www.ford.com

General Electric—*electronics, consumer products*
3135 Easton Turnpike
Fairfield, CT 06431-0001
Tel. 203/373-2211
Fax 203/373-3131
www.ge.com

General Instrument Corp.
electronic instruments
8770 W. Bryn Mawr Ave., Suite 130
Chicago, IL 60631
Tel. 773/695-1000
Fax 773/695-1001
www.gi.com

General Motors Corporation
auto manufacturer
3-251 GM Building
3044 West Grand Blvd.
Detroit, MI 48202
Tel. 313/556-7637
Fax 313/556-5108
www.gm.com

Gerber Products Co.
baby foods
445 State Street
Fremont, MI 49413
Tel. 616/928-2000
Fax 616/928-2819
www.gerber.com

Goodyear Tire & Rubber Co.
tire manufacturer
1144 East Market Street
Akron, OH 44316-0001
Tel. 330/796-7990
Fax 330/796-4099
www.goodyear.com

Guardian Industries Corp.
glass and insulation
2300 Harmon Road
Auburn Hills, MI 48326
Tel. 248/340-1800
Fax 248/340-9988
www.guardian.com

Helene Curtis Industries
cosmetics, hygiene products
325 W. Wells Street
Chicago, IL 60601

Tel. 312/661-0222
Fax 312/836-0125
www.yoursalon.com

Hewlett-Packard Co.
computers and electronics
3000 Hanover Street
Palo Alto, CA 94304-1185
Tel. 650/857-1501
Fax 650/857-5518
www.hp.com

H.J. Heinz Company
food products, sauces, spices
600 Grant Street
Pittsburgh, PA 15219
Tel. 412/456-5700
Fax 412/456-6128
www.heinz.com

Honeywell—*computers and automated systems*
Honeywell Plaza
2701 4th Avenue, South
Minneapolis, MN 55408-1746
Tel. 612/951-1000
Fax 612/951-2086
www.honeywell.com

IBM—*computers, electronics*
Old Orchard Road
Armonk, NY 10504-1783
Tel. 914/765-1900
Fax 914/765-6021
www.ibm.com

Ingersoll-Rand Co.
industrial machinery
200 Chestnut Ridge Road
Woodcliff Lake, NJ 07675
Tel. 201/573-3138
Fax 201/573-3168
www.ingersoll-rand.com

Intel Corporation
computer chips
3065 Bowers Avenue
Santa Clara, CA 95052
Tel. 408/765-8080
Fax 408/765-3979
www.intel.com

ITT—*communications, hotels, electronics, finance, wood*
1330 Avenue of the Americas
New York, NY 10019
Tel. 212/258-1000
Fax 212/258-1297
www.ittinfo.com

J.C. Penney Company, Inc.
household and consumer products
6501 Legacy Drive
Plano, TX 75024-3698
Tel. 214/431-1000
Fax 214/431-1315
www.jcpenney.com

Johnson & Johnson
health care products
1 Johnson & Johnson Plaza
New Brunswick, NJ 08933
Tel. 908/524-0400
Fax 908/214-0332
www.jnj.com

Johnson Controls, Inc.
plastic containers, auto seats and batteries, commercial facility control systems
P.O. Box 591
Milwaukee, WI 53201-0591
Tel. 414/228-1200
Fax 414/228-0118
www.jci.com

KFC Corporation
fast food restaurants
1441 Gardiner Lane

Louisville, KY 40232
Tel. 502/456-8393
Fax 502/454-2195
www.kentuckyfriedchicken.com

Kimberly-Clark Corp.
paper, disposable diapers
P.O. Box 619100
Dallas TX 75261-9100
Tel. 414/721-2000
Fax 414/721-4315
www.kimberly-clark.com

Kraft General Foods International
food products and consumer items
800 Westchester Avenue
Rye Brook, NY 10573
Tel. 914/335-2500
Fax 914/335-7144
www.kraftfoods.com/careers

Levi Strauss Associates, Inc.
clothing
1115 Battery Street
San Francisco, CA 94111
Tel. 415/544-6000
Fax 415/544-1468
www.levi.com

Litton Industries, Inc.
*electronics, resource exploration
equipment, industrial products*
21240 Burbank Blvd.
Woodland Hills, CA 91367
Tel. 818/598-5000
Fax 818/598-3313
www.littoncorp.com

Lockheed Martin Corporation
aircraft and aerospace
6801 Rockledge Drive
Bethesda, MD 20817
Tel. 301/897-6000
Fax 301/897-6083
www.lmco.com

Mattel, Inc.—*games and toys*
333 Continental Blvd.
El Segundo, CA 90245
Tel. 310/524-2000
Fax 310/524-3537
www.matelmedia.com

McCann-Erickson Worldwide
advertising
750 3rd Avenue
New York, NY 10017
Tel. 212/697-6000
Fax 212/867-5177
www.mccannerickson.com

Merck and Company, Inc.
chemicals, pharmaceuticals
1 Merck Drive
Whitehouse Station, NJ 08889-0100
Tel. 908/423-1000
Fax 908/423-2958
www.merck.com

**Minnesota Mining and
Manufacturing Co. (3M)**
chemicals and consumer products
3M Center, International Operations
St. Paul, MN 55144
Tel. 612/733-1110
Fax 612/736-2041
www.mmm.com

Monsanto Chemical Co.
chemicals
800 N. Lindbergh Blvd.
St. Louis, MO 63167-0001
Tel. 314/694-1000
Fax 314/694-7625
www.monsanto.com

Motorola, Inc.
electronics manufacturer
1303 E. Algonquin Road
Schaumburg, IL 60196-1079
Tel. 847/576-5000

Fax 847/538-3617
www.mot.com

Nike, Inc.—*footwear,*
apparel and accessories
One Bowerman Drive
Beaverton, OR 97005
Tel. 503/671-6453
Fax 503/671-6300
www.nike.com

Northrop Grumman Corp.
aircraft and aerospace
S. Oyster Bay Road
Bethpage, NY 11714
Tel. 516/575-3369
www.northrop-grumman.com

Ogilvy & Mather—*advertising*
309 W. 49th Street
New York, NY 10019
Tel. 212/237-4000
Fax 212/779-7717
www.*ogilvy.com*

Otis Elevator Co.—*elevators*
Ten Farm Springs Road
Farmington, CT 06032
Tel. 860/674-4000
Fax 860/676-5111
www.otis.com

Pepsico Food Services Intl.
beverage manufacturer
700 Anderson Hill Road
Purchase, NY 10057-0000
Tel. 914/253-2000
Fax 914/253-2070
www.pepsico.com

Pfizer International
pharmaceuticals and health care
235 East 42nd Street
New York, NY 10017

Tel. 212/573-2323
Fax 212/573-7851
www.pfizer.com

Philip Morris Companies, Inc.
tobacco and beverages
120 Park Avenue
New York, NY 10017-5592
Tel. 212/880-5000
Fax 212/878-2167

Phillips Petroleum Co.
oil and gas producer
4th & Keeler Street
5 D4 Phillips Building
Bartlesville, OK 74004-0001
Tel. 918/661-6600
Fax 918/662-5245
www.phillips66.com

Pitney Bowes, Inc.
office equipment and services
1 Elmcroft Road
Stamford, CT 06926
Tel. 203/356-5000
Fax 203/352-7681
www.pitneybowes.com

Pittway Corporation
publishing and security systems
200 S. Wacker Drive
Chicago, IL 60606
Tel. 312/831-1070
Fax 312/831-0828
www.pittway.com

Premark International
plastic containers
1717 Deerfield Road
Deerfield, IL 60015
Tel. 708/405-6000
Fax 708/405-6311
www.premarkintl.com

Primerica Corporation
finance and insurance
38 E. 29th Street
New York, NY 10016
Tel. 212/684-4115
Fax 212/696-0689
www.pfsnet.com

Procter & Gamble Co.
consumer products
1 Procter & Gamble Plaza
Cincinnati, OH 45201-0599
Tel. 513/983-1100
Fax 513/983-4381
www.pg.com

Ralston Purina Co.
pet products and batteries
Checkerboard Square
St. Louis, MO 63164-0001
Tel. 314/982-1000
Fax 314/982-1211
www.ralston.com

Raytheon Company—*high-tech
electronics producer*
141 Spring Street
Lexington, MA 02173-7899
Tel. 781/862-6600
Fax 781/860-2172
www.raytheon.com

Revlon Group—*cosmetics*
625 Madison Avenue
New York, NY 10022
Tel. 212/527-4000
Fax 212/527-4995

R. J. Reynolds Tobacco
tobacco products
401 N. Main Street
Winston-Salem, NC 27105
Tel. 336/741-5000
Fax 336/741-4328

Reynolds Metals Company
aluminum and plastic products
6601 W. Broad Street
Richmond, VA 23230
Tel. 804/261-2000
Fax 804/261-4160
www.rmc.com

Rockwell International Corp.
aviation and electronics
2201 Seal Beach Blvd.
Seal Beach, CA 90740-8250
Tel. 310/797-5066
Fax 310/797-5690
www.rockwell.com

Rubbermaid, Inc.
plastic and rubber products
1147 Akron Road
Wooster, OH 44691-6000
Tel. 330/264-6464
Fax 330/287-2739
www.rubbermaid.com

Russell Corporation
leisure and athletic apparel
P.O. Box 272
Alexander City, AL 35010
Tel. 256/329-4000
Fax 256/329-5045
www.russellcorp.com

Scott Technologies
security and fire protection
5875 Landerbrook Drive, Suite 250
Mayfield Heights, OH 44124
Tel. 440/446-1333

Shaklee
health and nutrition products
444 Market Street
San Francisco, CA 94111
Tel. 415/954-3000
Fax 415/986-0808
www.shaklee.com

Southland Corporation
convenience stores (7-11s)
2711 N. Haskell Avenue
Dallas, TX 75204-7011
Tel. 214/828-7011
Fax 214/828-7848
www.7-eleven.com

Sprint International
telecommunications
2330 Shawnee Mission Pkwy.
Westwood, KS 66205
Tel. 913/624-3000
Fax 913/624-3022
www.sprint.com

Texaco, Inc.—*oil producer*
2000 Westchester Avenue
White Plains, NY 10650-0001
Tel. 914/253-4000
Fax 914/253-7753
www.texaco.com

Texas Instruments, Inc.
computers and electronics
13500 N. Central Expressway
Dallas, TX 75243
Tel. 972/995-2011
Fax 972/995-4360
www.ti.com

Textron, Inc.—*finance, aerospace, commercial products*
40 Westminster Street
Providence, RI 02903
Tel. 401/421-2800
Fax 401/421-2878
www.textron.com

Toys "R" Us, Inc.—*toys*
461 From Road
Paramus, NJ 07652
Tel. 210/262-7800
Fax 201/262-8112
www.trus.com

Transocean Offshore, Inc.
offshore well drilling
Four Greenway Plaza
Houston, TX 77046
Tel. 713/871-7500
Fax 713/850-3817
www.deepwater.com

Triton Energy Corporation
oil and gas production/exploration
6688 N. Central Expressway
Dallas, TX 75206
Tel. 214/691-5200
Fax 214/987-0571
www.tritonenergy.com

TRW, Inc.—*electronics and equipment producer*
1900 Richmond Road
Cleveland, OH 44124-3760
Tel. 216/291-7000
Fax 216/291-7629
www.trw.com

Tyson Foods, Inc.
food products
P.O. Box 2020
Springdale, AR 72764
Tel. 501/756-4000
Fax 501/290-7903
www.tyson.com

Union Camp Corporation
paper, wood, and chemical products
1600 Valley Road
Wayne, NJ 07470
Tel. 201/628-2000
Fax 201/628-2592
www.unioncamp.com

Union Carbide—*chemical and plastics manufacturer*
39 Old Ridgebury Road
Danbury, CT 06817-0001

Tel. 203/794-2000
Fax 203/794-6104
www.unioncarbide.com

Unisys Corp.—*computers*
P.O. Box 500
Blue Bell, PA 19424
Tel. 215/986-4011
Fax 215/986-6810
www.unisys.com

Universal Foods Corporation
agricultural and tobacco products
P.O. Box 25099
Richmond, VA 23260
Tel. 804/359-9311
Fax 804/254-3584
www.universalcorp.com

VF Corporation
sports and occupational clothing
P.O. Box 1022
Reading, PA 19603
Tel. 215/378-5511
Fax 215/371-0749
www.threads.vfc.com

Wang Laboratories
information processing systems
600 Technology Park Drive
Billerica, MA 01821-4130
Tel. 508/967-5000
Fax 508/967-0436
www.wang.com

Weyerhaeuser Company
wood producer
33663 Weyerhaeuser Way
S. Tacoma, WA 98603
Tel. 253/924-2345
Fax 253/924-3756
www.weyerhaeuser.com

Whirlpool Corporation
home appliances
2000 M-63
Benton Harbor, MI 49022-2962
Tel. 616/926-5000
Fax 616/926-3568
www.whirlpool.com

Xerox Corporation
*computers, data processing,
office products*
800 Long Ridge Road
Stamford, CT 06902-1288
Tel. 203/968-3000
Fax 203/968-3508
www.xerox.com

BANKING AND FINANCE

Advent International
101 Federal Street
Boston, MA 02110
Tel. 617/951-9400
Fax 617/951-0566
www.adventinternational.com

Alliance Capital Management
1345 Avenue of the Americas
New York, NY 10105
Tel. 212/969-1000
Fax 212/969-1255
www.alliancecapital.com

Allied Irish Banks
405 Park Avenue
New York, NY 10022
Tel. 212/339-8000
Fax 212/339-8009
www.aibny.com

American Express Co., Inc.
International Bank
American Express Tower
New York, NY 10285-0001
Tel. 212/640-2000
Tel. 212/619-9802
www.americanexpress.com

Bank of America NT & SA
555 California St.
San Francisco, CA 94104
Tel. 415/622-3456
Fax 415/241-5080
www.bankamerica.com

Bank of Boston Corp.
100 Federal Street
Boston, MA 02110-1898
Tel. 617/434-5873
Fax 617/268-0635
www.bankboston.com

Bank of New York Co, Inc.
48 Wall Street
New York, NY 10286-0001
Tel. 212/495-1784
Fax 212/815-2203
www.bankofny.com

Bank of Tokyo Mitsubishi
1251 Avenue of the Americas
New York, NY 10020
Tel. 212/766-3400
Fax 212/782-6419

Bankers Trust Co.
280 Park Avenue
New York, NY 10017-1270
Tel. 212/250-2500
Fax 212/250-5353
www.bankerstrust.com

Banque Nationale de Paris
BNP International
Financial Services

499 Park Avenue
New York, NY 10022
Tel. 212/750-1400
Fax 212/750-9717
www.bnp.fr

Barclays Bank of New York
300 Park Avenue
New York, NY 10022-7455
Tel. 212/418-4600
www.barclays.com

Brown Brothers Harriman & Co.
59 Wall Street
New York, NY 10005-2818
Tel. 212/483-1818
Fax 212/493-7287
www.bbh.com

Charles Schwab & Co.
101 Montgomery Street
San Francisco, CA 94104
Tel. 415/627-7000
Fax 415/627-8538
www.schwab.com

Chase Manhattan Bank
270 Park Avenue
New York, NY 10017-2040
Tel. 212/270-6000
www.chase.com

Citicorp
399 Park Avenue
New York, NY 10043-0001
Tel. 212/559-7299
Fax 212/559-7373
www.citibank.com

Credit Agricole
520 Madison Avenue, 8th Floor
New York, NY 10022
Tel. 212/418-2200

Credit Lyonnais
Securities USA
CL Global Partners
1301 Ave. of the Americas, 37th Fl.
New York, NY 10019
Tel. 212/408-5700
Fax 212/261-2500

Credit Suisse
12 E. 49th Street
New York, NY 10017
Tel. 212/238-2000
www.ska.com

Creditanstalt-Bankverein
245 Park Avenue
27th Floor
New York, NY 10167
Tel. 212/856-1000
Fax 212/856-1414

Dai-Ichi Kangyo Bank
1 World Trade Ctr., Suite 4811
New York, NY 10048
Tel. 212/466-5200
Fax 212/524-0579
www.infowebor.jp/dkb/
welcome-e.html

Deutsche Bank North America
Holding Corp.
31 W. 52nd Street
New York, NY 10019-6160
Tel. 212/474-8000
Fax 212/474-8560
www.deutsche-bank.de/index_e.htm

Dillon, Read, and Co.
535 Madison Avenue
New York, NY 10022-4266
Tel. 212/906-7000
Fax 212/759-3755
www.wdr.com

Dresdner Bank
75 Wall St., 27th Floor
New York, NY 10005
Tel. 212/429-2000
Fax 212/429-2363
wwwdresdner-bank.com

Dresdner Kleinwort Benson Ltd.
75 Wall Street
New York, NY 10005
Tel. 212/429-2000
Fax 212/429-2127
www.dresdnerkb.com

European American Bank
90 Park Avenue
New York, NY 10016
Tel. 212/682-2726
Fax 212/697-9149
www.eab.com

Federal Reserve Bank
of New York
33 Liberty Street
New York, NY 10045-1011
Tel. 212/720-5000
Fax 212/720-6407
www.nj.frb.org

First Union Bank
Broad and Walnut
Philadelphia, PA 19109
Tel. 215/985-6000
www.firstunion.com

French American Banking
Corporation
200 Liberty Street
20th Floor
New York, NY 10281-1003
Tel. 212/978-5700
www.bmp.fr

Fuji Bank
2 World Trade Center
79th Floor
New York, NY 10048
Tel. 212/898-2400
Fax 212/321-9408

Goldman, Sachs & Co.
85 Broad Street
New York, NY 10004-2456
Tel. 212/902-1000
Fax 212/902-1513
www.gs.com

J.P. Morgan & Co., Inc.
60 Wall Street
New York, NY 10260-0060
Tel. 212/483-2323
Fax 212/235-4950
www.jpmorgan.com

Keefe, Bruyette, and Woods
2 World Trade Center
85th Floor
New York, NY 10048-0203
Tel. 212/323-8300
Fax 212/323-8306
www.kbw.com

Kidder Peabody and Co.
10 Hanover Square
New York, NY 10005-3592
Tel. 212/968-2600

Marine Midland Bank
One Marine Midland Center
Buffalo, NY 14203
Tel. 716/841-2424
Fax 716/841-4746

Mellon Bank Corporation
1 Mellon Bank Center
500 Grant Street
Pittsburgh, PA 15258-0001

Tel. 412/234-5000
Fax 412/234-4025
www.mellon.com

Merrill Lynch & Co., Inc.
250 Vesey Street
World Financial Center
New York, NY 10081
Tel. 212/449-9836
Fax 212/449-8665
www.ml.com

Merita Nordbanken
437 Madison Avenue, 21st Floor
New York, NY 10022
Tel. 212/381-9300
Fax 212/421-4420
www.meritany.com

Mitsubishi International Corp.
520 Madison Avenue
New York, NY 10022-4223
Tel. 212/605-2000
Fax 212/605-2597
www.mitsubishi.co.jp

**Morgan Guaranty Trust
Company of New York**
60 Wall Street
New York, NY 10260-0023
Tel. 212/483-2323
Fax 212/648-5283

Morgan Stanley Group, Inc.
1585 Broadway
New York, NY 10036
Tel. 212/703-4000
Fax 212/761-0086

Northern Trust
50 LaSalle Street
Chicago, IL 60675-0001
Tel. 312/630-6000
Fax 312/630-1779
www.ntrs.com

Paine-Webber Group
1285 Avenue of the Americas
New York, NY 10019-6093
Tel. 212/713-2000
Fax 212/713-1380
www.painewebber.com

PricewaterhouseCoopers
1301 Avenue of the Americas
New York, NY 10019
Tel. 212/259-1000
Fax 212/259-1301
www.pwcglobal.com

Republic New York Corporation
425 5th Avenue
New York, NY 10018-2790
Tel. 212/525-5000
Fax 212/525/5678
www.rnb.com

Salomon Brothers Inc.
7 World Trade Center
New York, NY 10048-1196
Tel. 212/783-7000
Fax 212/783-2520
www.saloman.com

Sanwa Bank California
444 Market Street
San Francisco, CA 94111-5381
Tel. 415/597-5000
Fax 415/596-5647
www.sanwa-bank-ca.com

Smith Barney, Inc.
388 Greenwich Street
New York, NY 10013
Tel. 212/816-6000
www.smithbarney.com

Sumitomo Bank of California
320 California Street
San Francisco, CA 94104

Tel. 415/445-8000
Fax 415/445-3886

Tokai Bank
300 S. Grand Avenue
Los Angeles, CA 90071
Tel. 213/972-0200
Fax 213/812-3541
www.tokai.com

Wells Fargo Bank
420 Montgomery St.
San Francisco, CA 94163
Tel. 800/411-4932
www.wellsfargo.com

CONSULTING

American Management Systems
4050 Legato Street
Fairfax, VA 22033
Tel. 703/267-8000
Fax 703/267-5111
www.amsinc.com

Andersen Consulting
69 Washington St., 35th Floor
Chicago, IL 60602
Tel. 312/372-7100
Fax 312/507-2548
www.andersencorp.com

Arthur D. Little Inc.
25 Acorn Park
Cambridge, MA 02140
Tel. 617/498-5000
Fax 617/498-2700
www.adlittle.com

Bain and Company
2 Copley Place
Boston, MA 02116
Tel. 617/572-2000

Fax 617/572-2427
www.bain.com

Booz, Allen, and Hamilton
8283 Greensboro Drive
McLean, VA 22102
Tel. 703/902-5000
Fax 703/902-3333
www.bah.com

Boston Consulting Group
1 Exchange Place
Boston, MA 02109
Tel. 617/973-1200
Fax 617/973-1339
www.bcg.com

Data Resources, Inc.
24 Hartwell Avenue
Lexington, MA 02173
Tel. 817/863-5100
Fax 817/860-6332

Deloitte and Touche
P.O. Box 820
Wilton, CT 06897
Tel. 203/761-3000
Fax 203/834-2200
www.dttus.com

Ernst and Young
787 7th Avenue, 20th Floor
New York, NY 10019
Tel. 212/773-3000
Fax 212/773-1996
www.ey.com

Frost and Sullivan
90 West Street, Suite 1301
New York, NY 10006
Tel. 212/233-1080
Fax 212/619-0831

Hay Group, Inc.
229 S. 18th Street
Rittenhouse Square
Philadelphia, PA 19103
Tel. 215/875-2300
Fax 215/875-2879
www.haygroup.com

Hewitt Associates
100 Half Day Road
Lincolnshire, IL 60015-3342
Tel. 847/295-5000
Fax 847/295-7634
www.hewitt.com

Hill and Knowlton
466 Lexington Avenue, 3rd Floor
New York, NY 10017
Tel. 212/885-0300
Fax 212/885-0570
www.hillandknowlotn.com

Jones Lang Wooton USA
101 E. 52nd Street
New York, NY 10022
Tel. 212/688-8181
Fax 212/308-5199

A.T. Kearney
222 W. Adams St., Suite 2500
Chicago, IL 60606
Tel. 312/648-0111
Fax 312/223-6200

KPMG Peat-Marwick
767 5th Avenue
New York, NY 10153
Tel. 212/909-5000
Fax 212/909-5863
www.us.kpmy.com

Kurt Salmon Associates
1355 Peachtree Street, NE, Suite 900
Atlanta, GA 30309

Tel. 404/892-0321
Fax 404/898-9590

McKinsey and Co. Inc.
55 E. 52nd Street
New York, NY 10022
Tel. 212/446-7000
Fax 212/446-8575
www.mckinsey.com

Mercer Consulting Group
1166 Avenue of the Americas
New York, NY 10036
Tel. 212/345-4500
www.mercer.com

Price Waterhouse
1177 Avenue of the Americas
New York, NY 10036
Tel. 212/819-5000
Fax 212/596-8910
www.pw.com/us

Theodore Barry & Associates
515 S. Figueroa Street, Suite 1500
Los Angeles, CA 90071
Tel. 213/689-0770
Fax 213/629-7580

Towers Perrin, Inc.
335 Madison Avenue
New York, NY 10017
Tel. 212/309-3400
Fax 212/309-3760

LAW

Cleary, Gottlieb, Steen, Hamilton
One Liberty Plaza
New York, NY 10006
Tel. 212/225-2000
Fax 212/225-3999

Coudert Brothers
1114 Avenue of the Americas
New York, NY 10036
Tel. 212/626-4400
Fax 212/626-4120

Covington and Burling
P.O. Box 7566
Washington, DC 20004
Tel. 202/662-6000
Fax 202/662-6291

Debevoise & Plimpton
875 Third Avenue
New York, NY 10022
Tel. 212/909-6000
Fax 212/909-6836

Gibson, Dunn, and Crutcher
333 S. Grand Avenue
Los Angeles, CA 90071
Tel. 213/229-7000
Fax 213/229-7520
www.gdclaw.com

Patton Boogs LLP
2550 M Street, NW, Suite 800
Washington, DC 20037
Tel. 202/457-6000
Fax 202/457-6315

Pennie and Edmonds
1155 Ave. of the Americas, 22nd Fl.
New York, NY 10036
Tel. 212/790-9090
Fax 212/869-9741
www.pennie.com

Sullivan & Cromwell
125 Broad Street
New York, NY 10004
Tel. 212/558-4000
Fax 212/558-3588

White and Case
1155 Avenue of the Americas
New York, NY 10036
Tel. 212/819-8200
Fax 212/354-8113
www.whitecase.com

COMMUNICATIONS, MEDIA, AND JOURNALISM

➤ BROADCASTING

ABC, Inc.
77 W. 66th St.
New York, NY 10023
Tel. 212/456-7777
Fax 212/456-2795
www.abctelevision.com

Cable News Network
P.O. Box 105366
Atlanta, GA 30348
Tel. 404/827-1500
Fax 404/827-1784
www.cnn.com

CBS Enterprises
51 W. 52nd Avenue
New York, NY 10019
Tel. 212/975-4321
Tel. 212/975-9387
www.cbs.com

NBC
30 Rockefeller Plaza
New York, NY 10012
Tel. 212/664-4444
Fax 212/664-3914
www.nbc.com

Radio Free Europe/Radio Liberty, Inc.
Production Center
1201 Connecticut Ave., NW
Suite 1100
Washington, DC 20036
Tel. 202/457-6900
Fax 202/457-6974
www.rferl.org

Turner Broadcasting System
One CNN Center
P.O. Box 105366
Atlanta, GA 30348
Tel. 404/827-1717
Fax 404/855-2262
www.turner.com

➤ MAGAZINES

Business Week
1221 Avenue of the Americas
New York, NY 10020
Tel. 212/512-2511
www.businessweek.com

Economist Magazine
111 W. 57th Street
New York, NY 10019
Tel. 212/541-5730
Fax 212/541-9378
www.economist.com

Forbes, Inc.
60 5th Avenue
New York, NY 10011
Tel. 212/620-2200
Fax 212/206-5126
www.forbes.com

Foreign Affairs Magazine
58 E. 68th Street
New York, NY 10021
Tel. 212/734-0400
Fax 212/861-1849

Fortune Magazine
Time and Life Building
Rockefeller Center
New York, NY 10020
Tel. 212/522-1212
Fax 212/246-3375
www.fortune.com

National Geographic
1145 17th Street, NW
Washington, DC 20036
Tel. 202/857-7000
Fax 202/775-6141
www.nationalgeographic.com

Newsweek, Inc.
251 W. 57th Street
New York, NY 10019
Tel. 212/445-4000
Fax 212/445-4120

Time, Inc.
Time and Life Building
Rockefeller Center
New York, NY 10020
Tel. 212/522-1212
Fax 212/522-0901

UNICEF News
United Nations, 3 UN Plaza
New York, NY 10017
Tel. 212/326-7000
Fax 212/888-7465
www.unicef.org

➤ MOTION PICTURES AND TV PRODUCTION

Columbia Pictures
10202 W. Washington Blvd.
Culver City, CA 90232
Tel. 310/280-8000
Fax 310/204-1300

Viacom International
1515 Broadway, 28th Floor
New York, NY 10036
Tel. 212/258-6000
Fax 212/258-6358
www.viacom.com

Warner Communications Co.
239 Lorraine Ave.
Upper Montclair, NJ 07043
Tel. 973/746-7900
Fax 973/746-4589

➤ Newspapers

Christian Science Monitor
1 Norway Street
Boston, MA 02115
Tel. 617/450-2000
Fax 617/450-7575
www.csmonitor.com

Gannett Co., Inc.
1100 Wilson Blvd.
Arlington, VA 22234
Tel. 703/284-6000
Fax 703/247-3294
www.gannett.com

Hearst Corporation
959 8th Avenue
New York, NY 10019
Tel. 212/649-2000
Fax 212/262-2680
www.hearstcorp.com

Knight-Ridder Inc.
One Herald Plaza
6th Floor
Miami, FL 33132
Tel. 305/376-3800
Fax 305/376-3865
http://kri.com

Los Angeles Times
Times Mirror Square
Los Angeles, CA 90053
Tel. 213/237-5000
Fax 213/237-4712
www.latimes.com

New York Times
229 W. 43rd St.
New York, NY 10036
Tel. 212/556-1234
Fax 212/556-4188
www.nytimes.com

Wall Street Journal
Dow Jones and Co.
200 Liberty St.
New York, NY 10281
Tel. 212/416-2000
Fax 212/416-2658
http://wsj.com

Washington Post
1150 15th St., NW
Washington, DC 20071
Tel. 202/334-6000
Fax 202/334-4344
www.washingtonpost.com

➤ NEWS SERVICES

Associated Press
50 Rockefeller Plaza
New York, NY 10020
Tel. 212/621-1500
Fax 212/621-1679
www.trib.com/NEWS/APwire.html

Foreign Press Association
110 E. 59th Street
New York, NY 10022
Tel. 212/826-4452
Fax 212/826-4657

United Press International
1510 H Street, NW, Suite 700
Washington, DC 20005
Tel. 202/898-8000
Fax 202/898-8057

TRAVEL

➤ ASSOCIATIONS

**American Society of
Travel Agents**
1101 King Street, Suite 200
Alexandria, VA 22314
Tel. 703/739-2782
Fax 703/684-8319
www.astanet.com

**Society of Incentive
Travel Executives**
21 W. 38th Street, 10th Floor
New York, NY 10018
Tel. 212/575-0910
Fax 212/575-1838
www.info-now.com/site/

➤ AIRLINES

American Airlines Inc.
P.O. Box 619616
DFW Airport
Dallas, TX 75261
Tel. 817/963-1234
Fax 817/931-6334
www.americanair.com

Continental Airlines, Inc.
2929 Allen Parkway, Suite 1501
Houston, TX 77019
Tel. 713/834-5000
Fax 713/520-6329
www.flycontinental.com

Delta Lines, Inc.
ATL International Airport
P.O. Box 20706
Atlanta, GA 30320
Tel. 404/715-2600
Fax 404/715-5494
www.delta-air.com

Northwest Airlines, Inc.
Minneapolis-St. Paul
International Airport
5101 Northwest Drive
St. Paul, MN 55111
Tel. 612/726-2111
Fax 612/726-3942
www.nwa.com

TWA, Inc.
515 N. 6th S.
1 City Center
St. Louis, MO 63101
Tel. 314/589-3000
Fax 314/589-3129
www.twa.com

United Airlines, Inc.
P.O. Box 66100
Chicago, IL 60666
Tel. 847-700-4000
Fax 847/700-2214
www.ual.com

Virgin Atlantic Airways
747 Belden Avenue
Norwalk, CT 06850
Tel. 203/750-2000
Fax 203/750-6400
www.fly.virgin.com/atlantic

➤ CRUISELINES

Clipper Cruise Line
7711 Bonhomme Avenue
St. Louis, MO 63105
Tel. 314/727-2929

Fax 314/727-6575
www.ecotravel.com/clipper

Commodore Cruise Line
4000 Hollywood Blvd.
South Tower, Suite 385
Hollywood, FL 33021
Tel. 954/967-2100
Fax 954/967-2147

Cunard Line, Ltd.
555 Fifth Avenue
New York, NY 10017
Tel. 212/880-7500
Fax 212/949-0915
www.cunardline.com

Norwegian Cruise Lines
95 Merrick Way
Coral Cables, FL 33134
Tel. 305/447-9660
Fax 305/529-6359

Royal Caribbean Cruise Line
1050 Caribbean Way
Miami, FL 33132
Tel. 305/379-2601
Fax 305/374-7354
www.royalcaribbean.com

➤ AUTO COMPANIES

**Avis Rent-A-Car
Systems, Inc.**
900 Old Country Road
Garden City, NY 11530-2181
Tel. 516/222-3000
Fax 516/222-4767
www.avis.com

Budget Rent-A-Car Corporation
4255 Naperville Road
Lisle, IL 60532
Tel. 708/955-1900

Fax 708/955-7799
www.budgetrentacar.com

Hertz Corporation
225 Brae Blvd.
Park Ridge, NJ 07656-1870
Tel. 201/307-2000
Fax 201/307-2644
www.hertz.com

Thrifty Rent-A-Car System, Inc.
5330 E 31st Street
Tulsa, OK 74135
Tel. 918/665-3930
Fax 918/669-2228
www.thrifty.com

➤ TRAVEL AGENCIES

Arrington Travel Center
55 West Monroe Street, Suite 3800
Chicago, IL 60603
Tel. 312/726-4900
Fax 312/726-1447

Austin Travel Corporation
265 Spiagnoli Road
Metville, NY 11747
Tel. 516/752-9100
Fax 516/293-7620

Corporate Travel Services
550 California Street, 3rd Floor
San Francisco, CA 94104
Tel. 415/433-4700
Fax 415/773-3440

Garber Travel Service, Inc.
1406 Beacon Street
Brookline, MA 02146
Tel. 617/734-2100
Fax 617/731-7521
www.garber.com

Morris Travel—Ask Mr. Foster
240 East Morris Avenue, Suite 400
Salt Lake, City, UT 84115
Tel. 801/487-9731
Fax 801/483-6677

Omega World Travel Inc.
3102 Omega Office Park Drive
Fairfax, VA 22032
Tel. 703/359-8888
Fax 703/359-8887
www.omegaworld.com

Rosenbluth Travel Inc.
2401 Walnut Street
Philadelphia, PA 19103
Tel. 215/977-4000
Fax 215/977-4023

Sunbelt Motivation & Travel
8150 Brookline Drive
Suite 5-400
Dallas, TX 75247
Tel. 214/638-2400
Fax 214/630-6642
www.sunlite.com

Travel and Transport Inc.
2120 S. 72nd Street
Commercial Federal Tower
Suite 300
Omaha, NE 68124
Tel. 402/399-4500
Fax 402/398-9950

➤ HOTELS

Clarion Hotels & Resorts
11555 Darnestown Road
Gaithersburg, MD 20878
Tel. 301/979-5000
Fax 301/979-6177
www.hotelchoice.com

Club Mediterranee (French)
40 West 57th Street
33rd Floor
New York, NY 10019
Tel. 212/977-2100
Fax 212/315-5392
www.clubmed.com

Hilton International Co.
1 Wall Street Court
10th Floor
New York, NY 10005
Tel. 212/820-1700
Fax 212/809-7595

Holiday Inn Worldwide
3 Ravinia Drive
Suite 2900
Atlanta, FL 30346
Tel. 404/604-2000
Fax 404/604-5403
www.holiday-inn.com

Hyatt Hotels Corporation
200 W. Madison
39th Floor
Madison Plaza
Chicago, IL 60606
Tel. 312/750-1234
Fax 312/750-8008

ITT-Sheraton
60 State Street
Boston, MA 02109-6002
Tel. 617/367-3600
Fax 617/367-5601
www.sheraton.com

Marriott International, Inc.
1 Marriott Drive
Washington, DC 20058
Tel. 301/380-3000
Fax 301/380-3090
www.marriott.com

Meridien Hotels
888 7th Avenue
27th Floor
New York, NY 10016-4895
Tel. 212/956-3501

Nikko Hotels International
1700 Broadway
38th Floor
New York, NY 10019
Tel. 212/765-4890
Fax 212/757-2091

Omni Hotels International
500 Lafayette Road
Hampton, NH 03842-3625
Tel. 603/926-8911
Fax 603/926-9122
www.omnihotels.com

Pan Pacific Hotels & Resorts
177 Post Street
Suite 800
San Francisco, CA 94108
Tel. 415/732-7747
Fax 415/732-5800
www.panpac.com/hotels/

Regent International Hotels
132 S. Rodeo Drive
Beverly Hills, CA 90212
Tel. 310/275-8858

Westin Hotels & Resorts
2001 6th Avenue
Seattle, WA 98121
Tel. 206/443-5000
Fax 206/443-8997
www.westin.com

➤ INCENTIVE TRAVEL WHOLESALERS

Carlson Marketing Group
12755 Highway 55
Minneapolis, MN 5000
Tel. 612/540-5000
Fax 612/550-4357

Maritz Travel
1395 N. Highway Drive
Fenton, MO 63099-0000
Tel. 314/827-4000
Fax 314/827-4336
www.maritz.com

FOREIGN FIRMS IN THE U.S.

BASF Corp. (German)
chemicals, paints, inks
3000 Continental Drive N.
Mount Olive, NJ 07828
Tel. 973/426-2600
Fax 973/426-2610
www.bsaf.com

**British Petroleum
Exploration, Inc.**—*oil*
200 W. Lake Blvd.
Houston, TX 77079
Tel. 281/560-8500
Fax 281/560-8114
www.bp.com

Casio Inc. (Japanese)—*watches,
computers, electronics*
570 Mt. Pleasant Avenue
Dover, NJ 07801
Tel. 201/361-5400
Fax 201/361-3819
www.casio-usa.com

**Daimler-Benz North
American Corp.**—*autos*
375 Park Avenue
Suite 3001
New York, NY 10152
Tel. 212/909-9700
Fax 212/826-0356
www.daimler-benz.com

Fiat USA (Italian)—*autos*
375 Park Avenue
Suite 2703
New York, NY 10152
Hasbrouck Heights, NJ 07604
Tel. 212/355-2600
Fax 212/308-2968
www.fiat.com

Heineken USA (Dutch)
beverages
50 Main Street
White Plains, NY 10606
Tel. 914/681-4100
Fax 914/681-4178
www.heineken.com

Hitachi (Japanese)
*electronics, chemicals,
construction*
Hitachi America, Ltd.
50 Prospect Avenue
Tarrytown, NY 10591
Tel. 914/332-5800
Fax 914/33-25834
www.hitachi.com

Hyundai Motor America (Korean)
*autos, ships, computers, and
construction*
P.O. Box 20850
Fountain Valley, CA 92728
Tel. 714/965-3000
Fax 714/965-3837
www.hmc.co.kr

Matsushita (Japanese)
electronics
9401 Grand Avenue
Franklin Park, IL 60131
Tel. 708/451-1200

Michelin North America (French)
rubber products and travel guides
Patewood Industrial Park
P.O. Box 19001
Greenville, SC 29602
Tel. 803/458-5000
Fax 803/458-6359
www.michelin.com

NEC (Japanese)-*computers
and electronics*
NEC America Inc.
Corporate Center Drive
Melville, NY 11747
Tel. 516/753-7000
Fax 516/753-7041
www.nec.com

Nestle USA, Inc. (Swiss)
coffee and food products
800 N. Brand Blvd.
Glendale, CA 91203
Tel. 818/549-6000
Fax 818/549-6952

Perrier Group (French)—*bottled
water and fitness equipment*
Great Waters of France
777 W. Putnam Avenue
Greenwich, CT 06836
Tel. 203/531-4100
Fax 203/863-0297
www.perrier.com

Sony (Japanese)—*electronics,
consumer products, and
motion pictures*
Sony Corporation of America
550 Madison Avenue
New York, NY 10022
Tel. 212/833-6800
Fax 212/833-7392
www.sony.com

Toshiba (Japanese)
*computers, electronics,
nuclear products*
Toshiba America, Inc.
1251 Avenue of the Americas
41st Floor
New York, NY 10020
Tel. 212/596-0600
Fax 212/593-3875
www.toshiba.com

Yamaha (Japanese)—*sports
goods, electronics, music*
Yamaha Corp. Of America
6660 Orangethorpe Avenue
Buena Park, CA 90620
Tel. 714/522-9011
Fax 714/522-9235
www.yamaha.com

6

Contracting and Consulting Firms in Development

The private contracting and consulting firms outlined in this chapter are the major recipients of government contracts and international funding. These firms provide technical assistance and other services to developing countries in Asia, the Pacific, Africa, Eastern Europe, the former Soviet Union, the Middle East, Latin America, and the Caribbean. They include everything from large construction and engineering firms involved in building roads, dams, and pharmaceutical plants to accounting firms, agricultural development specialists, health training groups, telecommunication consultants, and small business and financial development experts. Several of the businesses identified in Chapter 5, especially the consulting firms on pages 123-125, also do some government contract work abroad but not as exclusively as the firms identified in this chapter.

A Re-Invented Public-Private Partnership

While some of these firms—especially those in engineering, construction, and accounting—also operate in North America and Europe, most are oriented toward solving the infrastructural and managerial problems of developing Third and Fourth World countries. In contrast to government agencies and United Nations organizations, which are primarily involved in defining problems and funding projects, these firms are involved in the day-to-day implementation of projects at the local level. They build roads, construct factories, initiate health programs, experiment with new crops, organize agricultural cooperatives, develop legal and financial systems, promote privatization and small business enterprises, and provide technical assistance in developing information and communication systems.

Many of the firms examined in this chapter could be cross-listed in Chapter 5 as business firms operating abroad. In fact, many of these firms that grew up during the Cold War era used to primarily specialize in government contract work, with some having nearly 100 percent of their business dependent on government contracts. However, during the past decade, many of these firms have had to literally "reinvent" themselves in the face of cutbacks in government social spending for traditional development programs sponsored by the government's much troubled foreign aid agency —USAID. Forced to diversify their companies by operating more like private businesses rather than government contractors, many of these firms have flourished during the past decade by redefining their operations. Others have fallen on bad times due to their inability to transition to the private sector. Government contractors who have made successful transitions, such as Abt Associates, now have thriving businesses that include a healthy mix of government contract and private sector work.

> Many of these firms have had to literally "reinvent" themselves in the face of cutbacks in government social spending for traditional development programs sponsored by USAID.

The firms identified in this chapter more or less operate abroad. Some assign 70 percent of their staff abroad while others have 70 percent of their staff based in the United States.

New Contracting Frontiers

Most contractors and consultants identified in this chapter rely a great deal on public financing of foreign aid and international assistance programs. As a major funding source, the U.S. Agency for International Development (USAID) focuses most of its resources on Eastern Europe, the former Soviet republics, Latin America, Africa, and Asia. Each year

USAID awards over 5,000 contracts for a total value of over $7 billion. Most of these contracts go to private voluntary organizations, nonprofit organizations, education institutions, and many of the private contractors and consultants identified in this chapter.

During the past decade a great deal of U.S. government money has begun to flow into Eastern Europe and the former Soviet Union via U.S.-based contractors and consultants. These countries have been the new frontiers for international consulting work in the 1990s.

As parts of Eastern Europe and the former Soviet Union continued to disintegrate in the 1990s, more and more U.S. aid flowed into this part of the world. A larger number of contractors and consultants extended their operations into these newly developing countries.

Most of the contracts earmarked for Eastern Europe and the former Soviet Union focus on privatizing state owned industries; increasing the capacity of government ministries; installing new accounting and information processing systems; responding to emergencies; extending humanitarian assistance; restructuring agriculture; extending managerial expertise; developing legal systems; establishing investment programs; managing energy systems; and providing medical assistance. In other words, the aid has been aimed at promoting capitalist economies that would hopefully lead to increased economic and political stability in this part of the world. USAID and its cadre of contractors and consultants like to refer to this as a quest for "sustainable development."

Strategies

Getting a job with a contracting and consulting firm requires a thorough understanding of the organizations and their skill requirements. Many organizations, such as engineering, construction, and accounting firms, are primarily concerned with recruiting individuals who have specific technical skills relevant to the work of the organization rather than knowledge of specific countries, exotic foreign language abilities, or extensive international experience. Other firms, such as those specializing in tropical agriculture, community development, population planning, rural health systems, and education, tend to recruit individuals who have a great deal of international experience as well as knowledge of specific countries. Many of these firms require candidates to have exotic combinations of language and work skills and Third World experience.

Given the project-by-project nature of these firms' work, most contracting and consulting firms encourage individuals to directly submit information on their skills and qualifications. Most of the firms maintain resume banks, computerized personnel files, or "resource rosters". Information on qualified candidates is kept on file and referred to when staffing needs occur. Firms use these resource rosters frequently given the nature of the contracting business. Therefore, you may want to send your resume to several firms which appear to be relevant to your interests and skills. Since most of these firms have Web sites, be sure to visit their sites before contacting them by mail, phone, or fax. Most Web sites will include information on job vacancies and resume databases. For your convenience, we've included Web sites for most of these firms.

Many of the companies identified in this chapter compete with as well as work closely with counterpart organizations outlined in Chapters 7, 8, and 9. Private voluntary organizations (PVOs), nonprofit corporations, and university research centers share many of the same funding sources as the private contracting and consulting firms. Therefore, you may want to examine these firms in reference to the organizations in these other chapters. As you will quickly discover, the organizations in this and the next three chapters constitute an important "network" of international development organizations. Individuals who work for PVOs often find employment with nonprofit corporations and private contracting and consulting firms. After all, they engage in similar work and recruit individuals with similar international skills.

> **Most of the firms maintain resume banks, computerized personnel files, or "resource rosters". Check out their Web sites for information on job vacancies and resume databases.**

The abbreviations appearing in the descriptions of each firm refer to many of the organizations identified in Chapters 2 and 3 on the federal government and international organizations. As you will quickly discover, USAID is the major funding source for most of these organizations. United Nations agencies (United Nations Development Programme [UNDP], World Health Organization [WHO]), as well as the World Bank (IBRD), International Monetary Fund (IMF), and several regional financial institutions also provide funding for these firms. If you are serious about working for an international contractor, you should first understand the nature of their international work and the way they are funded. As we outlined in *The Complete Guide to International Jobs and Careers*, international contracting and consulting firms have their own peculiar way of hiring and managing staffs at home and abroad. They offer rich opportunities to work in some of the most exciting international job and work settings today.

The Organizations

ABB LUMMUS GLOBAL
1515 Broad Street
Bloomfield, NJ 07003
Tel. 973/893/1515 or Fax 973/893-2000
Web site: *abb.com/usa/lummus*

Previously known as Lummus Crest, Inc. Provides engineering and construction services relating to chemical, petrochemical, and refinery plants. Maintains a full-time staff in the U.S. of 1 and a long-term staff abroad of 1,800. Operates in Africa (Nigeria), Asia, Latin America, Middle East, Western and Eastern Europe, the USSR, and Japan. Major clients include governments and private companies.

ABT ASSOCIATES, INC.
4800 Montgomery Lane, Suite 600
Bethesda, MD 20814
Tel. 301/913-0500 or Fax 301/652-3618
Web site: *www.abtassoc.com*

Provides technical assistance in the areas of environment, agriculture, health, economic and urban development, law, and financial services. Operates projects in Africa, Asia, Latin America, the Caribbean, Middle East, North Africa, and Portugal. Major clients include: USAID, The World Bank, African Development Bank, CARE, United Nations, and foreign governments. Maintains overseas offices in South Africa and Egypt. Annual revenues exceed $100 million. Employs more than 800. Diversified in several major business areas.

ADVANCED SYSTEMS DEVELOPMENT, INC.
2800 Shirlington Road, Suite 800
Arlington, VA 22206
Tel. 703/998-3900 or Fax 703/824-5699
Web site: *www.asdinc.com*

Provides information management system, engineering, and computer services. Maintains a full-time U.S. staff of 90. Major client is the Department of Defense (Navy and Army).

AER ENTERPRISES
P.O. Box 6207
East Brunswick, NJ 08816
Tel. 732/254-6930
Fax 732/254-6812
Web site: *www.aerenterprises.com*

Specializes in conference planning relating to technology transfer. Maintains a full-time staff in the U.S. of 4.

AGUIRRE INTERNATIONAL
480 E. 4th Avenue, Unit A
San Mateo, CA 94401-3349
Tel. 650/373-4900 or Fax 650/348-0260

Provides technical assistance in the areas of policy and development analysis; project design, development, and evaluation; human resource development; and program implementation. Maintains a full-time staff in the U.S. of 35 and a long-term staff abroad of 7. Primarily operates in Latin America. Major clients include USAID, U.S. Department of Labor, U.S. Department of Education, and the U.S. Department of Energy.

ALLIED SIGNAL TECHNICAL SERVICES CORPORATION
1 Bendix Road
Columbia, MD 21045-1897
Tel. 410/964-7000 or Fax 410/730-6775
Web site: *www.alliedsignal.com*

A major international engineering firm providing comprehensive engineering, electronic, computer, and telecommunications services. Maintains a full-time staff in the U.S. of 6,600 and long-term staff abroad of 600. Operates in Asia, Latin America, Middle East, Europe, Australia, New Zealand, and Canada. Major clients include USAID, USIA, NASA, Department of Defense, Department of Energy, Federal Aviation Administration, U.S. Department of Agriculture, Defense Nuclear Agency, Government of Saudi Arabia, and numerous commercial firms.

AMEX INTERNATIONAL, INC.
1615 L Street, NW, Suite 340
Washington, DC 20036
Tel. 202/429-0222 or Fax 202/429-1867
Web site: *www.amexdc.com*

Provides consulting services in three major areas: international consulting, information technology, and procurement and shipping. Maintains offices in Ghana,

Guinea, Armenia, and Georgia. Major clients include USAID, the World Bank, and UNDP.

AMMANN & WHITNEY CONSULTING ENGINEERS, INC.
96 Morton Street
New York, NY 10014
Tel. 212/524-7200
Fax 212/524-7215

Specializes in the design, construction, and management of bridges, highways, airports, and mass transit facilities. Operates in Africa, Asia, Latin American, Middle East, North Africa, Western Europe, and Puerto Rico. major clients include the U.S. Department of State, U.S. Corps of Engineers, U.S. Information Agency, and several host country governments.

ARKEL INTERNATIONAL, LTD.
1048 Florida Boulevard
Baton Rouge, LA 70802
Tel. 225/343-0525
Fax 225/336-1849
Web site: *www.arkel.com*

Offers engineering, construction, and factory management services. Specializes in sugar production and refining, petro chemical industry, sulfur recovery from hydrocarbons, fertilizers, pulp and paper industry, alcohol production, agricultural development, material handling systems, and oil and gas transmission. Operates in Africa, Asia, North Africa, and Canada. Major clients include Export-Import Bank, USAID, U.S. Army Corps of Engineers, Government of Egypt, and private companies in Kenya, Philippines, Ivory Coast, and the Sudan.

ARTHUR ANDERSEN AND COMPANY
1666 K Street, NW
Washington, DC 20006
Tel. 202/862-3100
Fax 202/785-4689
Web site: *www.arthurandersen.com*

An international accounting firm providing accounting/audit services, management information consulting, tax analyses, and professional educational services. Maintains a full-time staff in the U.S. of over 25,000 and a long-term staff abroad of over 20,000. Operates 159 offices in 47 countries of Africa, Asia, Latin America, the Middle East, Australia, Canada, and Western Europe. Major clients include USAID, the World Bank, Asian Development Bank, African Development Bank, UNDP, and hundreds of banks, commercial firms, and government agencies.

ASSOCIATES IN RURAL DEVELOPMENT
110 Main Street, 4th Floor
Burlington, VT 05401
Tel. 802/658-3890 or Fax 802/658-4247
Web site: *www.ardinc.com*

Provides technical assistance in agriculture and rural development, natural resources management, environmental protection, energy planning and technology, management and institutional development, and water and sanitation. Major clients include USAID, World Bank, Asian Development Bank, Inter-American Development Bank, CARE, UNFAO, UNDP, UNOCF, and OECD. Operates projects in Africa, Asia, Latin America, the Caribbean, Middle East, North Africa, and Europe.

ATKINSON, GUY F. CONSTRUCTION CO.
1001 Bayhill Drive
Suite 200
San Bruno, CA 94066
Fax 415/876-1678
Web site: *www.atkn.com*

A major international construction firm involved in building tunnels, dams, power plants, harbor projects, highways, bridges, airports, transit systems, paper mills, and commercial and institutional buildings. Operates in Latin America, the Caribbean, Middle East, Australia, and Canada. Major clients are several private companies.

AURORA ASSOCIATES
1015 18th St., NW, Suite 400
Washington, DC 20036
Tel. 202/463-0950
Fax 202/659-2724

Specializes in providing assistance in two areas: management of computer services and automatic data processing facilities; and management of training programs for international students. Operates in Africa, Asia, and North Africa. Major clients include USAID, U.S. Department of Labor, U.S. Department of State, U.S. Department of Justice, and the U.S. General Accounting Office.

AUTOMATION RESEARCH SYSTEMS, LTD.
4480 King Street, Suite 600
Alexandria, VA 22302
Tel. 703/820-9000
Fax 703/820-9106
Web site: *www.arslimited.com*

Specializes in providing technical services in two areas: integrated computer systems and customized software; and engineering and technical support. Operates projects in the U.S., Korea, and Germany. Major international clients include USAID, Department of Defense (Army), and U.S. Department of State.

BECHTEL GROUP, INC.
50 Beale Street
San Francisco, CA 94105-1895
Tel. 415/768-1234
Fax 415/768-9038
Web site: *www.bechtel.com*

A major international construction firm specializing in all aspects of designing and constructing basic industrial plants—fossil and nuclear power, hydropower, mining and metals, petrochemical, refining, pipeline, chemical, food, and paper. Also involved in projects dealing with water use and conservation, pollution control, hazardous waste cleanup, asbestos abatement, rapid transit, airport development, hotels, factories, and commercial construction. Maintains a full-time staff in the U.S. of over 20,000. Operates worldwide, including Western and Eastern Europe and the former Soviet Union. Major clients include USAID, U.S. Trade and Development Program, World Bank, African Development Bank, EEC, OECF, European Investment banks, and host country governments.

R. W. BECK & ASSOCIATES
1001 Fourth Avenue
Suite 2500
Seattle, WA 98154
Tel. 206/441-7500
Fax 206/695-4701
Web site: *www.rwbeck.com*

A major engineering and construction firm providing a wide range of technical assistance services in the areas of civil, mechanical, electrical, sanitary, and structural engineering, computer systems, economics, environmental, and construction management. Maintains a full-time staff in the U.S. of nearly 6,000. Operates in Asia, Latin America, the Caribbean, the Middle East, Canada, and New Zealand. Major clients include host country governments.

LOUIS BERGER INTERNATIONAL, INC.
100 Halsted Street
East Orange, NJ 07019
Tel. 973/678-1960
Fax 973/672-4284
Web site: *www.louisberger.com*

Provides services in the areas of engineering and architectural design, economic analyses, agricultural and rural development, environmental and natural resources management, transportation, and irrigation systems. Maintains a full-time staff in the U.S. of 450 and a long-term staff abroad of 1260. Operates in Africa, Asia, Latin America, the Caribbean, Middle East, North Africa, and Europe. Major clients include USAID, World Bank, African Development Bank, UNDP, Asian Development Bank, Caribbean Development Bank, and Inter-American Development Bank.

BIRCH & DAVIS ASSOCIATES, INC.
8905 Fairview Road, Suite 200
Silver Spring, MD 20910
Tel. 301/589-6760
Fax 301/650-0398
Web site: *www.birchdavis.com*

U.S. staff of 150 and 3 abroad. Provides management consulting services in the areas of health and management information systems.

BLACK AND VEATCH LLP
8400 Ward Parkway
Kansas City, MO 64114
Tel. 913/458-2900
Fax 913/458-3730
Web site: *www.bv.com*

A major engineering-architectural firm providing electrical power generation, environmental engineering, and advanced energy technology services. Maintains a worldwide staff of over 3,000. Operates in Africa, Asia, Latin America, the Caribbean, Middle East, North Africa, Europe, the former Soviet Union, Japan, Australia, New Zealand, Greenland, and Canada. Major clients include USAID, World Bank, U.S. Export-Import Bank, and numerous host country governments and private companies.

BOOZ, ALLEN, AND HAMILTON, INC.
8283 Greensboro Drive
McLean, VA 22102
Tel. 703/920-5000
Fax 703/902-3333
Web site: *www.bah.com*

A major management consulting firm providing technical assistance in the areas of information systems, tax administration, transportation planning, banking, environment, financial management, public administration, private sector development, and labor force analysis. Maintains a full-time staff in the U.S. of 2700 and a long-term staff abroad of 1500. Operates in Africa, Asia, Latin America, the Middle East, and North Africa. International clients include USAID and host country governments.

JOHN T. BOYD COMPANY
4 Gateway Center, Suite 1900
444 Liberty Avenue
Pittsburgh, PA 15222
Tel. 412/562-1770
Fax 412/562-1953
Web site: *www.jtboyd.com*

Provides engineering, mining, environmental, and marketing, and financial services. Maintains a U.S. staff of over 50.

BOYLE ENGINEERING CORP.
1501 Quail Street, P.O. Box 3030
Newport Beach, CA 92658-9020
Tel. 949/476-3300
Fax 949/721-7141
Web site: *www.boyleengineering.com*

Provides complete engineering and architectural services in the areas of water supply, sewage, irrigation, and environment. Maintains a full-time staff in the U.S. of 500. Operates in Africa, Asia, Latin America, the Caribbean, the Middle East, Canada, and Western Europe. Major clients include host country governments and private firms.

BUCHART-HORN, INC.
445 West Philadelphia Street
York, PA 17404
Tel. 717/852-1400
Fax 717/852-1401
Web site: *www.bh-ba.com*

Offers engineering services in the areas of civil, sanitary, environmental, structural, electrical, mechanical engineering as well as architectural, land survey, landscape architecture, and solid/hazardous waste services. Maintains a full-time staff in the U.S. of nearly 400 and a long-term staff abroad of about 20. Operates in Columbia, Saudi Arabia, Germany, and Greece. Major clients include the U.S. Army Engineer Division, Europe.

BURNS AND ROE ENTERPRISES, INC.
800 Kinderkamack Road
Oradell, NJ 07649
Tel. 201/265-2000 or Fax 201/986-4459
Web site: *www.roe.com*

An architectural design and construction engineering firm focusing on electricity generation facilities. Maintains a full-time U.S. staff of 950 and a long-term staff abroad of 50. Operates in Asia, Latin America, the Caribbean, the Middle East, Australia, and Europe. Major clients include the Work Bank, USAID, U.S. Department of Defense, U.S. Department of Energy, Asian Development Bank, and host government agencies.

CACI INTERNATIONAL, INC.
1100 N. Glebe Road
Arlington, VA 22201
Tel. 703/841-7800
Fax 703/841-7882
Web site: *www.caci.com*

Specializes in providing information systems, advanced technologies, software development, and marketing services in the fields of defense, aerospace, communication, transportation, finance, and retailing. Maintains a full-time staff in the U.S. of 2,350 and a long-term staff abroad of 150, with 45 offices in North America and Europe. Operates projects Canada, Ireland, the Netherlands, Sweden, the United Kingdom.

CAMP DRESSER AND MCKEE INTERNATIONAL, INC.
One Cambridge Center
Cambridge, MA 02142
Tel. 617/621-8181 or Fax 617/577-7501
Web site: *www.cdm.com*

A major engineering firm specializing in water supply issues, wastewater, hazardous/industrial/solid wastes, agriculture and irrigation, utilities, and environmental planning. Maintains a full-time staff in the U.S. of 1900 and a long-term staff abroad of 36. Operates in Africa, Asia, the Pacific Islands, Latin America, the Caribbean, Middle East, North Africa, and Australia. Major clients include USAID, World Bank, Asian Development Bank, DECF, and the Government of Singapore.

CARTER & BURGESS, INC.
3880 Hulen Street
Ft. Worth, TX 76107
Tel. 817/735-6000 or Fax 817/735-6148
Web site: *www.ftp.c-b.com*

An engineering design and construction management firm providing technical assistance in the areas of mechanical, electrical, civil, and structural engineering, land use planning, landscape architecture, and surveying. Maintains a full-time staff in the U.S. of 215. Operates projects in Nigeria, Taiwan, Latin America, the Middle East, and Spain. Major clients include U.S. government agencies, host country governments, and corporations such as ARAMCO, General Dynamics, and IBM.

CBI INDUSTRIES, INC.
1501 N. Division Street
Plainfield, IL 60544-8984
Tel. 815/439-6000 or Fax 815/439-6010
Web site: *www.chicagobridge.com*

The Chicago Bridge and Iron Company (CBI) is a construction firm providing design, engineering, fabrication, project management, and general contracting services in the areas of forest product industries, water and wastewater treatment plant equipment, petrochemicals, oil, and gas. Maintains a full-time staff in the U.S. of 8,000 and a long-term staff abroad of 4,000. Operates in Africa, Asia, Latin America, the Middle East, Australia, Canada, and Western Europe.

CENTER FOR INTERNATIONAL RESEARCH, INC.
1815 N. Fort Myer Drive, Suite 600
Arlington, VA 22209
Tel. 703/527-5546 or Fax 703/527-4661
Web site: *air-dc.org*

Previously known as the American Institute For Research and the Institute For International Research. Provides technical assistance in the areas of education systems, communication, and human relations. Maintains a full-time staff in the U.S. of 40 and a long-term staff abroad of 5. Operates in Africa, Asia, Latin America, the Caribbean, Middle East, and North Africa. Main client is USAID.

CHECCHI AND COMPANY CONSULTING, INC.
1899 L Street, NW, Suite 800
Washington, DC 20036
Tel. 202/452-9700 or Fax 202/466-9070

Specializes in agricultural and rural development, management training, project planning, investment analysis, feasibility studies, and infrastructure appraisal. Operates in Africa, Asia, Pacific Islands, Latin America, the Caribbean, Middle East, and North Africa. Major clients include USAID, World Bank, Asian Development Bank, and the U.S. Department of Treasury.

CHEMONICS INTERNATIONAL
1133 20th Street, NW, Suite 600
Washington, DC 20036
Tel. 202/955-3300 or Fax 202/955-3400
Web site: *www.chemonics.com*

Provides technical assistance services to USAID in the areas of agriculture (policy and planning, farming systems research/extension, on-farm water management, rice production, livestock, seed technology, and agricultural engineering), agribusiness (food/fiber processing, marketing, agrochemicals, and business/financial management), natural resources (soil/water conservation/management, range management, and forestry), and rural development (infrastructure, cooperatives, information systems, and public administration).

CONSERVATION INTERNATIONAL
2501 M Street, NW, Suite 200
Washington, DC 20037
Tel. 202/429-5660 or Fax 202/887-5188
Web site: *www.conservation.org*

Provides technical assistance in the areas of marine resources and conservation. Major client is USAID.

CONSOER, TOWNSEND, AND ENVIRODYNE ENGINEERS, INC.
303 East Wacker Drive, Suite 600
Chicago, IL 60601
Tel. 312/938-0300 or Fax 312/938-1109

Provides engineering and construction services relating to water resources, wastewater collection and treatment, solid waste management, transportation, and architecture. Operates in Africa, Asia, Latin America, the Middle East, and France. Many clients include the U.S. Army Corps of Engineers, private firms, and host country governments.

CONSTRUCTION CONTROL SERVICES CORPORATION
115 West Main Street
Durham, NC 27701
Tel. 919/682-5741 or Fax 919/683-3072
Web site: *www.cipysearchcom/idu/ccsc*

Provides a full range of construction coordination and management services for clients. Operates in Chad, Mali, Afghanistan, India, Pakistan, Mexico, and Egypt. Major clients include USAID and the African Development Bank.

CREATIVE ASSOCIATES INTERNATIONAL, INC.
5301 Wisconsin Avenue, NW, Suite 700
Washington, DC 20015
Tel. 202/966-5804 or Fax 202/363-4771
Web site: *www.caii-dc.com*

U.S. staff of 50 and 200 abroad. Provides technical assistance in the several areas of educational development. USAID is major funding source.

DAMNES AND MOORE
7101 Wisconsin Avenue, Suite 700
Bethesda, MD 10814-4870
Tel. 301/652-2215
Fax 301/656-8059
Web site: *www.damnes.com*

Specializes in environmental and earth sciences, with emphasis on water resources development and environmental pollution control. Maintains a full-time staff in the U.S. of 2121 and a long-term staff abroad of 450. Operates projects in Africa, Asia, the Pacific, Latin America, the Caribbean, Middle East, North Africa, Western Europe, Australia, New Zealand, Antarctica, and Canada. Major clients include USAID, Inter-American Development Bank, World Bank, and numerous host country governments and private firms.

DELEUW, CATHER INTERNATIONAL LTD.
1133 15th Street, NW
Suite 800
Washington, DC 20005-2701
Tel. 202/775-3300
Fax 202/775-3422

A major international engineering and construction firm specializing in highways, railroads, rapid transit systems, marine and air terminals, parking garages, municipal water and sewage systems, community planning and development, and industrial and commercial complexes. Maintains a full-time staff in the U.S. of 893 and a long-term staff abroad of 269. Operates in Africa, Asia, Latin America, the Caribbean, Middle East, and North Africa. Major clients include USAID, Asian Development Bank, and World Bank.

DELOITTE AND TOUCHE
555 12th Street, NW, Suite 500
Washington, DC 20004-2505
Tel. 202/879-5600
Fax 202/879-5309
Web site: *www.dttus.com*

Provides technical assistance in the areas of management information systems, financial information management, private enterprise development, financial institutions development, marketing services, and agricultural and rural development. Maintains a full-time staff in the U.S. of 9500 and a long-term staff abroad of 17,000. Operates projects in Africa, Asia, Latin America, the Caribbean, Middle East, and North Africa. Major clients include USAID, World Bank, IMF, Overseas Private Investment Corporation, Canadian International Development Agency, Inter-American Development Bank, and the African Development Bank.

DEVELOPMENT ALTERNATIVES, INC.
7250 Woodmont Avenue, Suite 200
Bethesda, MD 20814
Tel. 301/718-8699 or Fax 301/718-7968
Web site: *www.dai.com*

A high quality consulting/contracting firm providing technical assistance services in the areas of agriculture, natural resources, finance, management, and economics. Maintains a full-time staff in the U.S. of 160 and a long-term staff abroad of 200. Operates in Africa, Asia, Latin America, the Caribbean, Middle East, Eastern Europe, and the former Soviet Union. Major clients include USAID, African Development Bank, Asian Development Bank, World Bank, European Bank for Reconstruction and Development, UN agencies, U.S. Department of Agriculture, foreign governments and private firms.

DEVELOPMENT ASSISTANCE CORPORATION
1413 11th Street, NW
Washington, DC 20001
Tel. 202/234-8842 or Fax 202/234-5878

Provides technical assistance in the areas of agricultural productivity, seed multiplication, and economic and social development. Maintains a full-time staff in the U.S. of 85 and a long-term staff abroad of 6. Major clients include USAID, U.S. Department of Defense (Army), and the U.S. Department of Health and Human Services. Operates projects in Africa, Asia, Latin America, and the Caribbean.

DEVELOPMENT ASSOCIATES, INC.
1730 North Lynn Street
Arlington, VA 22209
Tel. 703/276-0677
Fax 703/276-0432
Web site: *www.devassoci.com*

A well established and highly respected management and government consulting firm operating in Africa, Asia, the Pacific Islands, Latin American, the Caribbean, Middle East, and North Africa. Maintains a full-time staff in the U.S. of 100 and a long-term staff abroad of 11. Major clients include USAID, Department of Health and Human Services, Department of Education, Department of Agriculture, Department of Commerce, Department of Labor, Inter-American Bank, World Bank, United Nations, and many state and local governments, foundations, and foreign governments. Provides technical assistance in the areas of private sector promotion, health and nutrition, education, agriculture and rural development, public administration, urban and community development, drug and alcohol abuse problems, training development, population and family projects.

DILLINGHAM CONSTRUCTION CORPORATION
5960 Inglewood Drive
Pleasanton, CA 94588
Tel. 925/463-3300 or Fax 925/463-1571
Web site: *www.dillinghamconstruction.com*

A major engineering and construction firm providing a wide range of technical assistance services in the areas of highways, bridges, locks, dams, canals, hydro-electric projects, commercial and residential buildings, military bases and airfields, marine structures and dredging, oil storage facilities, pulp and paper mills. Maintains a full-time staff in the U.S. of 1,500 and a long-term staff abroad of 150. Nearly 25% of their projects are located outside the U.S. Operates in Africa, Asia, the Pacific Islands, Latin America, the Caribbean, Middle East, Europe, Russia, and Australia. Major clients are the U.S. Army Corps of Engineers, host countries, and private companies.

DPRA, INC.

200 Research Drive   1300 North 17th Street
Manhattan, KS 66502   Rosslyn, VA 22209
Tel. 785/539-3565   Tel. 703/522-3772
Fax 785/539-5353   Fax 703/524-9415
Web site: *www.dpra.com*

Specializes in conducting studies relating to economics, environment, financial and regulatory analysis, industrial assessments, marketing research and statistics. Has conducted projects in over 60 countries. Major clients include USAID and the Environmental Protection Agency. Provides technical assistance in the areas of environmental regulation, water resources, agriculture, industry, and trade. Maintains a full-time staff in the U.S. of 150 and long-term staff about of 3. Operates in Africa, Asia, Latin America, the Caribbean, the Middle East, North Africa, Australia, New Zealand, and Western Europe. Major clients include USAID, the World Bank, the United Nations, and several government agencies.

DUAL, INC.
1111 Jefferson Davis Highway, Suite 604
Arlington, VA 22202
Tel. 703/527-3500 or Fax 703/527-0829
Web site: *www.dualinc.com*

Specializes in providing services in the areas of program/project management and evaluation; family planning; management information systems; and automation planning, design, acquisition, and implementation. Maintains a full-time staff in the U.S. of 280. Primarily operates in Asia, Latin America, and the Caribbean but also does some work in Portugal and France. Major clients include USAID, U.S. Navy, NASA, and the National Science Foundation.

EARTH SATELLITE CORPORATION
6011 Executive Blvd., Suite 400
Rockville, MD 20852
Tel. 301/231-0660 or Fax 301/231-5020
Web site: *www.earthsat.com*

U.S. staff of 50. Provides technical services relating to the application of remote sensing and geographic information systems technology to agricultural land use and geological problems.

EMPIRE ACOUSTICAL/McKEOWN INDUSTRIES
36744 Constitution Drive
Trinidad, CO 81082
Tel. 719/846-2300 or Fax 719/846-7466
Web site: *www.empireacoustical.com*

U.S. staff of 20 and 20 abroad. Provides engineering services relating to water treatment and environmental protection.

ENGINEERING-SCIENCE, INC.
100 West Walnut Street
Pasadena, CA 91124
Tel. 626/440-4000 or Fax 626/440-6195
Web site: *www.parsons.com*

Provides engineering and construction services relating to urban infrastructure, water systems, sewage treatment, flood control, and wastewater management. Operates in Asia, Latin America, the Caribbean, the Middle East, North Africa, Greece, and Portugal. Major clients include USAID and host country governments.

ERNST & YOUNG
1225 Connecticut Avenue, NW
Washington, DC 20036
Tel. 202/327-6000 or Fax 202/327-6200
Web site: *www.ey.com*

One of the largest international accounting and business advisory firms representing the merger of two "Big Eight" firms in 1989: Arthur Young & Co. with Ernst and Whinney. Maintains a full-time staff in the U.S. of 7,700 and a long-term staff abroad of 23,500. Has branch offices in 400 cities of 72 countries. Operates worldwide with a major presence in both developing and developed countries, including Europe, Australia, Canada, and the U.S. (92 cities). Major clients include USAID, World Bank, Asian Development Bank, Inter-American Development Bank, and numerous governments and private firms.

FLUOR-DANIELS, INC.
3353 Michelson Drive
Irvine, CA 92730
Tel. 949/975-2000 or Fax 949/975-6549
Web site: *www.fluordaniels.com*

A major engineering, construction, and technical service company providing a broad range of international services relating to industrial, power, and hydrocarbon plant operations. Maintains a full-time staff in the U.S. of nearly 18,000. Operates in Asia, Latin America, the Middle East, Australia, Canada, and Western Europe. Major clients include numerous private firms and government agencies worldwide.

FOSTER WHEELER INTERNATIONAL CORPORATION
1667 K Street, NW, Suite 650
Washington, DC 20006
Tel. 202/296-9703
Web site: *www.fwc.com*

Offers engineering and construction services relating to industrial process plants such as petroleum refining, petrochemicals, chemicals, fertilizers, pulp and paper, and pharmaceuticals. Maintains a full-time staff in the U.S. of 1200 and a long-term staff abroad of 7000. Operates in Africa, Asia, Latin America, the Caribbean, the Middle East, North Africa, European, and the former Soviet Union. Major clients include the World Bank, USAID, Export-Import Bank, and numerous private companies.

FREDERIC R. HARRIS, INC.
300 East 42nd Street
New York, NY 10017
Tel. 212/973-2900 or Fax 212/953-0399
Web site: *www.frharris.com*

An engineering firm specializing in transportation and related systems. Maintains a full-time staff in the U.S. of 800 and a long-term staff abroad of 100. Operates in Africa, Asia, Latin America, the Caribbean, the Middle East, and North Africa. Major clients include USAID, the World Bank, African Development Bank, Inter-American Development Bank, and numerous U.S. and host country governments.

THE FUTURES GROUP, INC.
1050 17th Street, NW, Suite 1000
Washington, DC 20036
Tel. 202/775-9680 or Fax 202/775-9694
Web site: *www.tfgi.com*

Offers technical assistance services in the areas of family planning, health, and policy analysis. Operates in Africa, Asia, the Pacific Islands, Latin America, the

Caribbean, Middle East, and North Africa. Major clients include USAID and the United Nations.

GANNETT FLEMING ENGINEERS, INC.
P.O. Box 67100
Harrisburg, PA 17106-7100
Tel. 717/763-7211 or Fax 717/763-8150
Web site: *gannettfleming.com*

Provides architectural and engineering services relating to transportation, environmental control, water treatment, solid waste management, and rural development. Maintains a full-time staff in the U.S. of 1,000 and a long-term staff abroad of 30. Operates in Africa, Latin America, the Caribbean, and Saudi Arabia. Major clients include the World Bank, African Development Bank, United Nations, USAID, and numerous commercial firms and U.S. government agencies.

HARZA ENGINEERING COMPANY
233 South Wacker Drive
Chicago, IL 60606-6392
Tel. 312/831-3000
Fax 312/831-3999
Web site: *www.harza.com*

Provides technical assistance services relating to water resources (electrical power, irrigation, drainage, flood control, water supply, pollution abatement), municipal public works, transportation, tunnels, solid waste disposal, telecommunications, mining and environmental sciences. Maintains a full-time staff in the U.S. of 500 and a long-term staff abroad of over 100. Operates projects in Africa, Asia, Latin America, Middle East, and North Africa. Major clients include USAID, World Bank, InterAmerican Development Bank, Asian Development Bank, and host country governments and private firms.

HARZA NORTHEAST
181 Genesee Street
Utica, NY 13501
Tel. 315/797-5800
Fax 315/797-8143
Web site: *www.harzane.com*

Formerly known as Stetson-Harza. Provides architectural and engineering services relating to chemical, systems, building, civil, and water resources engineering. Maintains a full-time staff in the U.S. of 180. Operates in Korea, Italy, West Germany, and Puerto Rico. Major clients are U.S. Army Engineers and private companies.

HEERY INTERNATIONAL, INC.
999 Peachtree Street, NE
Atlanta, GA 30367
Tel. 404/881-9880 or Fax 404/875-1283
Web site: *www.heery.com*

Provides architectural, engineering, construction, and planning services for all types
of facilities—commercial, sports/recreation, educational, health, military, convention, and multi-use. Maintains a full-time staff in the U.S. of over 400 and a long-
term staff over 60. Operates in Asia, Latin America, the Middle East, Canada, and
Western Europe. Major clients include the U.S. Army Engineering Division, U.S.
Army Corps of Engineers.

HELLMUTH, OBATA, AND KASSABAUM, INC.
211 North Broadway, Suite 600
St. Louis, MO 63102
Tel. 314/421-2000 or Fax 314/421-6073
Web site: *www.hok.com*

Provides architectural and engineering services in numerous areas—facilities,
urban, site development, and environment. Maintains a full-time staff in the U.S.
of 930 and a long-term staff abroad of 9. Operates in Asia, Latin America, the
Caribbean, the Middle East, Australia, and Western Europe. Major clients include
host country governments.

ICF KAISER ENGINEERS GROUP, INC.
2101 Webster
Oakland, CA 94612
Tel. 510/419-6000 or Fax 510/419-5355
Web site: *www.icfkaiser.com*

Provides a wide range of management engineering, procurement, and construction
services for environmental, transportation, advanced technology, industrial, and
other infrastructure projects. Maintains a full-time staff in the U.S. of 1,550 and a
long-term staff abroad of 50. Operates in Asia, Latin America, Middle East, North
Africa, Europe, and Australia. Major clients include: U.S. government agencies,
host country governments, and private firms.

INSTITUTE FOR RESOURCE DEVELOPMENT
11785 Beltsville Drive
Calverton, MD 20705
Tel. 301/595-1757
Fax 301/572-0999

Provides technical assistance in the area of population planning and health. A
subsidiary of Westinghouse Electric Company. Maintains a full-time staff in the

U.S. of 80 and a long-term staff abroad of 5. Operates in Africa, Asia, Latin America, the Caribbean, Middle East and North America. Major client is USAID.

INTERNATIONAL RESOURCES GROUP
1211 Connecticut Avenue, NW
Washington, DC 20036
Tel. 202/289-0100
Fax 202/289-7601
Web site: *www.irgltd.com*

Provides technical assistance in the areas of energy planning and policy, finance, natural resources, conservation, wildlife systems, and health care. Maintains a full-time staff in the U.S. of 30 and a long-term staff abroad of 10. Operates in Africa, Asia, Latin America, the Caribbean, Middle East and North Africa. Major clients include USAID, World Bank, and the Asian Development Bank.

IONICS RESOURCES CONSERVATION COMPANY
3006 Northup Way
Bellevue, WA 98004-1407
Tel. 425/828-2400 or Fax 425/828-0526
Web site: *www.ionicsrcc.com*

U.S. staff of 85. Provides technical services relating to evaporative water treatment systems for recycling wastewater.

IRI RESEARCH INSTITUTE, INC.
169 Greenwich Avenue
Stamford, CT 06904-1276
Tel. 203/327-5985
Fax 203/359-1595
Web site: *www.iriresrch.com*

Specializes in providing technical assistance relating to agriculture: crop production, agribusiness, research, and marketing. Maintains a full-time staff in the U.S. of 10 and a long-term staff abroad of 8. Operates primarily in Latin America and the Caribbean but also has projects in Kenya, Bangladesh, Indonesia, Egypt, Oman, and Yemen Arab Republic.

JOHN SNOW, INC.
44 Farnswoth Avenue
Boston, MA 02111
Tel. 617/482-9485
Fax 617/482-0617

1616 N. Fort Myer Dr., 11th Fl.
Arlington, VA 22209
Tel. 703/528-7474
Fax 703/528-7480

Web site: *www.jsi.com*

One of the largest and most capable international companies providing technical assistance in developing countries relating to family planning, family health, nutrition, rural health systems, and education; water, sanitation, and tropical diseases; logistics and information systems; training and staff development; and research. Maintains a full-time staff in the U.S. of 120 and a long-term staff abroad of 20. Operates in Africa, Asia, Latin America, the Caribbean, Middle East, and North Africa. Engaged in joint contracts with PVOs and other private contractors. Major clients include USAID and UNHCR.

THE M.W. KELLOGG COMPANY
Three Greenway Plaza
Houston, TX 77046-0395
Tel. 713/960-2000 or Fax 713/960-2032

One of the world's oldest (1901) and largest international engineering and construction firms engaged in the design and construction of processing and manufacturing projects around the world: chemical, petrochemical, fertilizer, gas processing, refining, and computer integrated manufacturing. A subsidiary of Dresser Industries, Inc. Maintains a full-time staff in the U.S. of nearly 3,000 and a long-term staff abroad of 600. Has branch offices in London, Cayman Islands, Washington, DC, Buenos Aires, Singapore, Beijing, Jakarta, and Kuala Lumpur. Major clients include all major companies in the U.S. as well as both public and private companies and governments abroad. Operates projects in more than 30 countries, including Western and Eastern Europe, and on all but one continent.

KPMG PEAT-MARWICK
345 Park Avenue
New York, NY 10154-0102
Tel. 212/909-5000 or Fax 212/909-5200
Web site: *www.kpmg.com*

U.S. staff of 30,000 and 60,000 abroad. Provides tax and management services.

LABAT-ANDERSON, INC.
8000 West Park Drive, Suite 400
McLean, VA 22102
Tel. 703/506-9600 or Fax 703/506-4646
Web site: *labat.com*

Provides technical assistance services in agricultural research, analysis, and extension; natural resource and environmental planning; private sector and small enterprise strategy; resource development; health and child survival initiatives; and management information systems. Has 8(a) status. Maintains a full-time staff in the U.S. of 400 and a long-term staff abroad of 3. Major clients include USAID, Peace Corps, and the Department of State.

ARTHUR D. LITTLE
25 Acorn Park
Cambridge, MA 02140
Tel. 617/864-5770 or Fax 617/498-7200
Web site: *arthurdlittle.com*

Provides technical assistance in the areas of technology development, energy, financial planning, natural resource development, management, and infrastructure. Operates a full-time staff in the U.S. of 2,500. Operates in Africa, Asia, the Pacific Islands, Latin American, the Caribbean, Middle East, North Africa, Europe, Japan, and Canada. Major clients include USAID, World Bank, and host country governments.

ROY LITTLEJOHN ASSOCIATES, INC.
6856 Eastern Avenue, NW
Suite 317
Washington, DC 20012-2165
Tel. 202/722-2446
Fax 202/842-0215
Web site: *www.rlagroup*

Provides technical assistance in the areas of manpower/economic development, program design, applied research, data processing, technology, and applied science relating to labor, health, welfare, education, public administration, agriculture, and tourism. U.S. staff of 30 and 5 abroad.

LOGICAL TECHNICAL SERVICES CORPORATION
7250 Woodmont Avenue
Suite 340
Bethesda, MD 20814
Tel. 301/652-2121
Fax 301/951-9624
Web site: *www.ltscorporation.com*

Provides technical, software, and hardware support services relating to information services and technical publications. Maintains a full-time staff in the U.S. of 150. Operates projects in Africa, Asia, Latin America, and the Caribbean. Major clients include USAID.

MANAGEMENT SYSTEMS INTERNATIONAL
600 Water Street, SW
Washington, DC 20024
Tel. 202/484-7170 or Fax 202/488-0754

Provides technical assistance in the areas of small enterprise development, institutional strengthening, information utilization, and project design, implementation, and evaluation. Maintains a full-time U.S. staff of 65 and a long-term staff abroad of 3. Operates in Africa, Asia, Pacific Islands, Latin America, the Caribbean, Middle East, North Africa, Portugal, and Puerto Rico. Major clients include USAID, The World Bank, United Nations, and various U.S. government agencies.

MATHTECH, INC.
6402 Arlington Blvd., Suite 1200
Falls Church, VA 22042
Tel. 703/875-8866
Fax 703/875-8867
Web site: *www.mathtechinc.com*

U.S. staff of 60 and 1 abroad. Provides technical assistance on energy issues in developing countries.

MEDICAL SERVICE CORPORATION INTERNATIONAL
1716 Wilson Blvd.
Arlington, VA 22209
Tel. 703/276-3000
Fax 703/276-3017
Web site: none at present (email: msci@access.digex.net)

Provides technical assistance in the areas of health career management, information systems, training, vector borne disease control, and program management. Maintains a full-time staff in the U.S. of 50 and a long-term staff abroad of 20. Operates in Africa, Asia, Latin America, the Caribbean, Middle East, North Africa, Australia, and Hungary. Major clients include USAID, and the U.S. Department of Health and Human Services.

METCALF & EDDY INTERNATIONAL, INC.
P.O. Box 4071
Wakefield, MA 01880-5371
Tel. 781/246-5200
Fax 781/245-6293
Web site: *www.m-e.com*

Provides extensive capabilities in the areas of water and wastewater treatment, including the design and construction of wastewater systems, and defense communication systems. Maintains a full-time staff in the U.S. of nearly 1,500 and a long-term staff abroad of 50. Operates in Africa, Asia, Latin America, the Caribbean, Middle East, North Africa, Europe, Antarctica, Arctic, Australia, and Puerto Rico. Major clients include USAID, U.S. Air Force, and the Government of Egypt.

MMM DESIGN GROUP
229 West Bute Street
Norfolk, VA 23510
Tel. 757/623-1641 or Fax 757/623-5809
Web site: *www.mmmdg.com*

Provides a wide range of architecture, planning, and consulting engineering services. Maintains a full-time staff in the U.S. of 120 and a long-term staff abroad of 50. Operates in Africa, Asia, the Caribbean, the Middle East, North Africa, and Western Europe. Major clients include the World Bank, USAID, and several U.S. government agencies.

MONTGOMERY WATSON, INC
250 North Madison Avenue
Pasadena, CA 91101
Tel. 626/796-9141 or Fax 626/568-6318
Web site: *www.mw.com*

An international engineering and construction firm providing a full range of services involved in designing, constructing, and managing water and wastewater systems in more than 40 countries. Maintains a full-time staff in the U.S. of 1,130 and a long-term staff abroad of 11. Operates in Africa, Asia, Latin America, the Caribbean, Middle East, and Europe. Major clients include USAID, Asian Development Bank, IBRD, and numerous governments and private companies.

MORRISON-KNUDSEN CORPORATION
P.O. Box 73
Boise, ID 83729
Tel. 208/386-5000 or Fax 208/386-7186
Web site: *www.mk.com*

Provides a full range of engineering and construction services relating to transportation, water resources, defense systems, nuclear and hazardous wastes, power plants, railroads, and aircraft. Maintains a full-time staff in the U.S. of 13,500 and a long-term staff abroad of 500. Major clients include numerous host country governments.

MORRISON-MAIERLE/CSSA, INC.
910 Helena Avenue
Helena, MT 59601
Tel. 406/442-3050 or Fax 406/442-7862
Web site: *www.m-m.net*

Provides engineering consulting services in a variety of areas. U.S. staff of 125 and 3 abroad.

MULTI CONSULTANTS, INC.
8484 Georgia Avenue, Suite 320
Silver Spring, MD 20910
Tel. 301/565-4020 or Fax 301/565-5112
Web site: *www.multiconsult.com*

Previously known as Triton Corporation. Provides management consulting services relating to organizational infrastructure and social marketing of contraceptives. U.S. staff of 200 and 5 abroad.

ROBERT R. NATHAN ASSOCIATES, INC.
2101 Wilson Blvd., Suite 1200
Arlington, VA 22201-3062
Tel. 703/516-7700
Fax 703/351-6162
Web site: *www.nathanassoc.com*

Provides technical assistance in the areas of agricultural development, urban planning, small-scale enterprise development, macro-economic policy, and financial infrastructure. Maintains a full-time staff in the U.S. of 70 and a long-term staff abroad of 22. Operates in Africa, Asia, the Pacific Islands, Latin America, the Caribbean, Middle East, North America, and Europe. Major clients include USAID, UNDP, FAO, and the Asian Development Bank.

A. L. NELLUM AND ASSOCIATES
1900 L Street, NW, Suite 405
Washington, DC 20036
Tel. 202/466-4920
Fax 202/466-4745

Trains U.S. Peace Corps Volunteers as extension workers in natural resource and environmental conservation. Operates in Africa, the Caribbean, Latin America, and the Philippines.

NEW JERSEY MARINE SCIENCES CONSORTIUM
Building 22
Fort Hancock
Highlands, NJ 07732
Tel. 732/872-1300
Fax 732/291-4483

Provides technical assistance in the areas of marine and coastal science and technology. Maintains a full-time staff in the U.S. of 30. Operates primarily in the Middle East (Egypt and Israel). Major client is USAID.

ROBERT D. NIEHAUS, INC.
140 E. Carrillo Street
Santa Barbara, CA 93101
Tel. 805/962-0611 or Fax 805/962-0097

Provides economic and environmental consulting services to international development projects. U.S. staff of 10.

THE RALPH M. PARSONS COMPANY
100 W. Walnut Street
Pasadena, CA 91124
Tel. 626/440-2000 or Fax 626/440-2630
Web sites: *www.parsons.com* (main site)
www.jobsatparsons.com (lists job openings)

One of the largest international engineering and construction firms. Offers a full range of services to government, industry, and commerce. Has completed nearly 7,000 projects in more than 90 countries, from transportation systems to power plants. Maintains a full-time staff in the U.S. of nearly 3300 and a long-term staff abroad of 600. Operates in Africa, Asia, the Pacific Islands, Latin America, the Caribbean, Middle East, North Africa, Europe, the USSR, and Australia. Major clients include several U.S. government agencies as well as foreign governments and major corporations.

PARSONS BRINCKERHOFF INTERNATIONAL, INC.
One Penn Plaza
New York, NY 10119
Tel. 212/465-5000 or Fax 212/465-5096
Web site: *www.pbworld.com*

Provides planning, engineering, and architectural services relating to transportation, construction, industrial complexes, environmental protection, energy, water resources, urban and regional planning, and agricultural systems. Maintains a full-time staff in U.S. of 2,100 and a long-term staff abroad of 480. Operates in Africa, Asia, Latin America, the Caribbean, Middle East, North Africa, Europe, and the former Soviet Union. Major clients include USAID, the World Bank, and host country government.

PAYETTE ASSOCIATES INC.
285 Summer Street
Boston, MA 02210
Tel. 617/342-8200 or Fax 617/342-8202

Provides planning, design, construction services for research and health care projects. Maintains a full-time staff in the U.S. of 145. Operates in Guinea-Bissau, Korea, Pakistan, and Egypt. Major funding source is the Aga Khan Foundation.

PADCO, INC.
1025 Thomas Jefferson Street
Suite 170
Washington, DC 20007
Tel. 202/337-2326
Fax 202/944-2350

Provides technical assistance in the areas of housing and urban development, regional and rural development, financial management, human resource development, and project/program evaluation. Maintains a full-time staff in the U.S. of 20 and a long-term staff abroad of 7. Operates in Africa, Asia, Latin America, the Caribbean, Middle East, and North Africa. Major clients include USAID, Asian Development Bank, World Bank, and the United Nations.

PRAGMA CORPORATION
116 E. Broad Street
Falls Church, VA 22046
Tel. 703/237-9303
Fax 703/237-9326

Offers management consulting services in the areas of agriculture and rural development, family planning, health, financial management, private sector development, training/education, industrial development and finance, microcomputer applications, and information systems. Maintains a full-time staff in the U.S. of 30 and a long-term staff abroad of 27. Major clients include USAID, World Bank, InterAmerican Development Bank, IFAD, OAS, and Peace Corps. Operates in Africa, Asia, Latin America, the Caribbean, Middle East, and North Africa with its largest contacts for Burkina Faso, Burma, Zaire, Kenya, and Benin.

PRICEWATERHOUSECOOPERS

1301 Avenue of the Americas
New York, NY 10019
Tel. 212/259-1000
Fax 212/259-1301
Web sites: *www.pwcglobal.com*

1301 K Street, NW
Washington, DC 20005
Tel. 202/414-1000
Fax 202/414-1301
www.pricewaterhousecoopers.com

Formerly known as Coopers and Lybrand and Price Waterhouse (recently merged). Represents the merge of two of the oldest (since 1849 for Price Waterhouse and 1849 for Coopers and Lybrand) and most respected international firms specializing in audit, accounting, tax, information systems, business planning, and resource productivity. Maintains a full-time staff in the U.S. of nearly 30,000 and a long-term staff abroad of 70,000. Operates in over 100 countries. Major funding comes from USAID, World Bank, United Nations, Inter-American Development Bank, foreign governments, and private companies.

RAYTHEON ENGINEERING AND CONSTRUCTION
2 World Trade Center, 91st Floor
New York, NY 10048-0752
Tel. 212/839-1000 or Fax 212/839-3481
Web site: *www.raytheon.com*

Formerly EBASCO Overseas Corporation. A major engineering and construction firm providing project management, engineering design, quality assurance, construction management, and plant services worldwide. Involved in the design and construction of nuclear power facilities, hydroelectric power generation, roads, airports, hazardous waste remediation, petrochemical, commercial buildings, tunnels, piers, defense, aerospace, telecommunications, and pharmaceuticals. Operates in Africa, Asia, Latin America, the Caribbean, the Middle East, Europe, Australia, and Canada. Major clients include USAID, World Bank, U.S. Department of State, host country governments, and private firms.

RESOURCES MANAGEMENT INTERNATIONAL
1130 Connecticut Avenue, NW
Washington, DC 20036
Tel. 202/429-8615 or Fax 202/659-2926
Web site: *www.rmiinc.com*

Provides consulting services in a variety of areas, such as agriculture, education, and energy, primarily in Asia, Eastern Europe, and the former Soviet Union. U.S. staff of 4 and 60 abroad.

RONCO CONSULTING CORPORATION
1995 University Avenue, Suite 520
Berkeley, CA 94704
Tel. 510/526-8290 or Fax 510/848-1983
Web site: *www.roncoconsultingcorporation.com*

Specializing in providing a full range of agricultural, energy, private sector, human resource, family planning, and food aid services. Maintains a full-time staff in the U.S. of 20 and a long-term staff abroad of 25. Operates in Africa, Asia, Latin America, the Caribbean, Middle East, and North Africa. Major clients include USAID and UNFAO.

H. K. SCHUELER INTERNATIONAL, LTD.
432 Park Avenue South
New York, NY 10016
Tel. 212/725-5800 or Fax 212/725-2260
Web site: *www.hkschueler.com*

Procures and supplies medical and laboratory products for international health organizations, PVO's, and NGO's. U.S. staff of 6.

SHELADIA ASSOCIATES, INC.
15825 Shady Grove Road, Suite 100
Rockville, MD 20850
Tel. 301/590-3939
Fax 301/948-7174
Web site: *www.sheladia.com*

Provides technical assistance in the areas of water resources, transportation, and communication systems. Maintains a full-time U.S. staff of 186 and a long-term staff abroad of 23. Operates in Africa, Asia, Latin America, Middle East, and North Africa. Major clients include USAID, U.S. Department of State, and other consulting firms.

WILBUR SMITH ASSOCIATES, INC.
NationsBanc Tower—Gervais St. 1301/P.O. Box 92
Columbia, SC 29201
Tel. 803/252-8145
Fax 803/758-4610
Web site: *www.wilbursmith.com*

Provides international consulting services relating to engineering, architecture, planning, and economics. U.S. staff of 600 and 100 abroad.

SPARKS COMPANIES, INC.
889 Ridge Lake Blvd., Suite 300
Memphis, TN 38120
Tel. 901/766-4600
Fax 901/766-4402

Specializes in providing food and agriculture services. U.S. staff of 100.

STV ENGINEERS, INC.
205 W. Welsh Drive
Douglasville, PA 19518
Tel. 610/326-4600
Fax 610/385-8501
Web site: *www.stvinc.com*

A major international engineering, architectural, planning, construction management, management consulting, and interior design firm. Maintains a full-time staff in the U.S. of 1100 and a long-term staff abroad of 50. Operates in Africa, Asia, Latin America, the Caribbean, the Middle East, and Western Europe. Major clients include USAID, U.S. Department of State, numerous other U.S. government agencies, private firms, and host country governments.

TAMS CONSULTANTS, INC.
655 Third Avenue
New York, NY 10017
Tel. 212/867-1777
Fax 212/697-6354
Web site: *www.tamsconsultants.com*

A full service international engineering, architecture, planning, and environmental consulting firm specializing in projects relating to airports, natural resource management, highways, ports, transportation planning, urban development, waste, and water resources. Maintains a full-time staff in the U.S. of 450 and a long-term staff abroad of 25. Operates in Africa, Asia, Latin America, the Caribbean, the Middle East, North Africa, Australia, Portugal, and the Slovac Republic. Major clients include the World Bank, Inter-American Development Bank, USAID, and host country governments.

TRAINING RESOURCES GROUP
909 North Washington Street, Suite 305
Alexandria, VA 22314
Tel. 703/548-3535 or Fax 703/836-2415

Provides management training, train the trainers, and cross-cultural training services. U.S. staff of 25.

TROPICAL RESEARCH AND DEVELOPMENT, INC.
7001 SW 24th Ave.
Gainesville, FL 32607
Tel. 352/331-1886 or Fax 352/331-3284

Provides technical assistance in the areas of natural resource development, marine culture, fisheries and coastal management, crop, livestock and forest production, water resource management, and integrated regional development. Maintains a full-time U.S. staff of 37 and a long-term staff abroad of 7. Operates in Africa, Asia, Latin America, the Caribbean, Jordan, Italy, and Puerto Rico. Major clients include USAID, InterAmerican Development Bank, U.S. Navy, FUSADES, FAO, and universities.

UNIVERSITY RESEARCH CORPORATION
7200 Wisconsin Avenue, Suites 500 & 600
Bethesda, MD 20814
Tel. 301/654-8338 or Fax 301/941-8427

Provides technical assistance in the areas of family planning, health care, and rural health delivery systems. Maintains a full-time staff in the U.S. of 200 and a long-term staff abroad of 10. Operates in Africa, Asia, Latin America, the Caribbean, the Middle East, and North Africa. Major clients include USAID, United Nations, U.S.

Peace Corps, Organization of American States, and several U.S. government agencies.

WALKHAYDEL, INC.
12 Commerce Drive
Cranford, NJ 07016
Tel. 732/287-2111 or Fax 732/931-1797
Web site: *www.dcames.com* (parent company)

Also known as H-R International, Inc. Provides a full range of engineering and construction services in a variety of commercial development areas. Maintains a full-time staff in the U.S. of 400 and a long-term staff abroad of 25. Operates in the Philippines, Western Samoa, Aruba, Chile, Venezuela, Saudi Arabia, and the Virgin Islands. Major clients include numerous private companies and government agencies.

WASHINGTON CONSULTING GROUP (WCG)
6707 Democracy Blvd., Suite 1010
Bethesda, MD 20817
Tel. 301/581-3347
Fax 301/571-0960
Web site: *www.washcg.com*

Provides technical assistance in the areas of aviation, computer technology, quantitative studies, and technical publications. Maintains a full-time staff in the U.S. of 500. Operates projects in Africa, Asia, Latin America, the Caribbean, Middle East, and North Africa. Major clients include USAID, World Bank, UNDP, USDA, 8 other government departments, National Institutes of Health, and commercial clients.

WIMBERLY ALLISON TONG AND GOO
700 Bishop Street, Suite 1800
Honolulu, HI 96813
Tel. 808/521-8888
Fax 808/521-3888
Web site: *www.watg.com*

Provides architecture and planning services dealing with hotels, resorts, rapid transit, waterfront development, and environmental projects. Maintains a full-time staff in the U.S. of 180. Operates in Asia, the Pacific Islands, Middle East, Mexico, Australia, New Zealand, Western Europe, and the former Soviet Union. Major clients include private firms and host country governments.

7

Private Voluntary Organizations (PVOs/NGOs)

Private voluntary organizations (PVOs)—also frequently referred to as non-governmental organizations (NGOs)—function similarly to nonprofit corporations and contracting firms. Often competing for the same public and private funding source, they operate projects and manage staffs at the field level in poor Third and Fourth World countries. They primarily provide assistance to various disadvantaged groups in developing countries. They work in rural villages, urban slums, and remote areas.

Orientation

PVOs are especially noted for helping the poorest and most distressed groups in developing countries—groups government agencies, international organizations, businesses, and contracting firms are not well equipped to help. A disproportionate number of PVOs focus on child survival, refugee and disaster relief, self-help income generation, enterprise development, vocational training, agriculture and food production, population planning, communications, social welfare, environment and natural resource management, housing, health care, and community development, and women in development efforts for the very poor and destitute. Few if any are involved in creating physical infrastructure or managing technical and marketing programs, although many of their activities support these other efforts that are largely dominated by the private contracting and consulting firms outlined in Chapter 6.

Many of these organizations have religious affiliations, such as the Adventist Development and Relief Agency International, Catholic Relief Services, and Lutheran World Relief, Inc. These groups are closely linked to the missionary activities of U.S.-based Christian churches.

In many respects, PVOs are modern-day missionaries who are less motivated by an evangelical zeal to save souls than by a commitment to humanity—help the very poor move into the mainstream of development. These organizations appeal to a certain type of person who still has a missionary zeal to improve the conditions of poor people throughout the

> **PVOs are modern-day missionaries who are less motivated by an evangelical zeal to save souls than by a commitment to humanity—help the very poor move into the mainstream of development.**

world. Individuals working for PVOs tend to be dedicated to certain human values and committed to helping others; few are motivated by money. Working conditions for employees of these organizations can be difficult and pay is often low. Noted for people-to-people contact at the community level, PVO work tends to generate a certain sense of personal satisfaction and accomplishment that is hard to match in the counterpart work of businesses, government agencies, or international organizations.

While many of these groups are funded by individual and corporate contributions, most also receive contracts and grants from government agencies and foundations. Some of the more enterprising child survival groups, such as Save the Children Foundation, Foster Parents Plan, and Christian Children's Fund, also operate individual "sponsorship" programs for generating income.

PVOs are increasingly playing a major role in developing countries. Funding agencies view these groups as most capable of making a difference in developing countries. Given their great strengths—extensive field operations, commitment to change, adaptability, innovation, performance—PVOs have increasingly become favorite target organizations for key funding organizations such as USAID and the United

Nations. These organizations are committed to expanding the community-based operations of PVOs in Third and Fourth World countries. Consequently, many of these organizations may experience significant growth during the coming decade.

PVOs have traditionally operated in the poorest countries of Sub-Saharan Africa, Asia, the Caribbean, and Central and South America. Within the past eight years, however, many of these groups have extended their operations into the former communist countries of Eastern Europe and the former Soviet Union. For the first time in more than 50 years, numerous PVOs provide assistance in such familiar and unfamiliar places as Albania, Armenia, Belarus, Bosnia-Hercegovina, Bulgaria, Croatia, Czech Republic, Estonia, Georgia, Hungary, Kazakhstan, Kyrgyzstan, Latvia, Lithuania, Moldova, Poland, Romania, Russia, Serbia, Slovak Republic, Tajikistan, Turkmenistan, and the Ukraine.

Strategies

Many PVOs are headquartered in New York City and Washington, DC and operate field staffs throughout the developing world. In contrast to other types of organizations in development, PVOs tend to have a larger proportion of staff working in the field than at headquarters. Therefore, if you are interested in working on development projects in the poor countries of Asia, Africa, and Latin America, many of the PVOs outlined in this chapter may be your perfect choice for targeting a job search.

PVOs should be approached in the same manner as private contracting and consulting firms and nonprofit corporations: research the organizations by first visiting their Web sites; send a copy of your resume to their resource bank (usually operated by the Personnel or Human Resource Development Department); monitor job vacancy announcements appearing on their Web site as well as in major publications; and network for information, advice, and referrals amongst individuals related to the organization. As we note in Chapter 12, international nonprofit organizations have their own resources—from Web sites to publications—that can assist you with your job search.

In contrast to many other organizations operating in developing countries, it is often easier to break into the international job market via PVOs and nonprofit corporations than through government agencies, international organizations, businesses, and private contracting and consulting firms. Many of these organizations offer volunteer opportunities which enable inexperienced individuals to acquire valuable international experience which may turn into full-time employment. As we will see in Chapter 11, many of these same organizations offer internships.

The Organizations

ACCION INTERNATIONAL/AITEC

120 Beacon Street	733 15th St., NW, 7th Fl.
Somerville, MA 02143	Washington, DC 20005
Tel. 617/492-4930	Tel. 202/393-5113
Fax 617/876-9509	Fax 202/393-5115

Web site: *www.accion.org*

U.S. staff of 14 and 10 abroad. Dedicated to eliminating hunger and poverty in the Americas by promoting small-scale economic activities amongst low-income groups in South and Central American, the Caribbean, and the southwestern United States. Operates with a $4 million annual budget.

ADVENTIST DEVELOPMENT AND RELIEF AGENCY INTERNATIONAL

12501 Old Columbia Pike
Silver Spring, MD 20904
Tel. 301/680-6380 or Fax 301/680-6370
Web site: *www.adra.org*

Sponsored by the Seventh-Day Adventist Church. Provides technical assistance in the areas of education, agriculture, health care, community development, social welfare, and disaster relief in Africa, Asia, Latin America, and the Middle East. Maintains a full-time staff in the U.S. of 45 and a long-term staff abroad of 130. Funded through donations from individuals, corporations, and foundations as well as USAID.

THE AFRICAN-AMERICAN INSTITUTE

380 Lexington Ave., 42nd Fl.	1625 Mass. Ave., NW, Ste. 400
New York, NY 10168	Washington, DC 20036
Tel. 212/949-5666	Tel. 202/667-5636
Fax 212/682-6174	Fax 202/265-6332

Web site: *www.interaction.org/mb/aai.html*

U.S. staff of 80 and 46 abroad. Promotes development in Africa and greater understanding between Americans and Africans. Conducts programs on economic recovery and growth, education, policy analysis, outreach, and women in development. Its program representatives operate in 24 African countries. Operates with a $28 million annual budget.

AFRICAN WILDLIFE FOUNDATION
1400 16th Street, NW, Suite 120
Washington, DC 20036
Tel. 202/939-3333
Fax 202/939-3332
Web site: *www.awf.org*

U.S. staff of 11 and 30 abroad. Promotes wildlife preservation through education and training programs in Africa.

AFRICARE, INC.
440 R Street, NW
Washington, DC 20001
Tel. 202/462-3614
Fax 202/387-1034
Web site: *www.africare.org*

Provides assistance to Africa in the areas of water resources, agriculture and food production, education, construction, medical care, health services, and refugee assistance. Maintains a full-time staff in the U.S. of 35 and a long-term staff abroad of 90. Funded by USAID and numerous corporations, foundations, and host country governments. Operates with a $26.5 million budget.

AGA KAHN FOUNDATION
1901 L Street, NW, Suite 700
Washington, DC 20036
Tel. 202/293-2537
Fax 202/785-1752

U.S. staff of 6 and 120 abroad. Promotes social development among low-income groups in Asia and Africa. Supports programs in education, agriculture and food production, and public health. Operates with a $2.7 million annual budget.

ALAN FUTTMACHER INSTITUTE
120 Wall Street, 21st Fl.
New York, NY 10003
Tel. 212/248-1111
Fax 212/248-1951

1120 Connecticut Ave., NW, #460
Washington, DC 20036
Tel. 202/296-4012
Fax 202/223-5756

Web site: *www.agi-usa.org*

Conducts research, policy analysis, and public education programs to disseminate information on reproductive health rights. Supports family planning efforts. Operates with a $4.2 million annual budget.

AMERICA'S DEVELOPMENT FOUNDATION
101 North Union Street, Suite 200
Alexandria, VA 22314
Tel. 703/836-2717
Fax 703/836-3379
Web site: *www.adfusa.org*

Promotes the international development of democracy and respect for human rights. Provides technical assistance to private sector organizations. Sponsors programs on institutional development, civic education, electoral processes, and human rights.

AMERICAN FRIENDS SERVICE COMMITTEE (AFSC)
1501 Cherry Street
Philadelphia, PA 19102
Tel. 215/241-7000
Fax 215/241-7247
Web site: *www.afsc.org*

A Quaker organization committed to alleviating human suffering and promoting global peace. Programs focus on integrated community development, agricultural production, cooperative organization, construction, public health services and refugee assistance. Staff and volunteers in Africa, Latin America, the Middle East and Southeast Asia. Although no specific degrees are required, a minimum of a Bachelor's degree is generally expected. Work experience related to areas of programs, experience living/working in a developing country and a service ideal are most important. Primarily funded through private grants, contributions, bequests, and investments. Operates with a $27.7 million annual budget and a staff of 356.

AMERICAN JEWISH JOINT DISTRIBUTION COMMITTEE, INC.
711 Third Avenue, 10th Floor
New York, NY 10017-4014
Tel. 212/687-6200
Fax 212/682-7262
Web site: *www.ajc.org*

Provides relief, reconstruction, and rehabilitation and supports development projects in Europe and the developing world. Involved in community development, education, disaster relief, health care, refugee services, and social welfare projects. Supports the work of the United Nations in human rights, assists overseas Jewish communities, and helps Israel protect its existence. Conducts programs in Central and South America, Eastern Europe, Russia and the Commonwealth of Nations, Europe, Middle East, South Asia, Southeast Asia, and Sub-Saharan Africa. Operates field offices in Argentina, Austria, France, Israel, and Italy. Major funding comes through the United Jewish Appeal along with some government contracts and grants. A Master's degree in public administration, social work or areas relating to human services or planning and program management is preferred as is experience in Jewish community services. Language of the country in which one would be stationed plus previous work abroad may be required. Operates with a $186.6 million annual budget and a staff of over 400.

AMERICAN NEAR EAST REFUGEE AID, INC.
1522 K Street, NW
Suite 202
Washington, DC 20005
Tel. 202/347-2558
Fax 202/682-1637
Web site: *www.anera.org*

Provides direct financial and technical assistance to Palestinian refugees and other needy individuals in the Arab world. Supports economic and social development through education, public health, vocational training, and municipal and agricultural cooperatives. Includes field offices in Israel and Gaza. Operates with a $6 million annual budget.

AMERICAN RED CROSS INTERNATIONAL SERVICES
8111 Gatehouse Road
6th Floor
Falls Church, VA 22042
Tel. 703/206-7090
Web site: *www.redcross.org/intl/*

Provides relief to disaster victims and refugees, development assistance, primary health care and education, HIV/AIDS education, blood collection and processing, and capacity building assistance. Collaborates with 170 National Red Cross and Red Crescent societies throughout the world. Operates with a $1.5 billion annual budget and a staff of 28,323 (American Red Cross National Headquarters).

AMERICAN REFUGEE COMMITTEE
2344 Nicollet Avenue South
Suite 350
Minneapolis, MN 55404-3305
Tel. 612/872-7060
Fax 612/872-4309
Web site: *www.archq.org*

Provides medical care, training, and other assistance to refugees and other displaced persons. Operates programs in Southeast Asia, Sub-Saharan Africa, and Eastern Europe and field offices in Cambodia, Malawi, Somalia, Thailand, and Croatia. Operates with a $3.5 million annual budget.

AMERICARES FOUNDATION
161 Cherry Street
New Canaan, CT 06840
Tel. 203/966-6028
Fax 203/972-0116
Web site: *www.americares.org*

Provides international relief by soliciting donations of medicines, medical supplies, and other materials from American companies and delivering them to health and welfare professionals in the U.S. and 60 other countries. Also provides training and conducts research. Maintains a full-time staff in the U.S. of 20. Operates in the Caribbean, Central and South America, Sub-Saharan Africa, Asia, South Asia, Southeast Asia, Middle East, Eastern Europe, and the former Soviet Republics. Major funding sources are USAID, CARE, Knights of Malta, and private companies. Operates with a $330 million annual budget and a staff of over 1,000.

AMIGOS DE LAS AMERICAS
5618 Star Lane
Houston, TX 77057
Tel. 800/231-7796 or 713/782-5290
Fax 713/782-9267
Web site: *www.amigoslink.org*

Provides leadership and development opportunities for young people and public health assistance in Latin America with volunteers who focus on sanitation projects, human immunization, dental screening, and rabies inoculation for animals. Maintains a full-time U.S. staff of 15 and numerous volunteers abroad. Operates only in the Caribbean (Dominican Republic) and Latin America (Brazil, Costa Rica, Ecuador, Honduras, Mexico, Paraguay). Funded through private contributions. Operates with a $2 million annual budget.

BAPTIST WORLD ALLIANCE
6733 Curran Street
McLean, VA 22101
Tel. 703/790-8980
Fax 703/893-5160
Web site: *www.bwanet.org*

Works with Baptist communities throughout the world in extending assistance to poor and disadvantaged peoples. Sponsors programs in agricultural assistance, community development, disaster relief and rehabilitation, and fellowship. Operates programs in the Caribbean, Central and South America, Eastern Europe, former Soviet republics, Middle East, South and Southeast Asia, and Sub-Saharan Africa. Operates with a $2.5 million annual budget.

BREAD FOR THE WORLD
1100 Wayne Avenue
Suite 1000
Silver Spring, MD 20910
Tel. 301/608-2400
Fax 301/608-2401
Web site: *www.bread.org*

A 45,000-member Christian organization with a staff of 50 dedicated to fighting world hunger and poverty. Lobbies members of Congress, campaigns to reduce hunger, promotes peace and development, and conducts the Bread for the World program. Operates with a $2.5 million annual budget.

BROTHER'S BROTHER FOUNDATION
1501 Reedsdale Street
Pittsburgh, PA 15233
Tel. 412/321-3160
Fax 412/321-3325
Web site: *brothersbrother.com*

U.S. staff of 6. Promotes preventive medicine and provides medical care and emergency relief to disaster areas throughout the world. Donates medical, educational, agricultural, and nutritional resources. Operates programs in the Caribbean, Central and South America, Eastern Europe, former Soviet republics, Asia, and Sub-Saharan Africa. Operates with a $70 million annual budget.

CATHOLIC RELIEF SERVICES (CRS)
209 W. Fayette Street
Baltimore, MD 21201
Tel. 410/625-2220
Fax 410/685-1635
Web site: *www.devcap.org/crs*

The relief and development agency of the U.S. Catholic Church which is the official overseas aid and development agency of the United States Catholic Conference with an operating budget of $246 million. Operates relief and self-help development programs in 67 countries in the areas of community development, housing, education, agriculture, health care, and social welfare. Maintains a full-time staff in the U.S. of 180 and a long-term staff abroad of 1400. Operates in Africa, Asia, the Pacific Islands, Latin America, the Caribbean, the Middle East, North Africa, Italy, and Poland. Major funding sources include USAID, European Economic Community, National Council of Catholic Women, Church of Jesus Christ of Latter-Day Saints, foundations, corporations, and others.

CENTER FOR INTERNATIONAL DEVELOPMENT & ENVIRONMENT
World Resources Institute
1709 New York Avenue, NW, Suite 700
Washington, DC 20006
Tel. 202/638-6300 or Fax 202/638-0036
Web site: *www.wri.org*

Provides technical support and policy advice on sustainable development to developing countries desiring to better manage their natural resources. Disseminates information on development and environment issues. Operates programs in Central and South America, South and Southeast Asia, North Africa, and Sub-Saharan Africa. Operates with a $3 million annual budget.

CENTRE FOR DEVELOPMENT AND POPULATION ACTIVITIES
1717 Massachusetts Avenue, NW, Suite 200
Washington, DC 20036
Tel. 202/667-1142
Fax 202/332-4496
Web site: *www.cedpa.org*

Provides technical assistance in the areas of population and family planning, women in development, maternal health, child survival, and community development. Maintains a full-time staff in the U.S. of 36. Operates in Sub-Saharan Africa, North Africa, South Asia, Central and South America, the Middle East, and Eastern Europe. Major funding sources include USAID, INFPA, USA For Africa, and several foundations. Manages field offices in Egypt, India, Kenya, Nepal, and Romania. Operates with a $5 million annual budget.

CHILDREACH
155 Plan Way	P.O. Box 804
Warwick, RI 02886-1099	804 Quaker Lane
Tel. 401/738-5600	East Greenwich, RI 02818
Tel. 800/444-7918	Tel. 401/826-2500
Fax 401/738-5608	Fax 401/826-2680

Web site: *www.childreach.org*

The U.S. member of PLAN International, this is a sponsorship organization linking caring people in the U.S. with children and their families in developing countries. Assists needy children and their families. Promotes self-help programs in health, nutrition, education, livelihood, community development, construction, agriculture, enterprise development and management, social welfare, and population and family planning, and environment and national resource management. Provides assistance to more than 700,000 families, in 32 countries of Africa, Asia, Latin America, and the Caribbean, including the United States. Has regional offices in Ecuador, Guatemala, India, Kenya, the Philippines, and Senegal and works with over 100 field offices of PLAN International. Operates with a $117 million annual budget. Employs 587.

CHILDREN'S SURVIVAL FUND, INC.
P.O. Box 3127
Carbondale, IL 62902
Tel. 618/549-7873 or Fax 618/549-8320

Attacks hunger, disease, and suffering afflicting millions of children around the world. Sponsors programs in disaster and emergency relief, education, medicine, and public health. Operates programs in the Caribbean, Central and South America, Eastern Europe, the former Soviet republics, the Middle East, South and Southeast Asia, and North and Sub-Saharan Africa. Operates with a $4 million annual budget.

CHRISTIAN CHILDREN'S FUND, INC.
2821 Emerywood Parkway
Richmond, VA 23294-3725
Tel. 804/756-2700 or Fax 804/756-2718
Web site: *www.christianchildrensfund.org*

Provides monthly support through individual sponsors for more than 700,000 children in over 40 developing countries. Assistance focuses on disaster relief, community development, cooperatives, housing, family planning services, medicine, public health, education, agriculture, vocational and nutritional training, and social welfare. Maintains full-time staff in the U.S. of 160 and long-term staff abroad of 400. Operates projects and field offices in Sub-Saharan Africa, South and Southeast Asia, Central and South America, Eastern Europe, and the Caribbean. Major funding comes from sponsorships, private donations, and grants. Projects primarily involve sponsoring individual children. Operates with a $110 million annual budget.

CHURCH WORLD SERVICE
475 Riverside Drive
New York, NY 10115-0050
Tel. 212/870-2257 or Fax 212/870-2055
Web site: *http://ncccusa.org/cws/mainone.html*

Provides disaster relief, rehabilitation, agriculture, food productions, health, nutrition, education, family planning, housing, social welfare and community development assistance in Africa, Asia, the Pacific Islands, Latin America, the Caribbean, Eastern Europe, the former Soviet republics, and the Middle East. Maintains a staff of 130. Major funding sources include USAID, CARE, United Nations agencies, and private foundations and contributions. A graduate degree in business, medicine, or international affairs and expertise in development technology, water resources, forestry or cross cultural administration/management are preferred. Operates with a $41.9 million annual budget.

COMPASSION INTERNATIONAL
3955 Cragwood Drive
P.O. Box 7000
Colorado Springs, CO 80933-7000
Tel. 719-594/9900
Fax 719/594-6271
Web site: *www.ci.org*

An Inter-denominational organization focusing on child development through relief services. Primarily operates a monthly sponsorship program for needy children. Maintains a full-time staff in the U.S. of 170 and a long-term staff abroad of 274. Operates in Africa, Asia, the Pacific Islands, Latin America, and the Caribbean. Major funding comes from numerous individual and corporation donations.

COOPERATIVE FOR AMERICAN RELIEF EVERYWHERE, INC. (CARE)

151 Ellis Street	1625 K Street, NW, Suite 200
Atlanta, GA 30335	Washington, DC 20006
Tel. 404/681-2552	Tel. 202/223-2277
Fax 404/577-6271	Fax 202/296-8695

Web site: *www.care.org*

Provides emergency relief for disaster victims and sponsors programs to improve nutrition, health, employment, and education of the poor worldwide. Maintains a staff of 9,000 (most stationed abroad). Major funding sources include donations from numerous individuals, foundations, corporations, and others as well as grants from USAID. Operates projects in North Africa, Sub-Saharan Africa, Asia, the Pacific, Latin America, the Caribbean, Eastern Europe, former Soviet republics, and the Middle East. A Bachelor's degree and overseas work experience of Master's degree in an international field or experience in a project related area and speaking ability in a foreign language—usually French or Spanish—required. Conducts operations in 66 countries. Operates with a $454 million annual budget.

COOPERATIVE HOUSING FOUNDATION, INC.
8300 Colesville
Suite 420
Silver Spring, MD 20910
Tel. 301/587-4700
Fax 301/587-2626
Web site: *www.chfhq.com*

U.S. staff of 20 and 10 abroad. Provides technical assistance relating to shelter, community improvement, and employment generation programs for low-income groups in developing countries.

DIRECT RELIEF INTERNATIONAL
27 S. La Patera Lane
Santa Barbara, CA 93117-3251
Tel. 805/964-4767 or Fax 805/681-4838
Web site: *www.directrelief.org*

U.S. staff of 8. Provides medical supplies and personnel to health care programs worldwide. Assists victims of war, poverty, and natural and civil disasters through donations of pharmaceuticals, medical supplies, and medical equipment. Operates programs in the Caribbean, Central and South America, Eastern Europe, the former Soviet republics, the Middle East, Pacific Islands, East and Southeast Asia, and Sub-Saharan Africa. Operates with a $11 million annual budget.

ESPERANCA, INC.
1911 West Earl Drive
Phoenix, AZ 85015
Tel. 602/252-7772 or Fax 602/340-9197
Web site: *www.experanca.org*

U.S. staff of 6 and 20 abroad. Provides primary health, rural development, and community organization assistance.

FOOD FOR THE HUNGRY, INC.
7729 E. Greenway Road
Scottsdale, AZ 85260
Tel. 602/998-3100 or Fax 602/443-1420
Web site: *www.fh.org*

Provides assistance in the areas of rural development and food-for-work programs as well as relief and rehabilitation programs in emergency aid and disaster situations. Sponsors programs in community development, water resources, income generation, food production, and agriculture. Maintains a full-time staff in the U.S. of 12 and a long-term staff abroad of 525. Operates in Sub-Saharan Africa, Asia, Central and South America, Eastern Europe, and the Caribbean. Major funding from USAID and the UN High Commission for Refugees. $44.4 million budget.

FREEDOM FROM HUNGER
1644 DaVinci Court
Davis, CA 95617
Tel. 530/758-6200 or Fax 530/758-6241
Web site: *www.freefromhunger.org*

U.S. staff of 20. Supports programs relating to food, educational, nutritional, and community health problems in developing countries. Operates programs and field offers in Bolivia, Burkina Faso, Honduras, Ghana, Mali, and Thailand. Operates with a $3 million annual budget.

GLOBAL HEALTH COUNCIL
1701 K Street, NW, Suite 600
Washington, DC 20006
Tel. 202/833-5900
Fax 202/833-0075
Web site: *www.ncih.org* or *www.globalhealthcouncil.org*

Formerly known as the National Council For International Health. U.S. staff of 11.
This membership organization promotes international health through a wide range
of information and education activities. Conducts programs in education and
training for health professionals and serves as a public policy advocacy group.
Operates with a $1.4 million annual budget.

GOODWILL INDUSTRIES OF AMERICA, INC.
9200 Rockville Pike
Bethesda, MD 20814-3896
Tel. 301/530-6500 or Fax 301/530-1516
Web site: *www.goodwill.org*

Provides vocational rehabilitation services and employment opportunities through
technical assistance and training for people with disabilities and special needs.
Conducts programs for information exchange and referral, international visitors,
partnership with industry, and technical assistance. Supports programs in the
Caribbean, Central and South America, Asia, Eastern Europe, Russia, and Sub-
Saharan Africa. Operates with a $7 million annual budget.

HABITAT FOR HUMANITY INTERNATIONAL
121 Habitat Street
Americus, GA 31709
Tel. 912/924-6935 or Fax 912/924-6541
Web site: *www.habitat.org*

A Christian housing ministry involved in improving the housing conditions of poor
people in developing countries through construction, rehabilitation, and innovative
financing arrangement. Maintains a staff of 433. Operates in Africa, Asia, the
Pacific Islands, Latin America, and the Caribbean. Receive funding from private
donations. Annual budget of $65 million.

HEIFER PROJECT INTERNATIONAL, INC
1015 South Louisiana St., P.O. Box 808
Little Rock, AR 72203
Tel. 501/376-6836 or Fax 501/376-8906
Web site: *www.heifer.org*

Assists developing countries in establishing community-based livestock and poultry
operations. Activities include dairy projects, poultry cooperatives, marketing

training, veterinary training, and aquaculture models. Also sponsors projects for women in development, nutrition, community development, and environment and national resource management. Maintains a full-time staff in the U.S. of 125 and a long-term staff abroad of 10. Operates projects in Sub-Saharan, Africa, Asia, the Pacific, the Caribbean, Middle East, Central and South America, and Eastern Europe. Major funding comes through donations and USAID. A graduate degree in animal husbandry or veterinary medicine is required; knowledge of French, Spanish or Arabic is useful when working in developing countries. Operates with a $10 million annual budget.

HELEN KELLER INTERNATIONAL
90 Washington Street, 15th Floor
New York, NY 10006
Tel. 212/943-0890 or Fax 212/940-1220
Web site: *www.hki.org*

Offers technical assistance to governments that wish to integrate eye care into community-level health care. Emphasizes the prevention of nutritional blindness and trachoma, and the restoration of sight through cataract surgery. Maintains a full-time staff in the U.S. of 34 and a long-term staff abroad of 16. Operates in Africa, South and Southeast Asia, the Pacific Islands, South America, Mexico, the Caribbean, and Morocco. A degree in international affairs or public health or an MD, MPH or PhD are useful. Foreign language helpful and work experience in the Third World or in public health is required. Major funding provided by USAID and private donations. Operates with a $8.7 million annual budget.

HIAS (HEBREW IMMIGRANT AID SOCIETY)
333 Seventh Avenue
New York, NY 10001-5004
Tel. 212/967-4100 or Fax 212/967-4442
Web site: *www.hias.org*

Provides services for Jewish refugees and migrants. Also provides under contractual arrangements similar services for non-Jewish refugees and migrants. Operates programs in migration and refugee affairs and monitoring and advocacy. Has programs in the Caribbean, Central and South American, Europe, the former Soviet republics, and Middle East. Operates with a $14 million annual budget.

HIGH/SCOPE EDUCATIONAL RESEARCH FOUNDATION
600 North River Street
Ypsilanti, MI 48198
Tel. 313/485-2000 or Fax 313/485-0704
Web site: *www.highscope.org*

U.S. staff of 49. Promotes learning and development of children.

THE HUNGER PROJECT
15 E. 26th Street
New York, NY 10010
Tel. 212/532-4255 or Fax 212/532-9785
Web site: *www.thp.org*

Promotes leadership, youth, and information dissemination programs to end hunger throughout the world. Has field offices in Australia, Japan, Europe, South Asia, and Senegal. Operates with a $4.5 million annual budget.

INSTITUTE OF INTERNATIONAL EDUCATION
809 United Nations Plaza
New York, NY 10017-3580
Tel. 212/883-8200
Fax 212/984-5452
Web site: *www.iie.org*

Provides technical assistance in the area of educational development through the support of training and education efforts. Administers the Fulbright Program for USIA. Maintains a full-time staff in the U.S. of 329 and a long-term staff abroad of 40. Operates in Africa, Asia, Latin America, the Caribbean, and Egypt. Major clients include USIA, USAID, the World Bank, Inter-American Development Bank, and private foundations. Annual budget of 91.8 million.

INTERCHURCH MEDICAL ASSISTANCE, INC.
Blue Ridge Building
College Avenue, P.O. Box 429
New Windsor, MD 21776
Tel. 410/635-8720 or Fax 410/635-8726
Web site: *www.interchurch.org*

Staff of 7 in U.S. only. Procures and distributes medical supplies for overseas health care ministries of Protestant Churches and U.S. relief organizations. Operates programs in emergency and disaster assistance and medicine and public health. Has programs in the Caribbean, Central and South America, Eastern Europe, the former Soviet republics, the Middle East, Africa, the Pacific, and Asia. Operates with a $17 million annual budget.

INTERNATIONAL AID, INC.
17011 W. Hickory Street
Spring Lake, MI 49456
Tel. 616/846-7490 or Fax 616/846-3842
Web site: *www.internationalaid.org*

This Christian relief and development agency provides food, health, and hope to the needy through a network of more than 500 relief organizations, NGOs, and churches in over 140 countries. Conducts programs in disaster and emergency relief, medicine and public health, and material aid. Has programs in Central and South America, Europe, the former Soviet republics, the Middle East, the Pacific, Asia, and Sub-Saharan Africa. Operates with a $25 million annual budget.

INTERNATIONAL CATHOLIC MIGRATION COMMISSION
1319 F Street, NW, Suite 820
Washington, DC 20004
Tel. 202/393-2904 or Fax 202/393-2908
Web site: *www.interaction.org/mb/icmi.html*

Coordinates international Catholic assistance to refugees, migrants, and displaced persons through a network of 70+ national affiliates. Promotes the implementation of major programs for refugees, migrants, and displaced persons. Has programs in Central and South America, Europe, Russia, Turkey, North Africa, Asia, and Sub-Saharan Africa. Operates with a $25 million annual budget.

INTERNATIONAL CENTER FOR RESEARCH ON WOMEN
1717 Massachusetts Avenue, NW, Suite 302
Washington, DC 20036
Tel. 202/797-0007 or Fax 202/797-0020
Web site: *www.icrw.org*

Conducts research and disseminates information on the role of women in development. Has programs in the Caribbean, Central and South America, the Middle East, Africa, and Asia. Operates with a $3 million annual budget.

INTERNATIONAL DEVELOPMENT ENTERPRISES
10403 W. Colfax, Suite 500
Lakewood, CO 80215
Tel. 303/232-4336 or Fax 303/232-8346
Web site: *www.ide.org*

U.S. staff of 4 and 154 abroad (4 expats and 150 locals). Promotes projects for developing self-sustaining business enterprises amongst Third World entrepreneurs.

INTERNATIONAL EXECUTIVE SERVICE CORPS
8 Stamford Forum, P.O. Box 10005
Stamford, CT 06904-2005
Tel. 203/967-6000 or Fax 203/324-2531
Web site: *www.iesc.org*

Promotes the development of private enterprise in the host nation by upgrading management skills, improving basic technologies and increasing management skills, improving basic technologies and increasing the productivity of businesses in the developing world. Participants selected by IESC work on short-term assignments as unpaid volunteers, although travel and living expenses are paid. Maintains a full-time staff in the U.S. of 60 and a long-term staff abroad of 40. Operates in Africa, Asia, Latin America, the Caribbean, the Middle East, North Africa, Hungary, and Poland. Individuals must be retired experts in their business field and willing to share their knowledge on a volunteer basis. Major funding comes through USAID, 180+ corporate sponsors, and numerous private donors.

INTERNATIONAL EYE FOUNDATION
7801 Norfolk Avenue
Bethesda, MD 20814
Tel. 301/986-1830 or Fax 301/986-1876
Web site: *www.iefusa.org*

U.S. staff of 7 and 12 abroad. Assists developing countries in establishing health care systems that stress the prevention and cure of blindness. Has field offices and programs in the Caribbean, Central America, Sub-Saharan Africa, and Bulgaria. Operates with a $2.2 million annual budget.

INTERNATIONAL INSTITUTE OF RURAL RECONSTRUCTION
475 Riverside Drive, Room 1270
New York, NY 10115
Tel. 212/870-2992 or Fax 212/870-2981
Web site: *www.interaction.org/mb/iirr.html*

U.S. staff of 5 and 140 abroad. Conducts leadership training, field operations, applied research, and international extension. Conducts programs in agriculture and food production, community development, cooperatives and credit loans, development education, enterprise development and management, environment and natural resource management, medicine and public health, nutrition, and population and family planning. Has programs in Guatemala, China, India, Southeast Asia, and Sub-Saharan Africa. Operates with a $3 million annual budget.

INTERNATIONAL READING ASSOCIATION
800 Barksdale Road
Newark, DE 19711
Tel. 302/731-1600 or Fax 302/731-1057
Web site: *www.reading.org*

Functions as a clearinghouse for disseminating reading research and promoting literacy levels worldwide. Works with more than 1,200 councils and national affiliates in 90 countries. Operates with a $8 million annual budget.

INTERNATIONAL RESCUE COMMITTEE
122 E. 42nd Street
New York, NY 10165
Tel. 212/551-3000
Fax 212/551-3180
Web site: *www.interscom.org*

Provides emergency relief, public health, medical, educational, and resettlement programs for refugees and maintains health care programs in refugee camps with emphasis toward training of refugee health workers. Operates programs in Asia, Eastern Europe, Sub-Saharan Africa and Central America. Major funding through private donations. A graduate degree in medicine, nursing, public health, immunology, infectious diseases or nutrition is required. Medical personnel should have strong backgrounds in public health and experience in developing world health care is essential. A Third World language is useful, but not required. Operates with a $84.2 million annual budget. Employs 500.

INTERNATIONAL VOLUNTARY SERVICES, INC.
1901 Pennsylvania Avenue, NW
Suite 501
Washington, DC 20006
Tel. 202/387-5533
Fax 202/466-5669
Web site: *www.interaction.org/mb/ivs.html*

U.S. staff of 10 and 3 abroad. Volunteer technicians assist with community development, cooperatives, agriculture and food production, health care, and micro-enterprise development. Operates projects in Bolivia, Ecuador, Bangladesh, Thailand, Vietnam, and Zambabwe and field offices in Bangladesh and Ecuador. Operates with a $2 million annual budget.

LAUBACH LITERACY INTERNATIONAL
1320 Jamesville Ave.
P.O. Box 131
Syracuse, NY 13210
Tel. 315/422-9121
Fax 315/422-6369
Web site: *www.laubach.org*

Promotes the development of adult literacy programs in developing countries. Maintains a full-time U.S. staff of 110. Has projects in Haiti, Mexico, Guatemala, South America, South and Southeast Asia, and Sub-Saharan Africa. Major funding provided by U.S. Department of Education, American Library Association, and numerous private foundations. Operates with a $11 million annual budget.

LUTHERAN IMMIGRATION AND REFUGEE SERVICE

390 Park Avenue South	122 C Street, NW, Suite 125
New York, NY 10016	Washington, DC 20001
Tel. 212/532-6350	Tel. 202/783-7509
Fax 212/683-1329	Fax 202/783-7502

Web site: *www.lirs.org*

Promotes resettlement, advocacy, and immigration services for refugees and immigrants. Involved in recruitment and training, finding foster homes, processing refugees, and supporting programs for asylum seekers. Administered from the U.S. and Hong Kong. Operates with a $9 million annual budget.

LUTHERAN WORLD RELIEF, INC.
390 Park Avenue South
New York, NY 10016
Tel. 212/532-6350 or Fax 212/213-6081
Web site: *www.lwr.org*

Promotes integrated community development projects which are usually operated through counterpart church-related agencies in the areas of disaster relief, refugee assistance, and social and economic development. Has projects in water resources, reforestation, land reclamation, construction and engineering, small business development nutrition, medical assistance, health practices, disaster relief, education, public administration, social welfare, and family planning. Maintains a full-time staff in the U.S. of 26 and a long-term staff abroad of 17. Operates projects in Sub-Saharan Africa, Asia, Central and South America, and the Middle East. Major funding support comes from USAID, Lutheran churches, CROP, Interfaith Hunger Appeal, and many individual contributors. $20.9 million annual budget.

MAP INTERNATIONAL
2200 Glynco Parkway, P.O. Box 215000
Brunswick, GA 31521-5000
Tel. 912/265-6010 or 800/225-8550
Fax 912/265-6170
Web site: *www.map.org*

Helps developing countries design, implement, and evaluate community development projects focusing on food production, water resources, health services, nutrition education, and disaster and emergency relief. Maintains a staff of nearly 200. Operates in Sub-Saharan Africa, Asia, Central and South America, the Caribbean, Eastern Europe, the former Soviet republics, and the Pacific. A graduate degree in international public health, education or medicine useful. Foreign language, especially French or Spanish, are helpful, but not required. A minimum of three years work in medicine, health, or education in a developing country is necessary for employment. Major funding provided by private contributions. Operates with a $148.2 million annual budget.

MENNONITE CENTRAL COMMITTEE
21 South 12th St.
Akron, PA 17501
Tel. 717/859-1151
Fax 717/859-2171
Web site: *www.mennonitecc.ca/mcc*

Functions as the cooperative relief service, and development agency of North American Mennonite and Brethren in Christ churches. Provides disaster relief and development assistance in the areas of education, agriculture, housing, health care, and crafts development. Maintains a salaried staff in North America of 275 as well as 660 volunteers (289 overseas and 271 in North America). Operates in Africa, Asia, Latin America, the Caribbean, the former Soviet republics, the Middle East, Europe, and Canada. Major funding comes from individual and corporate contributions.

MERCY CORPS INTERNATIONAL
3030 SW First Avenue
Portland, OR 97201
Tel. 800/292-3355
Fax 503/796-6844
Web site: *www.mercycorps.org*

Provides agricultural development assistance, primary health care, education, and emergency relief services. Conducts programs in agriculture and food production, community development, development education, disaster and emergency relief, medicine and public health, and migration and refugee services. Operates in Central America, Eastern Europe, the former Soviet republics, the Middle East, Asia, and Sub-Saharan Africa. Operates with a $111 million annual budget. Employs more than 600.

NATIONAL COOPERATIVE BUSINESS ASSOCIATION
1401 New York Avenue, NW
Suite 1100
Washington, DC 20005
Tel. 202/638-6222
Fax 202/638-1374
Web site: *www.cooperative.org*

Provides technical assistance in the areas of income-generation, business development, agriculture, rural development, and cooperatives in developing countries. Maintains a full-time U.S. staff of 39 and a long-term staff abroad of 26. Operates in Africa, Asia, Latin America, the Caribbean, the Middle East, and North Africa. Major funding source is USAID.

NATIONAL WILDLIFE FEDERATION
8925 Leesburg Pike
Vienna, VA 22184
Tel. 703/790-4000
Web site: *www.nwf.org*

The world's largest organization of private citizens promoting the conservation of natural resources. Maintains a full-time staff of 400. Operates throughout the world. Major funding sources includes USAID, U.N. Environmental Programme, and many private foundations, corporations, and individuals. $96 million budget.

THE NATURE CONSERVANCY
1815 North Lynn Street, Suite 400
Arlington, VA 22209
Tel. 703/841/5300 or Fax 703/841-1283
Web site: *www.tnc.org*

Identifies, protects, and manages natural land areas for the purpose of preserving biological diversity. Maintains a full-time staff in the U.S. of 1,086 and a long-term staff abroad of 2. Operates in the Caribbean and Latin America. Major funding comes from USAID and private donations.

OIC INTERNATIONAL (Opportunities Industrialization Centers International)
240 West Tulpehocken Street
Philadelphia, PA 19144
Tel. 215/842-0220 or Fax 215/849-7033
Web site: *www.oicinternational.org*

Assists local communities and government in creating nonformal skills training institutions. Conducts programs in agriculture and food production, enterprise development and management, and vocational and technical training. Operates in Belize, Poland, United Kingdom, the Philippines, and several countries in Sub-Saharan Africa. Maintains a full-time U.S. staff of 26 and a long-term staff abroad of 5. Major funding provided by USAID, CIDA, United Nations agencies, U.S. Peace Corps, Japanese Overseas Volunteer Service, and numerous other volunteer and private groups.

OPERATION USA
8320 Melrose Avenue, Suite 200
Los Angeles, CA 90069
Tel. 213/658-8876 or Fax 213/653-7846
Web site: *www.opusa.org*

Provides disaster relief assistance, trains health workers, and supports health care and children's programs in the Caribbean, Central and South America, the Middle East, Asia, and Sub-Saharan Africa. Operates with a $4 million annual budget.

OPPORTUNITY INTERNATIONAL
360 Butterfield Road, Suite 110
Elmhurst, IL 60126
Tel. 630/279-9300 or Fax 630/279-3107
Web site: *www.opportunity.org*

U.S. staff of 13 and 20 abroad. Formerly known as the Institute for International Development. Promotes job-creation for the poor in Africa, Asia, and Latin America.

OXFAM AMERICA
26 West Street
Boston, MA 02111-1206
Tel. 617/482-1211 or Fax 617/728-2584
Web site: *www.oxfamamerica.org*

Promotes self-reliant, participatory development among poor people through community development, education, food production, agriculture, public health, and material aid projects. Provides emergency and disaster relief. Operates in Sub-Saharan Africa, South and Southeast Asia, the Caribbean, and Central and South America. Major funding comes from private contributions. Operates with a $14 million annual budget.

PACT
(Private Agencies Collaborating Together)
1901 Pennsylvania Ave., NW, Suite 501
Washington, DC 20006
Tel. 202/466-5666 or Fax 202/466-5669
Web site: *www.pactworld.org*

A consortium for improving the lives of low-income individuals. Focuses on strengthening the programs of PVOs and NGOs through education, information, humanitarian assistance, coalition building, small grants, training, and technical assistance. Operates programs in Central and South American, Romania, the former Soviet republics, Southeast Asia, and Sub-Saharan Africa. Operates with a $20 million budget and a staff of 40.

PARTNERS OF THE AMERICAS
(National Association of the Partners of the Americas, Inc.)
1424 K Street, NW, Suite 700
Washington, DC 20005
Tel. 202/628-3300 or Fax 202/628-3306
Web site: *www.partners.net*

U.S. staff of 42 and 3 abroad. Promotes Inter-American friendship and cooperation between the United States, Latin America, and the Caribbean through technical training programs and economic and social development activities. Helps raise funds and promote technical assistance services of 45 volunteer Partners of Americas' committees located in 45 states. Links 45 state committees with 60 similar committees in Latin America and the Caribbean. Sponsors programs on agriculture and food production, citizen and student exchange, development education, environment and natural resource management, human resource development, public health and nutrition, and technical training. Operates with a $11 million annual budget.

PATHFINDER INTERNATIONAL
9 Galen Street
Suite 217
Watertown, MA 02172-4501
Tel. 617/924-7200
Fax 617/924-3833
Web site: *www.pathfinder.org*

Promotes population planning through innovative efforts to make fertility services more effective, less expensive, and more readily available to people in developing countries. Maintains a staff of 170. Programs operate in the Caribbean, South American, Sub-Saharan Africa, Asia, and the Middle East. Most professional positions require a Master's Degree in public health or a Master's Degree in business with an emphasis in health. Related fields such as international affairs or geography would be considered for some positions. Preference given to candidates with experience in developing countries. Major funding provided by USAID and numerous private foundations. Operates with a $50 million annual budget.

PEOPLE TO PEOPLE HEALTH FOUNDATION, INC
(Project HOPE)
Health Sciences Education Center, Carter Hall
Millwood, VA 22646
Tel. 540/837-2100
Fax 540/837-1813
Web site: *www.projhope.org*

Provides education and training assistance in the areas of modern health science techniques, sanitation, nutrition, public health, biomedical engineering, and preventive medicine. Maintains a full-time staff in the U.S. of 140 and a long-term staff abroad of 250. Operates in Africa, Asia, Latin America, the Caribbean, Egypt, Poland, Portugal, Russia and the CIS. Major funding comes from USAID, Inter-American Development Foundation, Pan American Health Organization, and numerous foundations, corporations, and individual donors.

PHELPS-STOKES FUND
10 East 87th Street
New York, NY 10128
Tel. 212/427-8100 or Fax 212/876-6278
Web site: *www.pssdo.org*

U.S. staff of 20 in New York and Washington. Promotes improvement of education for Africans, African-Americans, American Indians, and poor white Americans through scholarship programs, and study tours.

PLANNED PARENTHOOD FEDERATION OF AMERICA
810 Seventh Avenue
New York, NY 10019
Tel. 212/541-7800 or Fax 212/245-1845
Web site: *www.plannedparenthood.org*

The international department, Family Planning International Assistance (FPIA), assists local organizations throughout the world design and initiate family planning projects, monitor project performance, and provide technical assistance. Maintains a full-time staff in the U.S. of 175 and a long-term staff abroad of 63. A Bachelor's degree is required; a graduate degree is preferred for employment. A specialization in public or business administration is desirable. Fluency in French, Spanish or Arabic is often required. Work experience in developing countries and involvement in family planning and community health programs is desirable for positions posted abroad. Funding provided by USAID, USIA, and the U.S. Department of Education.

PLANNING ASSISTANCE, INC.
1832 Jefferson Place, NW
Washington, DC 20036
Tel. 202/466-3290 or Fax 202/466-3293

U.S. staff of 6 and 13 abroad. Provides training and technical assistance services to help organizations design and manage more efficient development programs in the areas of health, population/family planning, and food security/food aid management. Has programs in Haiti, Central America, South American, Turkey, and Sub-Saharan Africa. Operates with a $3 million annual budget.

POPULATION ACTION INTERNATIONAL
1120 19th Street, NW, Suite 550
Washington, DC 20036
Tel. 202/659-1833 or Fax 202/293-1795
Web site: *www.populationaction.org*

This advocacy group promotes public awareness, understanding, and action toward reducing population growth rates in developing countries through voluntary family planning. Operates with a $4.5 million annual budget.

POPULATION COUNCIL
One Dag Hammarskjold Plaza
New York, NY 10017
Tel. 212/339-0500
Fax 212/755-6052
Web site: *www.popcouncil.org*

Primarily involved with population research and information dissemination, the Council assists decision makers and population professionals in developing countries to design, implement, and evaluate research and assistance programs. Maintains a full-time staff in the U.S. of 174 and a long-term staff abroad of 31. Operates projects in Africa, Asia, Latin America, the Caribbean, the Middle East, and North Africa. An advanced degree in demography, public health, economics, population or biomedicine is preferred; undergraduate work in public health, international relations, economics, sociology and demography is also useful. Previous work experience is usually required. Experience requirements vary with different departments. Major funding provided by USAID, CIDA, United Nations, and numerous private foundations, corporations, and individuals.

PROGRAM FOR APPROPRIATE TECHNOLOGY IN HEALTH
4 Nickerson St.
Seattle, WA 98109-1699
Tel. 206/285-3500 or Fax 206/285-6619
Web site: *www.path.org*

Promotes the availability, effectiveness, safety, and acceptance of health products and technologies in developing countries. Maintains a full-time staff in the U.S. of 115 and a long-term staff abroad of 50. Operates in Africa, Asia, Latin America, the Caribbean, and the Middle East. Major funding provided by USAID, United Nations, and numerous private foundations, corporations, and individuals.

PROJECT CONCERN INTERNATIONAL
3550 Afton Road
San Diego, CA 92123
Tel. 619/279-9690 or Tel. 619/694-0294
Web site: *www.serve.com/PCI*

U.S. staff of 44 and 15 abroad. Provides health care training and development programs in developing countries. Promotes basic, low-cost health care services. Operates programs in community development, development education, population and family planning services, and public health and nutrition. Operates in Guatamela, Nicaragua, Bolivia, Mexico, Romania, Papua New Guinea, and Indonesia. Operates with a $12 million annual budget.

SALVATION ARMY WORLD SERVICE OFFICE
615 Slaters Lane, P.O. Box 269
Alexandria, VA 22313
Tel. 703/684-5528
Fax 703/684-5536
Web site: *www.salvationarmy.org*

U.S. staff of 12. Provides financial and personnel assistance for programs in education, community centers, disaster relief, health and medical services, agriculture, community development, and spiritual ministry. Operates programs on agriculture ·and food production, communications, community development, construction, cooperatives, disaster relief and reconstruction aid, education, material aid, medicine and public health, and social welfare. Has programs in the Caribbean, Central and South America, Europe, Eastern Europe, former Soviet republics, the Pacific, and South and Southeast Asia. Operates with a $18 million annual budget.

SAVE THE CHILDREN FEDERATION, INC.
54 Wilton Road
Westport, CT 06880
Tel. 203/221-4000 or Fax 203/227-5667
Web site: *www.savethechildren.org*

Supports development projects aimed at helping children and their communities with programs in sustainable agriculture, natural resource management, education, economic opportunities, health care, emergency response. Maintains a full-time staff of 2,474. Operates in 35 countries in the Caribbean, Central and South America, the Middle East, Sub-Saharan and North Africa, Greece, and Asia. A Bachelor's degree, but preferably an advanced degree in an area pertinent to Third World development is useful. Ability to speak French, Spanish, or Arabic is required. Work experience abroad is essential for overseas based positions. Major funding provided by sponsorship program, USAID, private foundations, corporations, and individual donors. Operates with a $105 million annual budget.

THE SIERRA CLUB
85 2nd Street, 2nd Floor
San Francisco, CA 94105-3459
Tel. 415/977-5500 or Fax 415/977-5799
Web site: *www.sierraclub.org*

This membership group seeks to stop the abuse of wilderness lands, save endangered species, and protect the global environment through grassroots conservation efforts and an extensive publication and information dissemination program. Operates programs in education, environment and natural resource management, and public policy and advocacy. Operates with $43 million annual budget. Employs 294.

SISTER CITIES INTERNATIONAL
120 S. Payne St.
Alexandria, VA 22314
Tel. 703/836-3535
Fax 703/836-4815
Web site: *www.sister-cities.org*

U.S. staff of 10. Promotes the development of long-term relationships between sister cities as well as collaborate development efforts.

TECHNOSERVE
49 Day St.
Norwalk, CT 06854-3106
Tel. 800/999-6757
Fax 203/838-6717
Web site: *www.technoserve.org*

Helps low-income people develop their own community-based enterprises in the areas of primary agricultural production, crop processing, livestock development, and savings and credit programs. Operates in Central America, Peru, Poland, and Sub-Saharan Africa. Major funding source is USAID. Operates with a $8 annual budget. Employs 225.

THOMAS A. DOOLEY FOUNDATION/INTERMED—USA
420 Lexington Ave., Suite 2428
New York, NY 10170
Tel. 212/687-3620 or Fax 212/599-6137
Web site: *ourworld.compuserve.com/homepages/intermed*

U.S. staff of 10 and 5 abroad. Provides medical equipment, supplies, personnel, and training support for health services in developing countries with emphasis on self-help through education.

TOLSTOY FOUNDATION, INC.
104 Lake Road
Valley Cottage, NY 10989
Tel. 914/268-6722
Fax 914/268-6937
Web site: *www.tolstoyfoundation.org*

A humanitarian foundation that assists refugees and the elderly and infirm. Conducts Russian cultural and educational programs. Operates programs in South America, Europe, and Russia. Operates with a $2.6 million annual budget.

UNITARIAN UNIVERSALIST SERVICE COMMITTEE
130 Prospect Street
Cambridge, MA 02139-1813
Tel. 617/868-6600 or Fax 617/868-7102
Web site: *www.uusc.org*

U.S. staff of 37. Promotes self-reliant development in the areas of public health, emergency relief, water resource development, vocational planning, leadership development, family planning, and child care. Operates programs in development education, education and training, medicine and public health, population and family planning, food production and agriculture, and environment. Operates with a $4 million annual budget.

UNITED METHODIST COMMITTEE ON RELIEF
General Board of Global Ministries
The United Methodist Church
475 Riverside Drive, Room 330
New York, NY 10115
Tel. 212/870-3816 or Fax 212/870-3624

Focuses efforts on alleviating hunger and human suffering. Conducts programs in agriculture and food production, community development, nutrition, social welfare, disaster and emergency relief, migration and refugee services, and public policy and advocacy. Operates programs in the Caribbean, Central and South America, the Middle East, and Southeast Asia. Operates with a $16 million annual budget.

U.S. CATHOLIC CONFERENCE OFFICE OF MIGRATION AND REFUGEE SERVICES

3211 4th Street, NE   902 Broadway, 8th Fl.
Washington, DC 20017-1194   New York, NY 10010-6093
Tel. 202/541-3220   Tel. 212/614-1277
Fax 202/541-3399   Fax 212/614-1201
Web site: *www.nccbuscc.org/mrs*

Supports a network of 145 local Catholic diocesan resettlement offices in the United States that provide assistance for approximately one-third of all refugees admitted to U.S. annually. Operates with a $9 million annual budget.

U.S. FEED GRAINS COUNCIL
1400 K Street, NW, Suite 1200
Washington, DC 20005
Tel. 202/789-0789 or Fax 202/898-0522
Web site: *grains.org*

Provides technical assistance to create, develop, and promote overseas markets for U.S. feed grains. Maintains a full-time staff in the U.S. of 38 and a long-term staff abroad of 60. Operates programs in 55 countries through a network of 13 overseas offices. Major funding sources include associations of grain producers.

U.S. COMMITTEE FOR UNICEF

333 East 38th St., 6th Fl.	110 Maryland Avenue, NE
New York, NY 10016	Washington, DC 20002
Tel. 212/686-5522	Tel. 202/547-7946
Fax 212/779-1679	Fax 202/543-8144

Web site: *www.unicefusa.org*

Supports UNICEF programs in over 120 developing countries. Helps raise funds and disseminate information about the needs of children worldwide. Programs encompass development education, emergency relief and material aid, medicine and public health, child survival, nutrition, social welfare, and women in development. Operates programs in Sub-Saharan Africa, Cambodia, El Salvador, and Mexico. Operates with a $60 million annual budget. Employs 150.

VOLUNTEERS IN OVERSEAS COOPERATIVE ASSISTANCE

50 F Street, NW, Suite 1075
Washington, DC 20001
Tel. 202/626-8750
Fax 202/783-7204
Web site: *www.acdivoca.org*

Provides short-term technical assistance for agricultural development through a Cooperative Assistance Program and a Farmer-to-Farmer Program. Operates 23 offices in Africa, Asia, Latin America, and Eastern Europe. $12 million budget. Employs 150.

VOLUNTEERS IN TECHNICAL ASSISTANCE (VITA)

1600 Wilson Blvd., Suite 500
Arlington, VA 22209
Tel. 703/276-1800
Fax 703/243-1865
Web site: *www.vita.org*

Provides information and assistance on appropriate technology to help small businesses, farmers, community workers, and government agencies in Africa, Asia, the Caribbean and Latin America. Maintains a full-time staff in the U.S. of 25 and a long-term staff abroad of 11. A Bachelor's degree in a technical field such as engineering is useful for volunteers as is knowledge of energy systems, agriculture, sanitation, or construction. French or Spanish competency is preferred; work experience abroad is not required to become a volunteer. Major funding comes from USAID, the United Nations, and numerous private foundations and corporations.

WINROCK INTERNATIONAL INSTITUTE
FOR AGRICULTURAL DEVELOPMENT
38 Winrock Drive
Morrilton, AR 72110-9537
Tel. 501/727-5435
Fax 501/727-5242
Web site: *www.winrock.org*

Seeks to alleviate poverty and hunger worldwide through agricultural, rural development, and environmental resources management assistance. Provides training, education, consultation, and project design services. Maintains a full-time staff in the U.S. of 170 and a long-term staff abroad of 55. Operates in Sub-Saharan Africa, Southeast Asia, Central and South America, the Caribbean, and the former Soviet republics. Major funding provided by USAID, the World Bank, African Development Bank, Asian Development Bank, and several private foundations. Operates with a $36.8 million annual budget.

WORLD CONCERN
19303 Fremont Ave. North
Seattle, WA 98133
Tel. 206/546-7201
Fax 206/546-7269
Web site: *www.worldconcern.org*

A division of Crista Ministries, World Concern sends personnel, commodities, and funds to aid projects related to health, agriculture, animal husbandry, water development, education, economic development, refugee aid, community development, and emergency relief. Maintains a full-time staff in the U.S. of 40 and a long-term staff abroad of 125. Operates in Sub-Saharan Africa, Asia, the Pacific, Central and South America, the Caribbean, Europe, Eastern Europe, and the former Soviet republic. Major funding provided by CRISTA Ministries, USAID, and many corporations and individual donors. Operates with a $21 million annual budget.

WORLD COUNCIL OF CREDIT UNIONS
5710 Mineral Point Rd.
Madison, WI 53705
Tel. 608/231-7130 or Fax 608/238-8020
Web site: *www.woccu.org*

Promotes the development of credit unions in developing countries. Maintains a full-time U.S. staff of 33 and a long-term staff abroad of 15. Also maintains a computerized Talent Bank for personnel to fill short-term consultancy requests. Operates in Africa, Asia, Latin America, and the Caribbean. Major funding sources include USAID, Canadian Co-operative Association, and Deutsche Gesellschaft fur Technische Zusammenarbeit.

WORLD EDUCATION
44 Farnswort Street
Boston, MA 02210
Tel. 617/482-9485
Fax 617/482-0617
Web site: *www.tfi.com*

U.S. staff of 9. Provides training and technical assistance in nonformal education for adults with emphasis on income generation, employment, refugee orientation, community development, small enterprise development, literacy, food production, and family life education. Sponsors programs in education, information dissemination, institutional development and training, refugee assistance, and women in development. Operates in Yemen, South Asia, China, Southeast Asia, and Sub-Saharan Africa. Operates with a $4.2 annual budget.

WORLD NEIGHBORS, INC.
4127 NW 122 Street
Oklahoma City, OK 73120-8869
Tel. 405/752-9700 or 800/242-6387
Fax 405/752-9393
Web site: *www.wn.org*

This people-to-people organization focuses on eliminating hunger, disease, and poverty in Asia, Africa, and Latin America. Sponsors programs in community development, food production and agriculture, medicine and public health, reproductive health and family planning, communications, and development education. Operates in Haiti, Honduras, Mexico, South America, South and Southeast Asia, and Sub-Saharan Africa. Operates with a $4 million annual budget.

WORLD RELIEF CORPORATION
P.O. Box WRC
Wheaton, IL 60189
Tel. 630/665-0235
Fax 630/665-0129
Web site: *www.worldrelief.org*

The official relief and development agency of the National Association of Evangelicals. Promotes rural development, agriculture, community development, health, nutrition, vocation training, refugee relief, and resettlement programs. Maintains a full-time staff in the U.S. of 200 and a long-term staff abroad of 40. Major funding sources include USAID and private donations. Operates with a $20 million annual budget.

WORLD SHARE
6950 Friars Road
San Diego, CA 92108
Tel. 619/686-5818 or Fax 619/686-5815
Web site: *www.worldshare.org*

Promotes self supporting food and community development programs in 24 locations serving over 400,000 families each month. Secures food commodities from the U.S. government (Title II) and sells them to support programs of NGO coordination, maternal/child health, infrastructure development, agroforestry, and income generation. Operates in Mexico and Guatemala. Operates with a $48 million annual budget.

WORLD VISION RELIEF AND DEVELOPMENT, INC.
34834 Weyerhaeuser Way S.
Federal Way, WA 98001
Tel. 253/815-10000
Web site: *www.worldvision.org*

Provides disaster relief, primary health care and child survival, water development, natural resource management, microenterprise development, natural resource management, community leadership training, and development education. Maintains a full-time staff in the U.S. of 600, and a long-term staff abroad of over 3,000. Operates programs in the Caribbean, Central and South America, Greece, Egypt, the Middle East, the Pacific, Asia, and Sub-Saharan Africa. Graduate degrees in business, medicine, public, health or technical skills in related areas are most useful for employment. Knowledge of French or Spanish preferred; at least five years experience in development or related work usually required. Major funding sources include USAID, United Nations agencies, and numerous foundations, corporations, and individual donors. Operates with a $300 million annual budget.

WORLD WILDLIFE FUND/ THE CONSERVATION FOUNDATION
1250 24th St., NW
Washington, DC 20037
Tel. 202/293-4800 or Fax 202/293-9211
Web site: *www.wwf.org*

Promotes the protection of endangered wildlife and wildlands, with particular emphasis on the conservation of tropical forests. Operates programs in the Caribbean, Central and South America, Asia, the Pacific, and Sub-Saharan Africa. Major funding sources includes USAID and numerous foundations and corporations. Operates with a $156 million annual budget. Employs more than 600. Mass membership organization of 1.2 million members.

Y.M.C.A.—INTERNATIONAL DIVISION
101 N. Wacker Drive
Chicago, IL 60606
Tel. 312/977-0031
Fax 312/977-9063
Web site: *www.ymca.net*

Provides assistance to local YMCAs for promoting social and economic development programs. Maintains a full-time U.S. staff of 14. Operates in Sub-Saharan Africa, Asia, the Pacific Islands, Central and South America, the Caribbean, the Middle East, Greece, and Egypt. Major funding provided by private donations and USAID. Operates with a $37 million annual budget.

Y.W.C.A. OF THE U.S.A.

350 5th Ave., 3rd Fl.	624 9th Street, NW, 3rd Fl.
New York, NY 10118	Washington, DC 20001
Tel. 212/273-7800	Tel. 202/628-3636
Fax 212/465-2281	Fax 202/783-7123

Web site: *www.ymca.org*

Sponsors programs in community development, development education, enterprise development and management, public health, and social welfare. Operates in Jamaica, South America, Lebanon, India, Southeast Asia, the Pacific, and Sub-Saharan Africa. Operates with a $9 million annual budget.

ZERO POPULATION GROWTH
1400 16th Street, NW, Suite 320
Washington, DC 20036
Tel. 202/332-2200
Fax 202/332-2302
Web site: *www.zpg.org*

Produces and disseminates population planning information throughout the world. Includes programs in development education, information dissemination, public policy and advocacy. Operates with a $2 million annual budget.

8

Nonprofit Corporations

Not-for-profit corporations provide similar technical assistance services as private firms, private voluntary organizations (PVOs) or non-governmental organizations (NGOs), and many colleges and universities. Many of these corporations are closely linked to these other organizations in terms of mission, personnel, and funding sources. As nonprofit organizations, they have tax-exempt status.

Orientation

Most not-for-profit organizations conduct research or manage agricultural, rural development, health, population planning, energy, or educational projects in developing countries. Many work closely with counterpart PVOs and private contracting firms—often serving as either the prime contractor or subcontractor to these other organizations—and are largely indistinguishable from these organizations in all but corporate structure and tax exempt status. Several are university-based and thus provide many academic-relevant services, such as research, training, and educational development. Similar to private firms and PVOs, these nonprofit corporations compete alongside the other organizations for technical assistance contracts funded by USAID, World Bank, development banks, and private foundations.

While many of these organizations are large, receiving millions of dollars in contracts each year, none are involved in the design, construction, and implementation of large-scale infrastructure projects; few receive funding outside the network of public-oriented development agencies of government, international organizations, and private foundations.

Strategies

Nonprofit organizations offer numerous job opportunities for international specialists pursuing international careers rather than for individuals just looking for an international job. Many require higher education degrees, specialized training, exotic combinations of work skills, international experience, and foreign language capabilities. Operating similar to many private firms and PVOs, these organizations make up an intricate part of the job and career network of international specialists. They are especially appealing to individuals who wish to pursue development causes for alleviating the problems of Third World countries. Consequently, you may want to merge this list of organizations with the lists of private contractors and PVOs found in Chapters 4 and 5. Together, these organizations make up a major portion of organizations involved in spending billions of dollars in aid funds in the developing worlds of Asia, Africa, Middle East, Latin America, the Caribbean, Eastern Europe, and the former Soviet Union.

The Organizations

ACADEMY FOR EDUCATIONAL DEVELOPMENT
1875 Connecticut Avenue, NW
Washington, DC 20009
Tel. 202/884-8000 or Fax 202/884-8400
Web site: *www.AED.org*

Provides technical assistance in the areas of education, health care, technical training, agriculture, communications, computer science, and student services. Maintains a full-time staff in the U.S. of 600 and a long-term staff abroad of 150. Operates in Africa, Asia, the Pacific Islands, Latin America, the Caribbean, Middle East, North Africa, Australia, New Zealand, and Western and Eastern Europe. Major clients include USAID, World Bank, United Nations agencies, several development banks, and private foundations.

AGRICULTURAL CO-OP DEVELOPMENT INTERNATIONAL
50 F Street, NW, Suite 900
Washington, DC 20001
Tel. 202/338-4661
Fax 202/783-7204
Web site: *www.acdivoca.org*

Provides training, technical, and management assistance in the areas of agricultural cooperatives, farm credit, agribusiness, and marketing. Maintains a full-time staff in the U.S. of 28 and a long-term staff abroad of 24. Operates in Africa, Asia, Latin America, the Caribbean, Middle East, and North Africa. Major clients include USAID, World Bank, and host country governments and cooperatives.

AMERICAN PUBLIC HEALTH ASSOCIATION
1015 15 Street, NW, Suite 300
Washington, DC 20005
Tel. 202/789-5600
Fax 202/789-5661
Web site: *www.apha.org*

Membership organization providing health information and training services. U.S. staff of 60.

APPROPRIATE TECHNOLOGY INTERNATIONAL
1828 L Street, NW, Suite 1000
Washington, DC 20036
Tel. 202/293-4600 or Fax 202/293-4598

Specializes in providing appropriate technology services relating to agricultural production and wastes, local mineral resource development, and equipment and support for small farms. Maintains a full-time staff in the U.S. of 36 and a long-term staff abroad of 3. Operates in Sub-Saharan Africa, Asia, Central and South America, and the Caribbean. Major client is USAID. Operates with a $4 million annual budget.

AIR SERV INTERNATIONAL
P.O. Box 3041
Redlands, CA 92373-0993
Tel. 909/793-7008, 909/793-2627 or Fax 909/793-0226
Web site: *www.airserv.org*

Provides air transportation (small aircraft) for relief agencies, PVOs, and embassies in developing countries. U.S. staff of 13 and long-term staff abroad of 41. Operates with a $10 million annual budget.

ASIA FOUNDATION
465 California Street, 14th Floor
San Francisco, CA 94104
Tel. 415/982-4640
Fax 415/392-8863
Web site: *www.asiafoundation.org*

A major foundation providing assistance to Asian and Pacific government agencies, institutions, organizations, and individuals for promoting social and economic development in the areas of private and voluntary sector; representative government; public administration and government service; legal systems and human rights; education and national development; management, business, and economics; media, information, and communication; international relations; and regional cooperation. Maintains a full-time staff in the U.S. of 76 and a long-term staff abroad of 178. Operates throughout Asia and the Pacific Islands. Receives funding from private sources as well as the U.S. Congress and USAID. Major clients include government agencies, institutions, organizations, and individuals applying for assistance from the Asia Foundation.

ASSOCIATION FOR VOLUNTARY SURGICAL CONTRACEPTION, INC.
79 Madison Avenue
7th Floor
New York, NY 10016
Tel. 212/561-8000
Fax 212/779-9439
Web site: *www.avsc.org*

Provides technical assistance relating to voluntary sterilization, family planning, and maternal-child health care. Maintains a full-time staff in the U.S. of 90 and a long-term staff abroad of 30. Operates in Africa, Asia, Latin America, the Caribbean, Middle East, and North Africa. Major client is USAID.

ASSOCIATION OF UNIVERSITY PROGRAMS IN HEALTH ADMINISTRATION
1110 Vermont Avenue, NW
Suite 220
Washington, DC 20005-3500
Tel. 202/822-8550
Fax 202/822-8555
Web site: *www.aupha.org*

Consortium of 96 colleges and universities in North America and 65 universities in 34 other countries. U.S. staff of 20.

BATTELLE MEMORIAL INSTITUTE
505 King Avenue
Columbus, OH 43201-2693
Tel. 614/424-6424 or Fax 614/424-5263
Web site: *www.battelle.org*

This is the world's largest contract research firm specializing in the areas of biological and chemical sciences, engineering and manufacturing technology, electronic and engineering systems, biotechnology, advanced materials, and nuclear system. Maintains a full-time staff in the U.S. of 6,700 and a long-term staff abroad of 800. Operates worldwide. Major funding sources include USAID and numerous host country governments, and private firms.

BIOMEDICAL RESEARCH INSTITUTE
12111 Parklawn Drive
Rockville, MD 20852
Tel. 301/881-3300 or Fax 301/881-7640

Focuses on developing malaria and schistosomiesis vaccines for developing countries. U.S. staff of 65.

BOARD ON SCIENCE AND TECHNOLOGY FOR INTERNATIONAL DEVELOPMENT
2101 Constitution Avenue
Milton Harris Building, Room 476
Washington, DC 20418
Tel. 202/334-2639 or Fax 202/334-2660

Provides technical assistance for strengthening local scientific and technological capabilities in agriculture, environmental planning, energy, forestry, health, industrial development, natural resource management and conservation, and nutrition. Functions as a unit within the Office of International Affairs of the National Research Council. Maintains a full-time staff in the U.S. of 30 and a long-term staff abroad of 1. Operates in Africa, Asia, Latin America, Middle East, North Africa, and Portugal. Major clients include USAID, National Science Foundation, and several foundations.

CONSORTIUM FOR INTERNATIONAL DEVELOPMENT (CID)
6367 East Tanque Verde, Suite 200
Tucson, AZ 85715
Tel. 520/885-0055 or Fax 520/886-3244

A consortium of universities located in the west and southwest, such as Utah State, Oregon State, Washington State, California State Polytechnic, University of

Arizona, and the University of New Mexico. Maintains a full-time staff in the U.S. of 17 and a long-term staff abroad of 61. Operates in Africa, Asia, Latin America, Middle East, and North Africa. Major clients include USAID, World Bank, and the Government of the Arab Republic of Egypt.

EDUCATIONAL DEVELOPMENT CENTER, INC.
55 Chapel Street
Newton, MA 02158
Tel. 617/969-7100
Fax 617/224-3436
Web site: *www.edc.org*

Provides technical assistance in the areas of child development, K-12 education, health promotion, workforce preparation, learning technologies, and institutional reform. Maintains a full-time staff in the U.S. of 140 and a long-term staff abroad of 3. Operates in Africa, Asia, the Pacific Islands, Latin America, the Caribbean, Middle East, North Africa, and Western Europe. Major clients include USAID, World Bank, USIA, and United Nations agencies.

ENVIRONMENTAL RESEARCH INSTITUTE OF MICHIGAN
1975 Green Road
Ann Arbor, MI 48105
Tel. 313/994-1200
Fax 313/665-9956
Web site: *www.erim.org*

Designs, establishes, and operates remote sensing centers and provides assistance in agriculture, forestry, water resources, and geology. U.S. staff of 600.

FAMILY HEALTH INTERNATIONAL
P.O. Box 13950
Research Triangle Park, NC 27709
Tel. 919/544-7040
Fax 919/544-7261
Web site: *www.fhi.org*

Provides technical assistance relating to family planning and health care issues. Maintains a full-time staff in the U.S. of 173. Operates in Africa, Asia, Latin America, the Caribbean, Middle East, North Africa, Canada, Australia, and Western and Eastern Europe. Major clients include USAID, National Institutes for Health, and several foundations.

INSTITUTE FOR CONTEMPORARY STUDIES
720 Market Street, 4th Floor
San Francisco, CA 94102
Tel. 415/981-5353
Fax 415/986-4878

Serves as a forum for discussions between scholars and policymakers on key economic and development issues. U.S. staff of 10 and long-term staff abroad of 5.

INSTITUTE FOR DEVELOPMENT ANTHROPOLOGY
99 Collier Street
Binghamton, NY 13902
Tel. 607/772-6244
Fax 607/773-8993

Conducts studies on rural development, river basin development, natural resources, regional planning, social analysis, remote sensing, and cartography. U.S. staff of 14 and long-term staff abroad of 7.

INSTITUTE OF GAS TECHNOLOGY
1700 S. Mount Prospect Road
Des Plaines, IL 60018-1804
Tel. 847/768-0500
Fax 847/768-0501
Web site: *www.igt.org*

Provides technical assistance relating to energy planning, pricing, utilization, transmission, distribution, storage, and development. Maintains a full-time staff in the U.S. of 260 and a long-term staff abroad of 10. Operates in Africa, Asia, Latin America, Middle East, Africa, and Europe. Major clients include: World Bank, Asian Development Bank, USAID, and numerous national petroleum companies.

LASPAU—ACADEMIC AND PROFESSIONAL PROGRAMS FOR THE AMERICAS
25 Mount Auburn Street
Cambridge, MA 02138-6095
Tel. 617/495-5255
Fax 617/495-8990
Web site: *www.laspau.harvard.edu*

Affiliated with Harvard University, this organization designs, develops, and implements academic and professional programs on behalf of individuals and institutions in the U.S., Canada, Latin America, and the Caribbean. Administers scholarships, loans, and short-term training programs for national and international organizations, academic institutions, and government agencies. Maintains a full-time U.S. staff of 65. Primarily funded through USIA (Fulbright Academic Exchange Program), USAID, World Bank, Inter-American Development Bank, and several Latin American and Caribbean organizations.

MANAGEMENT SCIENCES FOR HEALTH
165 Allandale Road
Boston, MA 02130
Tel. 617/524-7799
Fax 617/524-2825

Provides technical assistance in several public health areas—human resource management, drug management, maternal and child health, health services, health financing, and management information systems. Maintains a full-time U.S. staff of 80 and a long-term staff abroad of 30. Operates in Africa, Asia, the Pacific Islands, Latin America, the Caribbean, Middle East, North Africa, and Portugal. Major client is USAID.

MEDICAL CARE DEVELOPMENT, INC.
1742 R Street, NW
Washington, DC 20009
Tel. 202/462-1920
Fax 202/265-4078

Provides technical services in a variety of health care areas. U.S. staff of 85 and long-term staff abroad of 20.

MIDAMERICA INTERNATIONAL AGRICULTURAL CONSORTIUM
1555 Food Sciences Building
Iowa State University
Ames, IA 50011
Tel. 515/294-5871
Fax 515/294-9790
Web site: *www.ssu.missouri.edu/miac*

A consortium of five major Midwest universities—Kansas State, Iowa State, Missouri, Nebraska, and Oklahoma State—providing agricultural development assistance to Third World countries. Maintains a full-time staff in the U.S. of 3 and a long-term staff abroad of 30. Operates in a few countries of Africa, Asia, Latin America, and North Africa. Major client is USAID.

MIDWEST UNIVERSITIES CONSORTIUM
FOR INTERNATIONAL ACTIVITIES
66 East 15th Avenue
Columbus, OH 43201
Tel. 614/291-9646 or Fax 614/291-9717
Web site: *www.mucia.ohio-state.edu*

Consortium of eight midwest universities provides a wide range of educational, training, and technical assistance programs involving everything from architecture, law, and nursing to public affairs and agricultural development. Maintains a full-time staff in the U.S. of 15 and a long-term staff abroad of 78. Operates in Africa, Asia, Latin America, the Caribbean, Middle East, and the USSR. Major clients include USAID, World Bank, Asian Development Bank, and host country governments.

NATIONAL ASSOCIATION OF SCHOOLS OF
PUBLIC AFFAIRS AND ADMINISTRATION (NASPAA)
1120 G Street, NW #730
Washington, DC 20005
Tel. 202/628-8965
Fax 202/626-4978
Web site: *www.unomaha.edu/~wwwpa/nashome.html*

An accrediting organization for schools of public affairs and public administration that also sponsors research on institutional development. U.S. staff of 10 and long-term staff abroad of 1.

POPULATION REFERENCE BUREAU
1875 Connecticut Avenue, NW, Suite 520
Washington, DC 20009
Tel. 202/483-1100 or Fax 202/338-3937
Web site: *www.prb.org*

Provides publications to communicate research findings on population issues relating to developing countries. U.S. staff of 40.

POPULATION SERVICES INTERNATIONAL
1120 19th St., NW, Suite 600
Washington, DC 20036
Tel. 202/785-0072 or Fax 202/785-0120
Web site: *www.psiwash.org*

Provides social marketing, information, education, and communication services relating to family planning, oral rehydration therapy, and AIDS prevention. Maintains a full-time staff in the U.S. of 30 and a long-term staff abroad of 500.

Operates in a few countries of Africa and Asia as well as in Haiti, Mexico, and Jordan. Major client is USAID.

RESEARCH TRIANGLE INSTITUTE
P.O. Box 12194
Research Triangle Park, NC 27709
Tel. 919/541-6000 or Fax 919/541-5945
Web site: *www.rti.org*

A contract research organization providing a wide range of technical capabilities in the areas of economic policy, development planning, urban finance, agriculture, women in development, regional planning, health, nutrition, family planning, and water sanitation. Maintains a U.S. staff of 1,400 and a long-term staff abroad of 12. Operates in Africa, Asia, Latin America, the Caribbean, Middle East, North Africa, and the United Kingdom. Major clients include USAID, World Bank, UN agencies, Asian Development Bank, and the Inter-American Development Bank.

SRI INTERNATIONAL
333 Ravenswood Avenue	1611 North Kent Street
Menlo Park, CA 94025-3493	7th Floor
Tel. 415/326-6200	Arlington, VA 22209
Fax 415/326-5512	Tel. 703/524-2053

Web site: *www.sri.com*

A major consulting and development firm involved in providing technical assistance in numerous areas—economic analysis, engineering, energy research, environmental management, health sciences, information sciences, management consulting, national security, physical sciences, and social sciences. Maintains a full-time staff in the U.S. of 2,700 and a long-term staff abroad of 900. Operates in Africa, Asia, the Pacific Islands, Latin America, the Caribbean, Middle East, North Africa, Western Europe, and Australia with branch offices in France, Italy, Japan, Philippines, Saudi Arabia, Singapore, Sweden, Switzerland, United Kingdom, West Germany, and Arlington, Virginia. Major clients include USAID and numerous government agencies and private firms.

URBAN INSTITUTE
2100 M Street, NW, 5th Floor
Washington, DC 20037
Tel. 202/833-7200 or Fax 202/429-0687
Web site: *www.urban.org*

A policy and research organization providing assistance with health policy, public finance, housing, human resources, population, and income policy. U.S. staff of 200. Annual budget of $21 million.

WORLD LEARNING, INC.
Kipling Road
P.O. Box 676
Brattleboro, VT 05302-0676
Tel. 802/257-7751 or Fax 802/258-3500
Web site: *www.worldlearning.org*

Founded in 1932, this is one of the oldest private international educational services in the world. It operates international exchange programs, conducts training programs, and provides technical assistance in the areas of agricultural and rural development, refugees, family planning, and water resources. A major force for cross-cultural training and ESL programs, it operates 260 programs in 70 countries. Operates the highly respected School for International Training. Maintains a full-time staff in the U.S. of 350 and a long-term staff abroad of 750. Operates in Africa, Asia, Latin America, the Caribbean, and the Middle East. Major clients include USAID, USIA, U.S. Department of State, United Nations agencies, CIDA, and host country governments.

WORLD RESOURCES INSTITUTE
1709 New York Avenue, NW, Suite 700
Washington, DC 20006
Tel. 202/638-6300
Fax 202/638-0036
Web site: *www.wri.org*

A policy research center providing assistance with major policy questions relating to development issues. U.S. staff of 90.

9

Colleges and Universities

olleges and universities play a significant role in developing countries. While these institutions are especially well organized to offer traditional education and training programs, many also operate similarly to consulting firms, nonprofit corporations, and private voluntary organizations—they conduct research, provide technical assistance, and manage projects. Indeed, colleges and universities compete alongside these other organizations for contracts, grants, and cooperative agreements dispensed by USAID, the World Bank, foundations, and other funding institutions involved in promoting development in Third World countries.

Major Strengths

Colleges and universities are especially strong competitors in five major research and technical assistance areas—agriculture, aquaculture, forestry, public health, and family planning. They are uniquely equipped to offer education and training services such as providing degree programs for foreign students, developing institutional linkages for developing programs in foreign universities, and exchanging faculty with counterpart institutions. Many operate interdisciplinary area studies programs which focus on conducting research on Europe, Asia, Africa, Latin America, and the Middle East.

Funding Sources

International contracts and grants acquired through government agencies and private foundations play an important role in the overall funding of many colleges and universities. Such funds also affect the allocation of faculty positions and determine workloads of faculty members. In some institutions, research "institutes," "centers," "programs," or "international offices"—especially those in agriculture and public health—operate like independent contractors. Organized to compete for outside contracts, most of their funding is dependent on receiving such contracts and grants; the college or university may provide little or no financial support since such operations are designed to be both self-supporting and income-generating for the college or university.

> In some institutions, research "institutes," "centers," "programs," or "international offices"—especially those in agriculture and public health—operate like independent contractors.

Full-time faculty may be directly hired by the institute/center/program/ office, or they are assigned to it by a department where they primarily engage in research and technical assistance activities. In other cases, a particular school, center, or institute, such as agriculture, health, population, marine science, engineering, health, or area studies, operate international programs independent of other international programs within the university or in cooperation with one another; a committee of deans or program administrators may more or less coordinate these diverse institutional efforts. In other cases, faculty members may receive part-time appointments and "release time" in order to work with such an institute/center/program or engage in research projects; their teaching loads are normally reduced in order to participate in such programs. This often leads to resentment and petty politics amongst other faculty members who usually take on additional teaching loads in order to make up for the "teaching slack" created by their "research" colleagues who are off engaging in more financially rewarding and professionally enhancing activities. And in still other cases, a college or university may provide little organizational support for such activities other than operate a small research and development office that helps procure and administer contracts acquired by enterprising faculty members.

However, the **academic department** remains the basic organizational unit from which all international programs and activities are developed. In this sense, international activities tend to be decentralized and fragmented within most higher educational institutions.

The Beneficiaries

Each year hundreds of colleges and universities receive billions of dollars in contracts and grants to conduct research, provide technical assistance, and operate university-based educational programs aimed at developing countries and foreign students. Agriculture, population, health, and education programs are the four major beneficiaries of contracts, grants, and cooperative agreements dispensed to colleges and universities by government agencies, international organizations, and private foundations. During the past 15 years, the major recipients of such largess were:

- Colorado State University
- Florida State University
- Georgetown University
- Harvard University
- Indiana University
- Johns Hopkins University
- Michigan State University
- North Carolina State University
- Ohio State University
- Oregon State University
- Purdue University
- State University of New York—System
- Texas A&M University
- University of Florida
- University of Hawaii
- University of Illinois
- University of Kentucky
- University of Minnesota
- University of Missouri
- University of Nebraska

As noted in Chapter 8, many colleges and universities also belong to consortia (Consortium For International Development, Midwest Universities Consortium For International Activities, MidAmerican International Agricultural Consortium, South-East Consortium For International Development) or are closely linked to other nonprofit corporations (Research Triangle Institute) and private firms (Development Alternatives, Inc.). The consortium are able to better mobilize the diverse resources of member institutions in organizing for large technical assistance projects. If you are primarily interested in pursuing international opportunities with the colleges and universities listed in this chapter, do keep in mind the consortia in Chapter 8 which also have their own full-time staffs in the U.S. and abroad.

Opportunities

Finding positions in colleges and universities to engage in international work takes two major paths. Entry into most institutions is still via the basic organizational unit—the academic department. You must possess the necessary academic credentials and professional experience to qualify for an academic position. The basic requirement is a Ph.D. although Masters' degrees are acceptable in some institutions. Opportunities to do international contract and grant work may arise from your own efforts to acquire a contract or grant or in conjunction with the activities of fellow faculty members, including an institute or center specifically organized for contract and grant work. In many institutions, you must first acquire an academic appointment in a department *before* you can participate in the activities of such an institute or center; you may also receive a joint appointment involving both an academic department and an institute or center. Your workload within the department versus the institute or center will be a matter of negotiation between you, your department chair, the dean, and institute/center personnel. In other colleges and universities, the institute or center operates like an independent contractor by directly hiring its own personnel. Positions may be strictly research or administrative in nature with no teaching or other academic responsibilities involved. Entry into these positions also requires advanced educational degrees (Masters' or Ph.D.). These positions place greater emphasis on contracting and grantsmanship skills as well as practical field and research experience than on scholarly credentials normally associated with academic departments.

The following list of academic institutions includes the major recipients of international contracts, grants, and cooperative agreements funded primarily by USAID, the World Bank, and private foundations. Many other educational institutions also have international programs, engage in international research, and provide technical assistance but on a smaller scale than the institutions listed here. While faculty in many departments may possess international expertise, engage in international research, or provide technical assistance, each institution tends to take on a particular international orientation, be it agriculture, health, public policy, area studies, or education and training.

Major Recipients

Alabama A&M University
P.O. Box 1177
Normal, AL 35762-0030
Tel. 205/851-5418
Fax 205/851-9157
ORGANIZATION: Office of International Programs
FOCUS: agriculture

University of Alabama—Birmingham
University Station, 315 Tim Howell
720 20th Street
Birmingham, AL 35294-0098
Tel. 205/934-8647
Fax 205/975-3329
ORGANIZATION: Office of International Programs, John Sparkman Center for International Public Health Education
FOCUS: public health

University of Alaska—Fairbanks
172 Arctic Health Research Bldg.
Fairbanks, AK 99775-0100
Tel. 907/474-7500
Fax 907/474-5379
ORGANIZATION: School of Agriculture and Land Resources Management
FOCUS: agriculture and land use

Alcorn State University
Rural Station, P.O. Box 690
Lorman, MS 39096
Tel. 601/877-6136

Fax 601/877-6219
ORGANIZATION: Agricultural Research and Applied Science
FOCUS: agriculture, animal science, nursing

American University
4400 Massachusetts Ave., NW
Washington, DC 20016-8071
Tel. 202/885-1600
Fax 202/885-2494
ORGANIZATION: School of International Service
FOCUS: U.S. foreign policy, international policy, international communication, peace studies, international development

Arizona State University
Box 874105
Tempe, AZ 85287-4105
Tel. 602/965-5965
Fax 602/965-4026
ORGANIZATION: Office of International Programs, Center for Asian Studies, Center for Latin American Studies
FOCUS: Asian and Latin American studies, rural credit, engineering, training

University of Arizona
Harville 151
Tucson, AZ 85721
Tel. 520/621-1900
Fax 520/621-7257
ORGANIZATION: Office of International Agricultural Programs, Middle East Center
FOCUS: agriculture, natural resources, environment, socio-economic analysis

University of Arkansas—Fayetteville
300 Hotz Hall
Fayetteville, AR 72701
Tel. 870/575-6857 or Fax 870/575-5055
ORGANIZATION: School of Agriculture
FOCUS: agriculture, aquaculture

University of Arkansas—Pine Bluff
Box 4990, 1200 North University
Pine Bluff, AR 71611
Tel. 870/543-8131 or Fax 870/543-8033
ORGANIZATION: School of Agriculture
FOCUS: agriculture, aquaculture, health/nutrition

Auburn University
International Programs
146 College of Business Bldg., Box P
Auburn, AL 36849-5159
Tel. 334/844-5766
Fax 334/844-6436
ORGANIZATION: Office of International Programs, International Center for Aquaculture, International Agricultural Programs.
FOCUS: agriculture, fisheries, education training.

Boston University
19 Deerfield St.
Second Floor
Boston, MA 02215
Tel. 617/353-3565
Fax 617/353-5891
ORGANIZATION: International Student Services Office, College of Communication, School of Education, Medical School, and Centers for African Studies, Asian Development, and Latin American Development.
FOCUS: training, education, health, and area studies.

Brigham Young University
Benson Institute 110 B-49
Provo, UT 84602
Tel. 801/378-2607 or Fax 801/378-5278
ORGANIZATION: Ezra Taft Benson Agriculture and Food Institute; David M. Kennedy Center for International Studies
FOCUS: agriculture, nutrition, rural development, archaeology, pharmacology, education and training.

California State University—Fresno
School of Agricultural Sciences & Technology
Fresno, CA 93740-0079
Tel. 209/278-5118
Fax 209/278-4496
ORGANIZATION: Office of International Agricultural Programs, International Business Programs, and Office of International Student Services and Programs
FOCUS: agriculture, business, education and training

University of California—Berkeley
College of Natural Resources
101 Gianinni Hall
Berkeley, CA 94720
Tel. 510/642-0542
Fax 510/642-4612

ORGANIZATION: College of Natural Resources; African Studies Center; South Asian Center; East Asian Center; Middle East Studies Center; Collaborative Research Support Program in Nutrition Sciences.
FOCUS: natural resource management, water and sanitary management, nutrition, agriculture, area studies, education and training.

University of California—Davis
424 2nd Street
Suite B
Davis, CA 95616
Tel. 916/752-7071
Fax 916/752-7523
ORGANIZATION: International Programs; Graduate Studies and Research
FOCUS: agriculture, engineering, management, and law

University of California—Los Angeles
10833 Le Conte
Los Angeles, CA 90024-1772
Tel. 310/825-4321 or Fax 310/206-8460
ORGANIZATION: School of Public Health, Office of International Students and Scholars, East Asia Center, Russian and East European Center, Latin American Center, Near Eastern Center, African Studies Center, Chinese Studies Center, Japanese Research and Exchange Program, Mexican Studies Center, Pacific Rim Studies Center
FOCUS: health, education, and training

Case Western Reserve University
10900 Euclid Ave.
Cleveland, OH 44106
Tel. 216/368-2000
Fax 216/368-4889
ORGANIZATION: Office of International Student Services, Medical School, International Health Center University Hospital
FOCUS: health, applied social sciences, and management

Clark Atlanta University
223 James P. Brawley Dr., SW
Atlanta, GA 30314
Tel. 404/880-6662
Fax 404/880-8654
ORGANIZATION: Research and Sponsored Programs; International Affairs and Development Program
FOCUS: health, child survival, human resource development, rural sanitation, education and training

Clark University
Program for International Development
950 Main Street
Worcester, MA 01610-1477
Tel 508/793-7201
Fax 508/793-8820
ORGANIZATION: International Development Program
FOCUS: resource management, population, rural development, energy

Clemson University
101 Barre Hall
Clemson, SC 29634-5201
Tel. 864/656-2357
Fax 864/656-4187
ORGANIZATION: International Programs
FOCUS: agriculture, resource management, education and training

Colorado State University
Office of International Programs
Fort Collins, CO 80523
Tel. 970/491-5917
Fax 970/491-5501
ORGANIZATION: International Programs
FOCUS: agriculture, water resource development, education and training

Columbia University
617 West 168th St., 3rd Floor
New York, NY 10032
Tel. 212/305-3927
Fax 212/305-6450
ORGANIZATION: School of Public Health and Administration Medicine, Center for Population and Family Health, School of International and Public Affairs, South Asian Institute, East Asian Institute, Latin American Institute, Middle East Institute
FOCUS: population, family health

University of Connecticut
1376 Storrs Road
Box U66
Storrs, CT 06269-4066
Tel. 860/486-2917 or Fax 860/486-5113
ORGANIZATION: College of Agriculture and Natural Resources, Latin American Center, Institute of Public Service International
FOCUS: agriculture, nutrition, natural resources, human resource management, computer systems, education and training

Cornell University
170 Uris Hall
Ithaca, NY 14853
Tel. 607/255-6370
Fax 607/254-5000
ORGANIZATION: Mario Einaudi Center for International Studies (International Agricultural Programs, Institute for African Development, Rural Development Committee, South Asia Program, Population and Development Program, International Nutrition Program)
FOCUS: agriculture, nutrition, rural development, law, population, education and training, area studies

Delaware State College
1200 N. Dupont Hwy.
Dover, DE 19901
Tel. 302/739-4924
ORGANIZATION: International Programs
FOCUS: agriculture, nutrition, family health education

University of Delaware
International Programs and Special Sessions
4 Kent Way
Newark, DE 19716
Tel. 302/831-2852
Fax 302/831-6042
ORGANIZATION: International Programs and Special Sessions, College of Agricultural Sciences
FOCUS: agriculture, engineering, marine resources, development administration, education and training

Duke University
2122 Campus Drive
Box 90404
Durham, NC 27708-0404
Tel. 919/684-2765
Fax 919/684-8749
ORGANIZATION: Center for International Studies, Center for International Development Research (Institute of Policy Science), School of Forestry and Environmental Studies
FOCUS: natural resources, ecology, area studies, international economics, migration issues

Eastern Michigan University
The World College
307 Goodison Hall
Ypsilanti, MI 48197
Tel. 734/487-2414 or Fax 734/485-1980
ORGANIZATION: The World College
FOCUS: education and training

East-West Center
1777 East West Road
Honolulu, HI 96848
Tel. 808/944-7111
Fax 808/944-7970
ORGANIZATION: Resource Systems Institute, Environment and Policy Institute, Population Institute, Institute of Culture and Communication, Pacific Islands Development Program, Student Affairs and Open Grants Program
FOCUS: environment, population, economic development, natural resources

Eastern Virginia Medical School
601 Colley Avenue
Norfolk, VA 23507
Tel. 757/446-5899
Fax 757/446-5905
ORGANIZATION: Contraceptive Research and Development Program
FOCUS: fertility and population planning

Florida A&M University
P.O. Box 338
Tallahassee, FL 32307
Tel. 850/599-3562
Fax 850/561-2587
ORGANIZATION: Technology Transfer and International Programs, College of Engineering, Sciences, Technology, and Agriculture
FOCUS: engineering, pharmacy, architecture, agriculture, institutional development

Florida International University
Latin America and Caribbean Center
University Park—DM353
Miami, FL 33199
Tel. 305/348-2894
Fax 305/348-3593
ORGANIZATION: Latin America and Caribbean Center
FOCUS: journalism, communication, business, education and training

Florida State University
Learning Systems Institute
4600 University Center, Building C
Tallahassee, FL 32306-4041
Tel. 850/644-2570 or Fax 850/644-3783
ORGANIZATION: Learning Systems Institute
FOCUS: education and training

University of Florida
3028 McCarty Hall
Gainesville, FL 32611
Tel. 352/392-1965
Fax 352/392-7127
ORGANIZATION: Institute of Food and Agricultural Sciences, Center for Tropical
Agriculture, Center for African Studies, Center for Latin American Studies,
Farming Systems and Small Farms Program, Agroforestry Program
FOCUS: agriculture, education and training

Fort Valley State University
1005 State College Drive
Fort Valley, GA 31030-3298
Tel. 912/825-6320
Fax 912/825-6376
ORGANIZATION: International Programs
FOCUS: agriculture, nutrition, health, rural development, communication, education
and training

Georgia Institute of Technology
Centennial Research Building
Atlanta, GA 30332
Tel. 404/894-2375 or Fax 404/894-7339
ORGANIZATION: Office of Interdisciplinary Programs, Research Institute, Con-
tinuing Education, Advanced Technology Development Center
FOCUS: institutional development, education and training

University of Georgia
111 Candler Hall
Athens, GA 30602-1773
Tel. 706/542-7889
Fax 706/542-7891
ORGANIZATION: International Development
FOCUS: agriculture, forestry, veterinary medicine, home economics, education and
training.

Harvard University
Harvard Institute for International Development
One Eliot St.
Cambridge, MA 02138
Tel. 617/495-2161 or Fax 617/495-0527
ORGANIZATION: Harvard Institute for International Development, Harvard School
of Public Health, Population Sciences and International Health Programs, John F.
Kennedy School of Government, Center for Middle Eastern Studies
FOCUS: health, agriculture, food, public policy, education and training

University of Hawaii
2565 The Mall
PSB 103
Honolulu, HI 96822
Tel. 808/956-6940 or Fax 808/956-5030
ORGANIZATION: College of Tropical Agriculture and Human Resources, International Programs, School of Public Health, School of Medicine
FOCUS: agriculture, health, engineering, management, education and training

University of Houston
One Main Street, Room 325 South
Houston, TX 77002
Tel. 713/221-8048 or Fax 713/221-8157
ORGANIZATION: International Business Programs, Madrid Business School Project,
Office of Overseas International Education, Office of International Student Office,
Language and Culture Center
FOCUS: business, education and training

Howard University
520 W St., NW
Washington, DC 20059
Tel. 202/806-6270 or Fax 202/806-7934
ORGANIZATION: College of Medicine, School of Education, School of Engineering,
Office of International Student Services, African Studies and Research
FOCUS: education and training

University of Idaho
216 Morrill Hall
Moscow, ID 83843
Tel. 208/885-8984 or Fax 208/885-6198
ORGANIZATION: International Trade and Development Office, College of
Agriculture and Forestry
FOCUS: agriculture, forestry, education and training

University of Illinois
109 Mumford Hall
1301 West Gregory Dr.
Urbana, IL 61801
Tel. 217/333-6420
Fax 217/244-6537
ORGANIZATION: Office of International Agriculture
FOCUS: agriculture, health, education and training

University of Illinois—Chicago
1033 West Van Buren
Chicago, IL 60607
Tel. 312/966-5455
Fax 312/413-7857
ORGANIZATION: International Programs Office, College of Pharmacy, College Nursing, Center for Research in Law and Justice, College of Business Administration
FOCUS: business, health, education and training

Indiana University
International Programs
Bryan Hall, Room 205
Bloomington, IN 47405
Tel. 812/855-7557
Fax 812/855-6884
ORGANIZATION: International Development Institute, International Programs, Center for African Studies
FOCUS: management, education and training

Iowa State University
117 Curtiss Hall
Ames, IA 50011
Tel. 515/294-1851 or Fax 515/294-9477
ORGANIZATION: International Agricultural Programs
FOCUS: agriculture, education and training

University of Iowa
120 International Center
Iowa City, IA 52242
Tel. 319/335-0335 or Fax 319/335-2021
ORGANIZATION: Office of International Education and Services, Center for International and Comparative Studies, Center for Asian and Pacific Studies
FOCUS: economics, social sciences, education and training

Johns Hopkins University

103 E. Mount Royal Ave., Suite 2B
Baltimore, MD 21202
Tel. 410/659-4108
Fax 410/659-4118
ORGANIZATION: School of Hygiene and Public Health, Department of Population
Dynamics, Department of International Health, Institute for International Programs,
Center for Communications Programs, School of Advanced International Studies,
School of Medicine, JHPIEGO, International Center for Epidemiology and Preventive Ophthalmology
FOCUS: health, population, area studies, education and training

Kansas State University

Manhattan, KS 66506
Tel. 785/532-5990 or Fax 785/532-6550
ORGANIZATION: International Programs
FOCUS: agriculture, business, education and training

University of Kansas

International Studies & Programs
300 Strong Hall
108 Lippincott Hall
Lawrence, KS 66045
Tel. 785/864-4141
Fax 785/864-4555
ORGANIZATION: International Studies and Programs
FOCUS: nutrition, area studies, education and training

Kentucky State University

Atwood Research Facility
Frankfurt, KY 40601
Tel. 502/227-6178 or Fax 502/227-6381
ORGANIZATION: Cooperative Extension and Community Research
FOCUS: aquaculture, rural development, nutrition, education and training

University of Kentucky

Office of International Affairs
212 Bradley Hall
Lexington, KY 40506
Tel. 606/257-4067 or Fax 606/323-1026
ORGANIZATION: International Agricultural Programs
FOCUS: agriculture, engineering, medicine, nutrition, business, education and
training

Langston University
P.O. Box 730
Research Building
Langston, OK 73050
Tel. 405/466-3836 or Fax 405/466-3138
ORGANIZATION: American Institute of Dairy Goat Research
FOCUS: agriculture and animal health

Lincoln University
202 Soldiers Hall
Jefferson City, MO 65101
Tel. 573/681-5360
Fax 573/681-5596
ORGANIZATION: International Programs
FOCUS: agriculture, animal science, nutrition

Louisiana State University
P.O. Box 16090
Baton Rouge, LA 70893
Tel. 504/388-6963
Fax 504/388-6775
ORGANIZATION: International Programs, LSU Agricultural Center
FOCUS: agriculture, aquaculture, forestry, home economics, food and nutrition, business

University of Maine—Orono
Office of International Research and Education Programs
204 Roger Clapp
Orono, ME 04469-0102
Tel. 207/581-3433 or Fax 207/581-2920
ORGANIZATION: International Programs
FOCUS: agroforestry and wildlife management, education and training

University of Maryland—College Park
145 Tydings Hall
College Park, MD 20742
Tel. 301/314-7703
Fax 301/314-9256
ORGANIZATION: College of Agriculture, College of Life Science, Consortium for International Crop Protection, Center for International Development and Conflict Management
FOCUS: agriculture, aquaculture, economics, water resources, management, education and training

University of Maryland—Eastern Shore
Office of Graduate Studies
Early Childhood Research Center
Princess Anne, MD 21853
Tel. 410/651-6080 or Fax 410/651-6085
ORGANIZATION: International Programs
FOCUS: agriculture, aquaculture, education and training

Massachusetts Institute of Technology
Center for International Studies, MIT E38-648
Cambridge, MA 02139-8093
Tel. 617/253-8093
Fax 617/253-9330
ORGANIZATION: Center for International Studies, MIT-Japan Science and Technology Program, Technology and Development Program
FOCUS: engineering, technology, economics, politics, education and training

University of Massachusetts
Center for International Education
285 Hills House South
Amherst, MA 01003
Tel. 413/545-0465 or Fax 413/545-1263
ORGANIZATION: International Programs Office, Center for International Education, Center for International Agriculture, African Studies Program, Japanese Work Experience Program
FOCUS: education and training, agriculture

Meharry Medical College
1005 D.B. Todd, Jr. Blvd.
Nashville, TN 37208
Tel. 615/327-6947 or Fax 615/327-6948
ORGANIZATION: International Medical Center
FOCUS: health

University of Miami
P.O. Box 248123
Coral Gables, FL 33124-3010
Tel. 305/284-4303 or Fax 305/284-4406
ORGANIZATION: Graduate School of International Studies, North-South Center, Rosenstiel School of Marine and Atmospheric Sciences, International Business and Banking Institute, School of Business Administration, International Student and Scholar Services
FOCUS: marine sciences, fisheries, oceanography, business, law, medicine, education and training

Michigan State University
209 International Center
East Lansing, MI 48824-1035
Tel. 517/355-2350
Fax 517/353-7254
ORGANIZATION: International Studies and Programs
FOCUS: agriculture, health, business, communication, education and training

University of Michigan
Division of Research Development
    and Administration
3003 S. State Street
Ann Arbor, MI 48109-1275
Tel. 313/764-5500
Fax 313/764-8510
ORGANIZATION: Center for Research on Economic Development, Institute for Public Policy Studies, School of Natural Resources, Department of Population Planning and International Health
FOCUS: economics, agriculture, natural resources, health, population planning, education and training

University of Minnesota
190 Coffe Hall
1420 Eckles Avenue
St. Paul, MN 55108
Tel. 612/624-3221
Fax 612/625-3111
ORGANIZATION: International Agricultural Programs
FOCUS: agriculture

Mississippi State University
P.O. Box 9733
Mississippi State, MS 39762
Tel. 601/325-3204 or Fax 601/325-4561
ORGANIZATION: Office of International Programs, Seed Technology Laboratory
FOCUS: agriculture, education, and training

University of Missouri
2-69 Agriculture Building
Columbia, MO 65211
Tel. 573/882-7740 or Fax 573/882-0388
ORGANIZATION: College of Agriculture
FOCUS: agriculture, education and training

Montana State University
400 Cobertson Hall
Bozeman, MT 59717
Tel. 406/994-4031
Fax 406/994-1619
ORGANIZATION: Office of International Programs
FOCUS: agriculture, education and training

Morehouse School of Medicine
720 Westview Drive, SW
Atlanta, GA 30310-1495
Tel. 404/752-1500
Fax 404/755-7505
ORGANIZATION: Sponsored Programs
FOCUS: health, nutrition

Morgan State University
Cold Spring Lane and Hillen Road
Baltimore, MD 21251
Tel. 410/319-3078
Fax 410/319-3256
ORGANIZATION: International Studies Program, Institute for Urban Research, Office of International Student Affairs
FOCUS: education and training

Murray State University
Center for International Programs, Box 9
Murray, KY 42071-0009
Tel. 502/762-4152
Fax 502/762-3237
ORGANIZATION: Center for International Programs
FOCUS: education and training

University of Nebraska—Lincoln
110 Agriculture Hall
Lincoln, NE 68583-0706
Tel. 402/472-2758
Fax 402/472-2759
ORGANIZATION: International Program Division, Institute of Agriculture and Natural Resources
FOCUS: agriculture, animal science, education and training

University of Nevada
4505 Maryland Parkway
Las Vegas, NV 89154
Tel. 702/739-3011
Fax 702/739-3850
ORGANIZATION: Office of International Programs, International Student Services
FOCUS: hotel administration, area studies, education and training

University of New Hampshire
316 James Hall
Durham, NH 03824
Tel. 603/862-1234
Fax 603/862-2030
ORGANIZATION: Center for International Perspectives
FOCUS: agriculture, education and training

New Mexico State University
Box 30001, Dept. 3567
Las Cruces, NM 88003-8001
Tel. 505/646/3199
Fax 505/646-2558
ORGANIZATION: Center for International Programs
FOCUS: agriculture, rural development, education and training

University of New Mexico
Earth Data Analysis Center
2500 Yale Center Southeast, Suite 100
Albuquerque, NM 87131-6031
Tel. 505/277-3622
Fax 505/277-3614
ORGANIZATION: International Programs
FOCUS: remote sensing, education and training

State University of New York—System
SUNY Plaza
International Programs and Development Group
Albany, NY 12246
Tel. 518/443-5124
Fax 518/443-5126
ORGANIZATION: International Programs and Development Group
FOCUS: economic growth, health care service, education and training, agriculture, management and public administration, natural resources, health care financing

North Carolina State University
Box 7112
Raleigh, NC 27695-7112
Tel. 919/515-3201
Fax 919/515-6835
ORGANIZATION: International Programs
FOCUS: agriculture, forestry, veterinary medicine

University of North Carolina—Chapel Hill
207 Caldwell Hall
Chapel Hill, NC 27519-3130
Tel. 919/962-2211 or Fax 919/962-3094
ORGANIZATION: Center for International Studies, School of Medicine, School of Public Health, Population Center
FOCUS: medicine, health, family planning, education and training

North Dakota State University
State University Station
Box 5636
Fargo, ND 58105
Tel. 701/231-8011
Fax 701/231-8802
ORGANIZATION: Department of Agricultural Economics, Northern Crops Institute
FOCUS: agriculture

Northwestern University
633 Clark Street
Evanston, IL 60208
Tel. 847/491-3741
Fax 847/467-1645
ORGANIZATION: Medical School, Program of African Studies, Transportation Center, International Office
FOCUS: medicine, area studies, education and training

Ohio State University
2120 Fyffe Road
Columbus, OH 43210
Tel. 614/292-6446 or Fax 614/292-4818
ORGANIZATION: International Programs in Agriculture, Research Foundation
FOCUS: agriculture, rural development, education and training

Ohio University
Center for International Studies
56 E. Union St.
Athens, OH 45701
Tel. 740/593-1840 or Fax 740/593-1837
ORGANIZATION: Center for International Studies, College of Education, ITM/BBA
Program
FOCUS: education and training

Oklahoma State University
Office of International Programs
307 Center for International Trade Development
Stillwater, OK 74078-0437
Tel. 405/744-6535
Fax: 405/744-7529
ORGANIZATION: International Programs, English Language Institute
FOCUS: agriculture, engineering, education and training

Oregon State University
Office of International Research and Development
Snell 400
Corvallis, OR 97331-1641
Tel. 541/737-0123
Fax 541/737-2400
ORGANIZATION: Office of International Research and Development
FOCUS: natural resources, agriculture, human resources, fisheries, education, and
training

Pennsylvania State University
222 Boucke Building
University Park, PA 16802
Tel. 814/865-7681
Fax 814/865-3336
ORGANIZATION: Office of International Programs, International Agricultural
Programs
FOCUS: agriculture, business, health, engineering, education and training

University of Pennsylvania
International Programs
133 Bennett Hall
Philadelphia, PA 19104-6275
Tel. 215/898-4661
Fax 215/898-2622
ORGANIZATION: Office of International Programs, Joseph H. Lauder Institute of
Management and International Studies, PENN/PACIE Institute, South Asian

Studies Center, Near East Studies Center, Center for International Management
FOCUS: business, management, area studies, education and training

University of Pittsburgh
4040 Forbes Quadrangle
230 South Bouquet St.
Pittsburgh, PA 15260
Tel. 412/648-7390
Fax 412/648-2199
ORGANIZATION: Center for International Studies
FOCUS: health, rural development, area studies, education and training

Prairie View A&M University
P.O. Box 4079
Prairie View, TX 77446-0608
Tel. 409/857-3311 or Fax 409/857-3225
ORGANIZATION: Institute for International Agribusiness Studies
FOCUS: agriculture, animal science, education and training

Princeton University
Woodrow Wilson School
Robertson Hall
Princeton, NJ 08544-1013
Tel. 609/258-4831 or Fax 609/258-2809
ORGANIZATION: Woodrow Wilson School of Public and International Affairs,
Center of International Studies, Middle East Center
FOCUS: international relations, economic development, biomass conversion techniques, forestry, education and training

University of Puerto Rico
Box 5000
Mayaguez, PR 00708
Tel. 787/832-4142 or Fax 787/832-3413
ORGANIZATION: College of Agricultural Sciences
FOCUS: agriculture

Purdue University
Agricultural Administration Building
West Lafayette, IN 47907
Tel. 765/494-8459 or Fax 765/494-9613
ORGANIZATION: International Programs in Agriculture
FOCUS: agriculture, education and training

University of Rhode Island
128 Woodward Hall
Kingston, RI 02818
Tel. 401/874-1000
Fax 401/874-5523
ORGANIZATION: International Center for Marine Resource Development
FOCUS: marine sciences

Rutgers University
Cook College
109 Martin Hall
New Brunswick, NJ 08903
Tel. 732/932-1766
Fax 732/932-6769
ORGANIZATION: University International Programs, Remote Sensing Center, Center for Advanced Food Technology, Center for Agricultural Molecular Biology
FOCUS: agriculture, food technology, remote sensing

Sam Houston State University
Box 2088
Huntsville, TX 77341
Tel. 409/294-1111
Fax 409/294-1597
ORGANIZATION: International Programs
FOCUS: education and training

San Diego State University
Career Services
San Diego, CA 92182-0578
Tel. 619/594-1982
Fax 619/594-5642
ORGANIZATION: Office of International Programs, SDSU Foundation, Office for International Student Services
FOCUS: agriculture, education and training

South Carolina State University
300 College St., NE
Orangeburg, SC 29117
Tel. 803/536-8393
Fax 803/536-8429
ORGANIZATION: International Programs, School of Business
FOCUS: agribusiness, nutrition, home economics, education and training

University of South Carolina
Byrnes International Building, Suite 123
Columbia, SC 29208
Tel. 803/777-7461 or Fax 803/777-0462
ORGANIZATION: James F. Byrnes International Center, Belle W. Baruch Institute
for Marine Biology and Coastal Research, International Business Programs, Earth
Sciences and Resources Institute, School of Public Health, Institute of International
Studies
FOCUS: education and training

South Dakota State University
Office of International Programs
Administration Building
Brookings, SD 57007
Tel. 605/688-4431 or Fax 605/688-4443
ORGANIZATION: International Programs, College of Agriculture and Biological
Science, College of Engineering, Office of Remote Sensing, Student Affairs
FOCUS: agriculture, remote sensing, area studies, education, training

University of Southern California
University Park, VKC #330
Los Angeles, CA 90089-0043
Tel. 213/740-6278 or Fax 213/742-0281
ORGANIZATION: International Public Administration Center, School of International Relations, Center for International Studies, Office of International Students
and Scholars
FOCUS: administration, management, health, education and training

Southern Illinois University
910 S. Forest Street
Carbondale, IL 62901-6514
Tel. 618/453-5774 or Fax 618/453-7660
ORGANIZATION: International Students and Scholars, Office of International
Agriculture, Center for English as a Second Language
FOCUS: agriculture, applied technologies, business, education and training

Southern University A&M College
P.O. Box 10596
Baton Rouge, LA 70813-2004
Tel. 504/771-2004 or Fax 504/771-2026
ORGANIZATION: International Development Programs, Small Farm Research
Center
FOCUS: agriculture, education and training

Stanford University
Encina Hall
Room 200
Stanford, CA 94305-6055
Tel. 650/723-4581
Fax 650/725-2592
ORGANIZATION: Institute for International Studies, Stanford Project on International and Cross Cultural Education, Latin American Center, Center for East Asian Studies, African Studies Center, Food Research Institute
FOCUS: area studies, education and training

Syracuse University
310 Walnut Place
Syracuse, NY 13244-2380
Tel. 315/443-2457
Fax 315/443-3091
ORGANIZATION: Maxwell School of Citizenship and Public Affairs, Office of International Services, Foreign and Comparative Studies, South Asia Center
FOCUS: public administration, management, education and training

University of Tennessee
404 Andy Holt Tower
Knoxville, TN 37996-0140
Tel. 423/974-2475
Fax 423/974-2708
ORGANIZATION: Agricultural Experiment Station, International Agricultural Programs
FOCUS: agriculture, education and training

Texas A&M University at Kingsville
Campus Box 156
Kingsville, TX 78363
Tel. 512/593-2111 or Fax 512/593-2195
ORGANIZATION: College of Agriculture and Human Sciences, Office of International Programs
FOCUS: agriculture, home economics

Texas A&M University
International Agricultural Programs
College Station, TX 77843-2477
Tel. 409/845-4164 or Fax 409/845-5663
ORGANIZATION: International Agricultural Programs
FOCUS: agriculture, education and training

Texas Southern University
3100 Cleburne St.
Houston, TX 77004
Tel. 731/313-7896
Fax 731/313-1876
ORGANIZATION: Office of International Affairs, Office of International Student Affairs
FOCUS: education and training

Texas Tech University
ICASALS, P.O. Box 41036
Lubbock, TX 79409-1036
Tel. 806/742-2218
Fax 806/742-1954
ORGANIZATION: International Center for Arid and Semiarid Land Studies
FOCUS: agriculture, natural resources, education and training

University of Texas—Austin
International Office, Drawer A
Austin, TX 78713-7206
Tel. 512/471-1211
Fax 512/471-8848
ORGANIZATION: International Office, East European Studies Center, Center for Latin American Studies, Middle East Studies Center, Center for South Asian Studies
FOCUS: area studies, education and training

Tufts University
Packard Hall
Medford, MA 02155
Tel. 617/627-3152 or Fax 617/726-3971
ORGANIZATION: Tufts Programs Abroad, International Programs Development, Fletcher Program in International Resources and Development, School of Veterinary Medicine, School of Dental Medicine, School of Medicine
FOCUS: medicine, health, dentistry, education and training

Tulane University
1501 Canal St., Suite 1300
New Orleans, LA 70112
Tel. 504/584-3655 or Fax 504/584-3653
ORGANIZATION: International Communication Center, Center of Resource Development and Department of International Health and Development
FOCUS: family planning, public health, education and training

Tuskegee University
219 Kresge Center
Tuskegee, AL 36088
Tel. 334/727-8011
Fax 334/727-8451
ORGANIZATION: International Programs, Carver Research Foundation, School of Agriculture and Home Economics
FOCUS: agriculture, veterinary medicine, health, education and training

Utah State University
UMC 9500
Logan, UT 84322
Tel. 801/797-1124
Fax 801/797-3522
ORGANIZATION: International Programs and Studies
FOCUS: agriculture, education and training

University of Vermont
Area and International Studies
506A Old Mill
Burlington, VT 05405
Tel. 802/656-1096
Fax 802/656-1376
ORGANIZATION: Area and International Studies, Office of International Education Services
FOCUS: agriculture, health, education and training

Virginia Polytechnic Institute and State University
1060 Litton Reaves Hall
Blacksburg, VA 24061-0334
Tel. 540/231-6338
Fax 540/231-6741
ORGANIZATION: Office of International Research and Development
FOCUS: agriculture, education and training

Virginia State University
Box 9416
Petersburg, VA 23803
Tel. 804/524-5613
Fax 804/524-5638
ORGANIZATION: International Agriculture Programs
FOCUS: agriculture

University of Washington

Office of International Programs, PA-10
Seattle, WA 98195
Tel. 206/543-9272 or Fax 206/685-3511
ORGANIZATION: International Programs, Institute of Marine Studies, College of Forest Resources, School of Public Health, Institute of Food Science and Technology, Jackson School of International Studies, East Asian Studies Center, Middle East Studies Center, International Studies Center, South Asia Center, Southeast Asian Center
FOCUS: forestry, marine sciences, health, area studies, education and training

Washington State University

French Administration Building No. 328
Pullman, WA 99164-1034
Tel. 509/335-2541
Fax 509/335-1060
ORGANIZATION: International Program Development
FOCUS: agriculture, rural development

Western Carolina University

Center for Technical Assistance Programs
Cullowee, NC 28723
Tel. 828/227-7492 or Fax 828/227-7422
ORGANIZATION: International Economic Development Programs, International Programs and Services, Center for Improving Mountain Living
FOCUS: rural development, agriculture

Western Virginia University

Box 6108
2112 Agricultural Sciences Bldg.
Morgantown, WV 26506-6957
Tel. 304/293-2041 or Fax 304/293-3740
ORGANIZATION: College of Agriculture and Forestry
FOCUS: agriculture, forestry, education and training

University of Wisconsin—Madison

International Agriculture Programs
240 Agriculture Hall
1450 Linden Dr.
Madison, WI 53606-1562
Tel. 608/262-1271 or Fax 608/262-8852
ORGANIZATION: International Agriculture Programs
FOCUS: agriculture, rural development, area studies

University of Wyoming
P.O. Box 3228 University Station
Laramie, WY 82071
Tel. 307/766-5193
Fax 307/766-4053
ORGANIZATION: International Programs, International Agriculture
FOCUS: agriculture, education and training

Yale University
Yale Station
New Haven, CT 06520
Tel. 203/432-4771
Fax 203/432-1323
ORGANIZATION: Tropical Resources Institute, Economic Growth Center, Center for International and Area Studies, African Studies Center
FOCUS: forestry, natural resources, public policy, area studies

10

Teaching Abroad–Jobs For People Who Love to Travel

I f you lack international skills and experience, or if you are primarily interested in gaining short-term (1-2 years) international work experience that satisfies your curiosity for travel and living abroad, this may be the perfect chapter for you—become a teacher. This is one of the easiest and quickest ways to enter the international employment arena. Indeed, thousands of individuals choose this employment route each year, especially if they are looking for short-term jobs rather than long-term professional employment. It's a good way to acquire international experience without having to invest a great deal of time in acquiring specialized skills and education required by many of the employers identified in previous chapters.

Opportunities Galore

Numerous teaching opportunities exist in schools throughout the world. Many of these jobs are for certified teachers who teach in the U.S. Department of State schools, U.S. Department of Defense schools, or international schools. Teaching jobs with these schools include all subject matters as well as administrative positions. These teaching positions pay comparable to teaching positions in the United States. Moving from one country to another every three to six years, many teachers decide to make a career of teaching in these overseas schools. Others may only teach in these schools for two to five years.

However, the largest number of overseas teaching positions are for teachers of English who work in local schools, institutes, or universities on either a short- or long-term basis. While few of these positions require teaching experience or teacher certification, some type of teacher training will be helpful for landing such teaching positions. Several universities in the United States, for example, offer special training as well as overseas placements for individuals interested in teaching English as a foreign language. Earnings for these types of teaching positions vary greatly. Most such positions are low paying or volunteer positions, but earnings can be very good in such countries as Japan, Korea, or Taiwan.

Teaching English As a Foreign Language

If you are willing to teach English as a foreign language, you can easily find a job abroad. Indeed, the worldwide demand for English language teachers remains high and the jobs are plentiful. Most recently, the demand for English teachers has increased substantially in Eastern Europe, Russia, and the former Soviet republics.

> **If you are willing to teach English as a foreign language, you can easily find a job abroad.**

The first thing you need to do is to understand the language of this particular occupational group. Teachers of English language usually refer to themselves and their training programs in the following abbreviated terms:

➢ **TEFL or TFL:** teaching English as a foreign language
➢ **TESL or TSL:** teaching English as a second language
➢ **TESOL:** teaching English to speakers of other languages
➢ **RSA/Cambridge CELTA:** Cambridge/RSA Certificate Course in English Language Teaching to Adults
➢ **CTEFL:** Certificate in Teaching English as a Foreign Language

Several universities in the United States and abroad provide degree programs in TEFL or TESOL, and many others offer teacher training courses in TEFL or TESOL. You are well advised to participate in such a program. After all, teaching English as a foreign language involves specific methodologies you should be familiar with before venturing into this field. Fortunately you can participate in several short intensive TEFL or TESOL training programs which will get you up and running quickly for English language teaching.

You basically have two approaches to landing an English language teaching position abroad—either apply through a U.S.-based organization specializing in the training and placement of English language teachers or apply directly to an overseas school, institute, or university. It is probably easiest to work through a U.S.-based organization since most handle placements and arrange other details such as visas, work permits, housing, and transportation. A third option is to become a freelance teacher of English, offering your services to individuals and groups at an hourly rate.

During the past 37 years the U.S. Peace Corps has trained thousands of volunteers to teach English in many Third and Fourth World countries throughout the world. While today's Peace Corps places volunteers in many technical and business fields, it still recruits volunteers to teach English and other subjects in nearly 100 countries, including most recently the Peoples' Republic of China. In fact, nearly 40 percent of all volunteers serve in the field of education; most are English teachers. Volunteer assignments are for two years. Since the Peace Corps is in the process of expanding its volunteer presence abroad by more than 50 percent over the next three years—increasing the number of volunteers from 6,500 in 1998 to 10,000 by the year 2002—more teaching opportunities should be available with the Peace Corps. For more information on the Peace Corps program, contact:

Peace Corps
1111 20th Street, NW
Washington, DC 20526
Tel. 1-800-424-8580
Web site: *www.peacecorps.gov*

Several private, nonprofit, and educational organizations also recruit, train, and place college graduates who are interested in teaching English and other subjects abroad. Many are volunteer positions similar to internships while others are salaried positions. Contact the following organizations for information on their placement programs:

➤ **BRETHREN VOLUNTEER SERVICES**
1451 Dundee Ave., Elgin, IL 60120, Tel. 708/742-5100, 800/323-8039, or Fax 847/742-6103. Places English teachers (volunteers) for two-year assignments primarily in China and Poland, but also includes a few other countries. Provides expenses. Includes other types of overseas volunteer experiences, including health care, peacekeeping, and environment.

➤ **CENTRAL EUROPEAN TEACHING PROGRAM**
Beloit College, Box 242, 700 College Street, Beloit, WI 53511-5594, Tel. 608/363-2619, Fax 608/363-2689, or email: mullenm@beloit.edu. Handles placements in 75 state schools in Hungary, Romania, Poland, and Latvia. $1,000 placement fee.

➤ **ENGLISH FOR EVERYBODY**
Iva Brozova, 655 Powell Street, Suite 505, San Francisco, CA 94108, Tel. 415/789-7641 or Fax 415/433-4733. Handles teaching positions in Eastern Europe, Russia, and Austria. $450 placement fee.

➤ **FANDANGO OVERSEAS PLACEMENT**
1613 Escalero Road, Santa Rosa, CA 95409, phone or fax 707/539-2722. Arranges teacher placements in client schools of the Czech Republic, Hungary, France, Baltic States, Russia, Poland, and Japan. Charges a $375 placement fee for graduates of Transworld Teachers, Inc. (San Francisco) or $450 for graduates of a comparable 100-hour teacher training program.

➤ **INTEREXCHANGE**
161 6th Avenue, New York, NY 10013, Tel. 212/924-0446, Fax 212/974-0575, or email: interex@earthlink.net. English teacher placements in the Czech Republic, Hungary, and Finland. $250 -$450 placement fees.

➤ **INTERNATIONAL SCHOOLS SERVICES**
P.O. Box 5910, Princeton, NJ 08543, Tel. 609/452-0990, Fax 609/452-2690, or email: edustaffing@iss.edu. Web site: *www.iss.edu*. The New Perspectives program places teachers without previous teaching experience but who have teacher certification. Places over 500 teachers and administrators in 580 international and American schools around the world each year primarily in the fields of math, science, computers, library science, and elementary teaching. Requires as $200 application fee. Individuals must have two years of current teaching experience (no certification required). Math and science teachers with certification but no experience are eligible for consideration. Holds recruitment fairs in February and June which require a $125 fee per fair. Publishes the authoritative annual directory to international schools: *The ISS Directory of Overseas Schools* (see order form at end of this book).

➤ **JET PROGRAM**
JET Office, Embassy of Japan, 2520 Massachusetts Ave., NW, Washington, DC 20008, Tel. 202/939-6772, 202/939-6773, or email: eojjet@pop.erols. com. Also, contact your local Japanese Consulate or call 1-800-INFO-JET.

This popular Japanese government-sponsored program places English teachers in Japanese schools and government offices throughout Japan for one-year assignments. Application deadline is early December for positions beginning in July of the following year. May also want to visit an unofficial JET Web page: *http://wacky.ccit.arizona.edu/~susd/jet.html*

➤ **KOREA SERVICES GROUP**
147-7 Bum Jeon Dong Jin-Ku, Pusan 614-064, Korea, Tel. 011-82-51-817-3611 or Fax 011-82-51-817-3612. Provides native speaking instructors for more than 120 Korean foreign language institutes. Hires a large number of foreign instructors each year. Some hires can expect to start within 60 days. Recruits extensively amongst former U.S. Peace Corps Volunteers. Places about 400 instructors each year.

➤ **NEW WORLD TEACHERS**
1-800-655-5424. Claims to be the largest US TEFL certificate training program. Conducts 4-week teacher training courses every month in five locations worldwide: San Francisco, Boston, Budapest (Hungary), Phuket (Thailand), and Puerto Vallarta (Mexico). Includes lifetime job placement assistance. Graduates currently teaching in over 45 countries. Call for free information packet.

➤ **OVERSEAS PLACEMENT SERVICE FOR EDUCATORS**
University of Northern Iowa, Student Services Center #19, Cedar Falls, IA 50614-0390, Tel. 319/273-2311 or Fax 319/273-6998. Visit their Web site: *www.uni.edu/placement/student/internat.html*. Sponsors an annual job fair in February ($5 registration) for international teachers and administrators attended by more than 100 overseas schools. Publishes a fact book and newsletter ($30 if not registered for the job fair) which include listings of overseas teaching vacancies.

➤ **PRINCETON-IN-ASIA**
224 Palmer Hall, Princeton, NJ 08544, Tel. 609/458-3657, Fax 609/258-5300, or email: pia@phoenix.princeton.edu. Web site: *www.princeton.edu/~pia*. Operates one- and two-year teaching programs in China, Korea, Hong Kong, Japan, Thailand, Singapore, Malaysia, Indonesia, Vietnam, and Kazakhstan. Application deadline is December 1. Requires a $30 application fee and a $300 participant fee.

➤ **PROJECT HARMONY**
6 Irasville Common, Waitsfield, VT 05673, Tel. 802/496-4545, Fax 802/496 4548, email: pharmony@igc.apc.org. Handles placement in Russia, the Baltics, and the Central Asian republics. $1,850 program fee which includes airfare and housing stipend.

➤ **TESOL INC.**
Teachers of English to Speakers of Other Languages, 1600 Cameron St., Suite 300, Alexandria, VA 22314, Tel. 703/836-0774. This 23,000 member nonprofit organization includes a placement service for its members.

Membership dues are $69 for regular members or $48.50 for students. A basic membership also is available for $38. The placement service costs an additional $20 in North American and $30 abroad.

➤ **WORLDTEACH**
Harvard Institute for International Development, 14 Story Street, Cambridge, MA 02138, Tel. 617/495-5527, Fax 617/495-1239, email: info@ worldteach.org. Web site: *www.worldteach.org*. Each year places nearly 200 volunteer teachers in the local schools of Costa Rica, Ecuador, Namibia, Poland, Thailand, China, Russia, Mexico, Honduras, and South Africa. Positions are for one year. Participants pay a fee of $3,600-$5,650 which covers the cost of airfare, health insurance, training, and administration. Local employers provide room and board and a small stipend.

Two organizations sponsor job fairs for teachers: International Schools Services (*www.iss.edu*) and the University of Northern Iowa's Overseas Placement Service (*www.uni.edu/placement/student/internat.html*).

Training Programs to Get You Up and Running

The best qualified candidates possess teacher certification and are skilled in teaching English as a foreign language. Ideally, you should have a bachelor's or master's degree in TEFL or in a substantive academic field. If you lack such qualifications, don't worry. You can easily establish your teaching credentials and land an overseas teaching job by enrolling in a TEFL program that also has a good placement record. In fact, we do not recommend looking for an English language teaching position unless you have completed a TEFL program. You will quickly discover these programs have several advantages. Many use the highly respected RSA/University of Cambridge and Trinity College London teaching methods for qualifying participants.

In the United States most TEFL programs are integrated into regular university academic programs which are usually part of an undergraduate or graduate Applied Linguistics program. A few universities and private institutes now offer intensive four-week TEFL programs modeled after the British 100-hour intensive TEFL teacher certification programs. These intensive four-week programs quickly prepare you for overseas teaching positions and thus save you time and money in the process of getting ready for an overseas job. Many of these programs also provide job assistance through their employment contacts with schools, institutes, and universities abroad.

Within the United States, several public and private organizations provide training for teachers of English as a foreign language. The following universities offer degree programs, many through traditional Applied Linguistics, English, or Education departments, that require two to four years preparation; some offer graduate degrees in TEFL/TESOL:

- ➤ Ball State University (Muncie, IN)
- ➤ Brigham Young University (Laie, HI)
- ➤ Fairleigh Dickinson University (Teaneck, NJ)
- ➤ Georgetown University (Washington, DC)
- ➤ Hawaii Pacific University (Honolulu, HI)
- ➤ Portland State University (Portland, OR)
- ➤ University of California (Irvine, CA)
- ➤ University of Delaware (Newark, DE)
- ➤ University of Georgia (Athens, GA)
- ➤ University of Illinois (Urbana, IL)
- ➤ University of New Hampshire (Durham, NH)
- ➤ Wright State University (Dayton, OH)

Many other private institutes offer certification through intensive four- to eight-week training programs. The major such programs include:

➤ **AEON**
203 N. LaSalle St., #2100, Chicago, IL 60601, Tel. 301/251-0900 or Fax 312/251-0901; 9301 Wilshire Blvd., #202, Beverly Hills, CA 90210, Tel. 310/550-0940 or Fax 310/550-1463; or 230 Park Avenue, Suite 1000, New York, NY 10169, Tel. 212/808-3080 or Fax 212/599-0340. Web site: *www.aeonet.com*. This is a private language school which places English teachers in 220 schools in Japan. Applicants need a bachelor's degree and are required to pay one-way airfare. Places about 20 percent of all applicants. Teachers earn around 250,000 yen ($2,300) per month. Send resume and an essay on why you would like to teach in Japan.

➤ **AMERICAN ENGLISH PROGRAMS OF NEW ENGLAND INC.**
17 South Street, Northampton, MA 01060, Tel. 1-800-665-2829, 413/582-1812, or e-mail: info@teflcertificate.com. Web site: *www.teflcertificate. com*. Offers 4-week TEFL certificate programs. Costs $1,800.00.

➤ **CENTER FOR ENGLISH STUDIES/INTERNATIONAL HOUSE**
330 Seventh Avenue, New York, NY 10001, Tel. 212/629-7300, Fax 212/736-7950, e-mail: Cesnewyork@cescorp.com. Web site: *www.cescorp. com*. Offers a four-week intensive course ten times a year: Cambridge/RSA Certificate Course in English Language Teaching to Adults (CELTA). Costs $2,225.00.

➤ **CHINA TEACHING PROGRAM**
Western Washington University, Old Main 530A, Bellingham, WA 98225-9047, Tel. 360/650-3753, Fax 360/650-2847, or email: ctp@cc.wwu.edu. Offers six-week course in TESL, Chinese, and culture. Places program participants. $1,500 program fee.

➤ **ENGLISH INTERNATIONAL**
655 Sutter St., Suite 200, San Francisco, CA 94102, Tel. 415/749-5633, Fax 415/749-5629, or e-mail: teflusa@compuserve.com. Visit their Web site: *www.english-international.com*. Excepting December, each month this organization offers an intensive four-week TEFL course. Participants become RSA/University of Cambridge certified TEFL teachers. Includes professional job guidance both during and after training. Tuition is $2,750.00.

➤ **HAMLINE UNIVERSITY**
Saint Paul, Minnesota. Tel. 1-800-888-2182, 612-523-2900, Fax 612/523-2987, or e-mail: gradprog@gw.hamline.edu. Offers several TEFL program options, from intensive 4-week course to semi-intensive 12-week course. Includes career counseling assistance.

➤ **INTERNATIONAL HOUSE—TEACHER TRAINING USA**
200 SW Market Street, #111, Portland, OR 97201, Tel. 503/224-1960 or Fax 305/224-2041; or 320 Wilshire Blvd., 3rd Fl., Santa Monica, CA 90401, Tel. 310/394-8618 or Fax 310/394-2708. Email: celta@ih-portland.com. Associated with the highly respected International House in London.

➤ **THE LADO CERTIFICATE PROGRAM**
Washington, DC. Tel. 202/333-4222 or Fax 202/337-1118. Web site: *www.Lado.com/home-t.htm*. Includes 4-week intensive and 12 week semi-intensive TEFL courses. Includes job search assistance.

➤ **SEATTLE UNIVERSITY**
School of Teaching English as a Second Language, 2601 NW 56th Street, Seattle, WA 98107, Tel. 206/781-8607, Fax 206/781-8922, or e-mail: tulare@seattleu.edu. Web site: *www.seattleu.edu/soe/stesl*. Offers a variety of training programs: intensive 4-week sessions; monthly employment seminars; MA or MEd in TESOL; post-Master's certificate in TESOL. For Master's program, visit this Web site: *www.seattleu.edu/soe/tesol.html*

➤ **ST. GILES LANGUAGE TEACHING CENTER**
One Hallidie Plaza, Suite 350, San Francisco, CA 94102, Tel. 415/788-3552 or Fax 415/788-1923. Web site: *www.stgiles-usa.com*. Offers a four-week intensive RSA/University of Cambridge teacher training certificate course. Requires a $35 application fee. Tuition is $1,690.

➤ **WORLDWIDE TEACHERS DEVELOPMENT INSTITUTE**
266 Beacon Street, Boston, MA 02116, Tel. 1-800-875-5564, Fax 617/262-0308, E-mail: BostonTEFL@aol.com. Web site: *www.bostontefl.com*.

Offers a variety of Teaching English as a Foreign Language courses, including an accredited distance learning option. Includes placement guidance.

Numerous other teacher training programs are offered by universities and private institutes in Canada, England, Ireland, France, Germany, Greece, Hong Kong, Malaysia, Spain, Turkey, and Australia. The oldest, largest, and most highly respected TEFL training program awarding the RSA/University of Cambridge Certificate is in England. For detailed information on their programs, contact:

INTERNATIONAL HOUSE TEACHER TRAINING
International House, 106 Piccadilly, London W1V 9FL, United Kingdom, Tel. (011) 44-171-491-2410, Fax (011) 44-171-491-2679, or email: ih_staff unit@compuserve.com.

This four-week (110 hour) program costs about $2,500. International House offers courses at Teacher Training Centers in its affiliated schools in Barcelona, Budapest, Cairo, Krakow, Lisbon, Madrid, New York, Paris, Poznan, Rome, San Sebastian, and Vienna. It also recruits nearly 200 teachers each year for its network of over 100 schools in 23 countries. If you want premier training in TEFL, enroll in this well established program. For more information on TEFL training programs in these and other countries, consult Susan Griffith's latest edition of *Teaching English Abroad.*

Job Listing Services For Teachers

Several organizations offer current job vacancy listings for teachers interested in overseas positions. The most popular such publications include:

➤ *International Educator*. TIE, P.O. Box 513, Cummaquid, MA 02637, Tel. 508/362-1414, Fax 508/362-1411, or email: tie@capecod.net. $25. Published quarterly as a 50-page newspaper. Each issue includes an "Educators Wanted" section that includes ads from international schools (mainly K-12 grades).

➤ *Overseas Academic Opportunities*. 72 Franklin Avenue, Ocean Grove, NJ 07756, Tel/Fax 732/774-1040. Monthly bulletin for K-12 teachers. $42 per year.

➤ *TESOL Placement Bulletin*. TESOL Inc., 1600 Cameron St., Suite 300, Alexandria, VA 22314, Tel. 703/836-0774, Fax 703/836-6447, or e-mail: place@tesol.edu. Must be a member of TESOL Inc. ($38-$60) in order to subscribe to this publication. $20 per year if mailed to addresses in the U.S., Canada, Mexico; $30 per year for all other countries.

Several enterprising companies sell country-by-country listings of schools for $10 to $20 per country. One of the most popular such publications is *Overseas Teaching Opportunities* which is available through Friends of World Teaching (P.O. Box 1049, San Diego, CA 92112-1049, Tel. 800/503-7436 or 619/299-1010, $20 for first three countries and $4 for additional countries). This publication includes over 1,000 schools in 100+ countries of interest to Americans and Canadians. However, much of this same information is readily available through several other less expensive resources, such as Susan Griffith's *Teaching English Abroad*, Transition Abroad's *Work Abroad*, the International School Service's annual *ISS Directory of Overseas Schools,* and the free directories available through the U.S. Department of Defense and the U.S. State Department. You may want to consult these directories before purchasing similar lists.

Other Teaching Opportunities

If you teach at the university level, you may find opportunities to teach and conduct research abroad through your present institution, through a regional international consortium or through special programs such as the Fulbright Program (Council for International Exchange of Scholars). You should also monitor the job vacancy announcements appearing in The *Chronicle of Higher Education* as well as in professional journals and newsletters of your academic discipline. Occasionally overseas university vacancy announcements appear in *The New York Times, Washington Post, Wall Street Journal, National Business Employment Weekly,* and a few other major newspapers. Major international magazines, such as *The Far Eastern Economic Review* and *The Economist,* regularly list university vacancy announcements.

Enterprising job seekers don't limit their search to established teaching programs, training institutes, and placement and job listing services. Numerous other teaching opportunities are available by directly applying to local schools in each country without the assistance of a U.S.-based organization or with a U.S.-sponsored school. While salaries may appear low in many of these schools, such teaching positions often come with free housing and they do offer an opportunity to gain experience in living and working abroad. They enable you to work in a truly international environment where you get to know faculty members and become a member of the local community—important international experiences which are sometimes best acquired by living off the local economy at the level of fellow faculty members.

Take, for example, one of our favorite universities abroad with which we have been involved for years as both advisory board members and donors. If you are interested in teaching English in Thailand, you might consider applying directly to Yonok University in Northern Thailand. We know this college very well since we have been closely involved with its evolution since 1973. One of Thailand's newest and most beautiful private universities located in a delightful provincial town near the famous city of Chiangmai, Yonok University offers an excellent English language program for its nearly 3,000 students who are studying for bachelor's degrees in business, arts, and the sciences. Yonok University has an on-going exchange program with the faculty and students of Baylor University in Waco, Texas as well as welcomes applicants from other educational institutions. Numerous Americans have taught English here for periods of one to five years. If you are interested in working at Yonok University, send a cover letter and resume to:

Director of International Relations
YONOK UNIVERSITY
Lampang-Denchai Road
Lampang 52000, Thailand
Email: iac@yn1.yonok.ac.th
Web site: *www.yonok.ac.th*

Be sure to first visit their Web site for information about the university, including vacancy announcements. Indicate in your letter what you would like to do and when you are available. If you email, be sure to include your resume in the body of your email message; do not include it as an attachment. Yonok University also welcomes applications from individuals with experience in university administration.

Key Resources On Teaching

The following books and directories provide useful information on teaching abroad:

➤ *China Bound: A Guide to Life in the PRC*. Anne Thurston. National Academy Press, 2101 Constitution Ave., NW, Washington, DC 20055, Tel. 1-800-624-6242. Web site: *www.nap.edu*. $24.95 plus $4 shipping. 1994.

➤ *The ELT Guide*. Teachers of English to Speakers of Other Languages, 1600 Cameron Street, Suite 300, Alexandria, VA 22314, Tel. 703/836-0774, Fax 703/836-6447. Web site: *www.tesol.edu*. $19.95. 1998. Provides country-by-country information on recruitment, schools, and training.

➤ *The ISS Directory of Overseas Schools*. International Schools Service, P.O. Box 5910, Princeton, NJ 08543, Tel. 609/452-0990, $34.95 plus $3.00 shipping. Also available through Peterson's and Impact Publications. Organized by country, this guide provides detailed information on overseas schools attended by American and international students in expatriate communities in 133 countries.

➤ *Now Hiring! Jobs in Asia*. Jennifer Dubois, Steve Gutman, and Clarke Canfield. Perpetual Press, P.O. Box 30414, Lansing, MI 48909-7914, Tel. 800-807-3030 or Fax 517/335-1625. $17.95. Focuses on English teaching jobs in Japan, South Korea, and Taiwan.

➤ *Now Hiring! Jobs in Eastern Europe*. Clarke Canfield. Perpetual Press, P.O. Box 30414, Lansing, MI 48909-7914, Tel. 800-807-3030 or Fax 517/335-1625. $14.95. Focuses on English teaching jobs in the Czech Republic, Hungary, Poland, or Slovakia.

➤ *Teaching English Abroad*. Susan Griffith, Vacation Work, 9 Park End St., Oxford OX1 1HJ, England. $16.95 (from Peterson's or Impact Publications). This classic annual directory includes thousands of short- and long-term teaching positions for both certified and uncertified teachers. Organized by country. Includes information on training and job search.

➤ *Teaching English Directories*. This series of 200+ page directories is published in England and geared toward non-U.S. citizens:

- *Teaching English in Eastern and Central Europe*
- *Teaching English in Italy*
- *Teaching English in Japan*
- *Teaching English in South and Central America*
- *Teaching English in Southeast Asia*
- *Teaching English in Spain*

Can be ordered directly from the publisher: In Print Publishing, 38 Ship Street, Brighton BN1 1AB, United Kingdom, Tel. (011) 44-1273-205599 or Fax (011) 44-1273-739737. $14.95 each.

➤ *Teaching English in Asia: Finding a Job and Doing It Well*. Galen Harris Valle. Pacific View Press, P.O. Box 2657, Berkeley, CA 94702, Tel. 510/849-4213. Email: pvp@sirius.com. Includes lots of teaching tips on teaching English in East and Southeast Asia. Not much contact information. $19.95 plus $3.00 shipping.

➤ *Work Abroad: The Complete Guide to Finding Work Overseas*. Transitions Abroad Publishing, P.O. Box 1300, Amherst, MA 01004-1300, Tel. 1-800-293-0373. Web site: *www.transitionsabroad.com*. Filled with informative articles and resources on teaching abroad. $15.95

The U.S. government publishes useful information on teaching opportunities with the U.S. Department of State and Department of Defense Dependents schools

➤ *Overseas American-Sponsored Elementary Schools Assisted By the U.S. Department of State*. Office of Overseas Schools, U.S. Department of State, Rm. 245, SA-29, Washington, DC 20522-2902, Tel. 703/875-7800 or Fax 703/875-7979. Free brochure on 192 private overseas K-12 schools. Also, visit the Department's Web site for more information: *www.state.gov*. Look under the sections on "Services," "Living Overseas," and "Overseas Schools."

➤ *Overseas Employment Opportunities For Educators*. Department of Defense, Office of Dependent Educational Activity, Office of Personnel, Dependents Schools, 4040 N. Fairfax Drive, 6th Floor, Alexandria, VA 22203, Tel. 703/696-1352. Free. Includes application for K-12 teaching positions in over 200 Department of Defense schools servicing U.S. military bases abroad.

If you are a university or college faculty member, you may want to apply for an international Fulbright teaching, research, or administration position. Contact the Council For International Exchange of Scholars for application information:

Council For International Exchange of Scholars
3007 Tilden Street, NW, Suite 5L
Washington, DC 20008-3009
Tel. 202/686-7877 or Fax 202/362-3442
Email: scholars@cies.iie.org
Web site: *www.iie.org/cies*

Application deadlines vary depending on the particular award: August 1 (lecturing and research awards); November 1 (international education administrators); and January 1 (NATO scholars).

11

International Internships

One of the best ways to break into the international employment arena is to acquire an international internship in the United States or abroad. With an internship you may gain valuable international work experience as well as develop important contacts for gaining full-time international employment. Many internships also provide unique opportunities to study and travel while working abroad. Sponsoring internship organizations normally arrange all the details for placement, travel, and accommodations. Upon completing the internship, participants can expect the sponsoring organization to arrange for letters of recommendation from the interns' employers.

The World of Internships

International internships come in several forms. Ideally, most people would like to find paid internships with organizations overseas that might lead to being hired on a full-time basis. Some internships come in this form, especially those for business, engineering, and science majors sponsored by the International Association of Students in Economics and Business Management (AIESEC) and the International Association for the Exchange of Students of Technical Experience (IAESTE). These are the two premier international internship organizations that offer paid internships with major international companies.

Most internships, however, tend to be nonpaid, volunteer positions sponsored by colleges and universities or nonprofit organizations. Many of these internships require enrollment, tuition, or program fees to participate in the program. Some of these internship experiences are basically study abroad programs which include a short work experience. Most such programs are designed for students in linguistics, social sciences, and the humanities. If sponsored by a college or university, students can usually earn academic credits while participating in the internship program. A three to twelve-month internship program may cost participants between $4,000 and $8,000, including international transportation, insurance, visas, and room and board. Like many volunteer positions, these internships may involve basic living and working conditions, such as participating in homestays and workcamps.

> **Most internships tend to be nonpaid, volunteer positions sponsored by colleges and universities or nonprofit organizations.**

Other international internships are based in the United States with nonprofit public interest, education, and research organizations. While these groups give interns an opportunity to work with important international organizations and issues, they involve little or no international travel. Many of these internships will involve basic research, copyediting, and clerical tasks, but they also offer opportunities to attend seminars, conferences, and make important international contacts.

Many internships are for two to three-month periods while others run for six to twelve-months or coincide with regular or summer college semester programs. Others may be flexible, depending on the individual intern's interests and skills. Many internships can lead to full-time employment with the sponsoring organization.

Most international internship programs tend to be centered in Washington, DC, the center for hundreds of government, nonprofit, and consulting organizations involved in international affairs.

Internship programs typically have application deadlines and several charge both application and placement fees. Some require an application package consisting of a resume, transcript, writing sample, recommendations, and a letter of availability and interest. Be sure to check Web sites first for detailed information and then call, fax, or write the organization for current application details.

If you are interested in an internship or volunteer position with an organization involved in the international arena, do not restrict your search efforts only to the organizations included in this chapter. You should be creative, aggressive, and persistent. Many of the organizations and employers listed in previous chapters, especially nonprofit organizations and consultants, are open to enterprising individuals who approach them with a proposal for an internship. In other words, you can create your own internship by directly approaching an organization with a detailed proposal. Do your homework on the organization. Identify what knowledge and skills you can bring to such a position as well as the experience you hope to acquire from such an experience. You may be surprised how many employers will be interested in your proposal. In the process you will gain invaluable international work experience specifically tailored to your needs and long-term international career goals.

Major Internship Organizations and Programs

The following businesses, government agencies, nonprofit organizations, and educational institutions offer a variety of internship experiences throughout the world. Many of the internships are based in the United States while others involve working overseas.

ACCESS: AN INTERNATIONAL AFFAIRS INFORMATION SERVICE
1701 K Street
11th Floor
Washington, DC 20006
Tel. 202/223-7949
Web site: *www.4access.org*

A computerized database clearinghouse that assists educators, researchers, journalists, and other interested groups in acquiring information on international affairs. Has three internship positions which pay $50 per week: inquiry/speakers referral intern; outreach intern; and publications intern. Positions require good communication, research, marketing, and coordination skills and a strong background in international affairs. Contact the Internship Coordinator.

ACCION INTERNATIONAL
120 Beacon Street
Summerville, MA 02143
(no phone calls please)
Web site: *www.accion.org*

A nonprofit group operating in Central and Latin America for the purpose or reducing poverty and improving the employability of the poor. Offers all types of internships, both paid and unpaid. Internships open to college undergraduates, graduates, graduate students, and those with work experience. Positions require good organization and communication skills. Send a resume and cover letter to the Communications Specialist.

AFRICA NEWS SERVICE
Internship Program
P.O. Box 3851
Durham, NC 27702
Tel. 919/286-0747
Fax 919/286-2614

Offers 10 internships for students of journalism and African affairs. Work involves research, writing, and clerical duties. These are unpaid internships, but the Africa News Agency will assist in finding inexpensive living accommodations in Durham, NC. Applicants must summit an approach letter, letters of recommendations, transcripts, and a writing sample.

AIESEC-U.S.
135 W. 50th Street
17th Floor
New York, NY 10020-1202
Tel. 212/757-3774
Fax 212/757-4062
Web site: *www.us.aiesec.org*

One of the premier international internship organizations (International Association of Students in Economic and Business Management) managed by students for students majoring in economics and business. Operates with local chapters on 73 member campuses throughout the U.S. Focuses on international management. Approximately 300 internships available each year with such companies as AT&T, IBM, and Unisystem. Exchanges encompass 87 member countries. These are paid internships ($200-$400 a week). Most internships last from 6 weeks to 18 months. Applicants must apply through campus chapters. Most applicants are college juniors or seniors who have completed at least two years of basic business and language courses. Application fee is $450.00.

AMERICAN INSTITUTE FOR FOREIGN STUDY, COLLEGE DIVISION
102 Greenwich Avenue
Greenwich, CT 06830
Tel. 203/869-9090
Fax 203/869-9615
Web site: *www.aifs.com*

This organization arranges the international exchange of high school and college students and adults. Its field of operations encompasses 10 campuses in Mexico, Europe, Asia, and Australia. It offers about 40 internships each year for a duration of 12 to 15 weeks each. Participants combine academic classes with work experience. These are unpaid, voluntary internships for college juniors, seniors, and graduate students. Requires a $50 applicant processing fee.

THE AMERICAN-SCANDINAVIAN FOUNDATION
725 Park Avenue
New York, NY 10021
Tel. 212-879-9779
Fax 212/249-3444
Web site: *www.amscan.org*

This nonprofit organization promotes educational and cultural exchanges between the United States and Denmark, Finland, Iceland, Norway, and Sweden. Designed for college juniors and seniors, this program offers 50-100 summer internships for engineers, computer specialists, chemists, agriculturalists, and horticulturalists. These are paid internships in which participants receive a stipend. Participants are expected to pay from $120 and $385 each month for housing. Application deadline is December 15. Requires a $50 applicant processing fee and a resume.

AMNESTY INTERNATIONAL USA
322 8th Avenue
New York, NY 10001
Tel. 212/807/8400
Fax 212/627-1451
Web site: *www.amnesty-usa.org*

This global nonprofit organization focuses on the release of prisoners of conscience. It lobbies international organizations and governments as well as focuses media attention on the release of political prisoners and the end of torture and executions. It offers 10 unpaid internships each year for a minimum of 10 weeks each. Applicants must be high school graduates.

THE ARMS CONTROL ASSOCIATION
1726 M Street, NW
Suite 201
Washington, DC 20036
Tel. 202/463-8270
Fax 202/463-8273
Web site: *www.armscontrol.org*

This nonprofit research organization focusing on educating the public about arms control and related issues. Offers several unpaid full-time and part-time internships each year involving research, writing, proofreading, editing, layout, and general clerical work. Open to college sophomores, juniors, seniors, college graduates, and graduate students. Application deadline is May 15. Contact the Intern Coordinator for details. Send a cover letter, resume, and a brief writing sample.

ASHOKA: INNOVATORS FOR THE PUBLIC
1700 North Moore St.
Suite 1920
Arlington, VA 22209
Tel. 703/527-8300
Fax 703/527-8300
Web site: *www.ashoka.org*

This nonprofit organization awards fellowships for innovation ideas related to social change in Africa, Asia, and Latin America. Offers 15 unpaid internships each year related to publications, press relations, publicity, fundraising, and fellowship relations. Duration of internships varies. Contact the Intern Coordinator for information and application procedures.

ASSOCIATION TO UNITE THE DEMOCRACIES
1506 Pennsylvania Avenue, SE
Washington, DC 20003
Tel. 202/544-5150
Fax 202/544-3742

This association promotes world order and democracy through educational programs, publications, and conferences. It offers paid internships ($250 per month) for periods of 4-6 months each. Candidates should have an interest in international relations, demonstrate a good command of English, and have good computer and foreign language skills. Applicants must submit a resume, writing sample, transcript, recommendation, and a letter explaining their interest in working for AUD. Application deadline is January 1 for spring, May 1 for summer, and August 1 for fall.

THE ATLANTIC COUNCIL OF THE UNITED STATES
910 17th Street, NW, 10th Floor
Washington, DC 20006
Tel. 202/463-7226 or Fax 202/463-7241
Web site: *www.gopher.nato.int*

This nonprofit, nonpartisan organization formulates policy recommendations for the developed democracies of the European and Asian communities. Offers several 8-12 week nonpaid internships. Most internships involve program development, policy research and recommendations, special projects, fundraising, and publication support. Open to college juniors, seniors, graduates, and graduate students. Contact the Internship Coordinator for further information.

BEAVER COLLEGE CENTER FOR EDUCATION ABROAD
Beaver College, 450 S. Easton Road
Glenside, PA 19038
Tel. 888/232-8379 or 215/572-2174
Web site: *www.beaver.edu/cea*

Beaver College arranges junior-senior year study abroad programs for numerous colleges and universities. Internships run for one semester. Candidates must be currently enrolled in an accredited American college or university with a GPA of 3.0 and at least a 3.3 in three courses in the internship discipline. Interns receive academic credit for courses taken during the internship period. Open to college juniors and seniors. Requires a $35 application fee. Application deadlines are October 15 for spring; April 20 for fall; and March 10 for summer London program (nonacademic). Contact the Program Coordinator for further information.

BRETHREN VOLUNTEER SERVICE
1451 Dundee Avenue
Elgin, IL 60120
Tel. 847/742-5100 or Fax 847/742-6103
Web site: *www.brethren.org/genbad/bvs/indix.htm*

Sponsored by the Church of the Brethren, this organization promotes peace, justice, and human and environmental welfare through numerous programs in 20 countries. Offers over 100 domestic and overseas internships. Domestic internships run for 1 year. Overseas internships require a 2-year minimum commitment and involve working in one of 34 projects in such countries as China, El Salvador, France, Germany, Israel, the Netherlands, Nicaragua, Nigeria, Northern Ireland, and Poland. Internships pay $45.00 per month and include free room and board. Candidates for overseas internships should be college graduates, Christians, at least 21 years of age, and in good health. Candidates for domestic internships should be high school graduates, Christians, and at least 18 years of age. Application deadlines are July 1 for fall, January 1 for spring, and May 1 for summer. Contact the Recruiter.

CDS INTERNATIONAL, INC.
330 7th Avenue
19th Floor
New York, NY 10001-5010
Tel. 212/497-3500
Fax 212/497-3535
Web site: *www.cdsintl.org*

CDS combines language training and work experience for over 1,000 individuals each year from the United States, Germany, France, Spain, the Netherlands, Sweden, Japan, China, and more than 30 other countries. Offers different types of 3, 6, 12, and 18 month paid internships. Requires an in-person interview. Open to college juniors, seniors, and graduates. Favors individuals with majors in a business, technical, or agricultural field. Application deadline is five months prior to starting the internship. Contact the Program Officer for detailed information on different internship programs. Program costs range from $200.00 to $400.00.

CENTER FOR THE STUDY OF CONFLICT
5846 Bellona Avenue
Baltimore, MD 21212
Tel. 410/323-7656

This is a research and education organization dedicated to the study and application of conflict resolution methods. Offers two unpaid internships each year. Length of internship is flexible. Interns perform research, copyediting, and general office work. Open to high school seniors, high school graduates, college students, college graduates, graduate students, and others. Contact the Director with a resume, names and addresses of two references, a one-page writing sample, and a letter of interest.

COMMITTEE FOR NATIONAL SECURITY
1901 Pennsylvania Avenue, NW
Suite 201
Washington, DC 20009
Tel. 202/745-2450
Fax 202/667-0444
Web site: *www.lawscns.org*

This nonprofit educational research group focuses on the study of arms control, defense budgets, and chemical and biological weaponry. It offers three unpaid research and legislative tracking internships lasting 3-4 months each. Open to college sophomores, juniors, seniors, and graduate students. Apply to the Program Coordinator with a letter, resume, transcripts, and recommendations. Final selection requires an in-person interview. Application deadlines are May 1 for summer, August 1 for fall, and December 1 for spring.

COUNCIL ON INTERNATIONAL
EDUCATIONAL EXCHANGE (CIEE)
205 E. 42nd Street
New York, NY 10017-5706
Tel. 1-888-COUNCIL
Web site: *www.ciee.org*

For college students and recent graduates. Administers a wide variety of work, volunteer, intern, study, and travel programs. Each year nearly 25,000 students worldwide (6,000 from U.S.) become involved in CIEE's programs. The Council's Work Abroad program involves up to six months of work experience in France, Ireland, Canada, Spain, Germany, Australia, New Zealand, Costa Rica, and China (teaching). Jobs range from waiting tables in a hopping pub in Dublin to helping customers as a sales clerk at a funky boutique in Sydney, or even interning at an architect's office in Frankfurt. $20 application fee.

DELEGATION OF THE EUROPEAN COMMISSION
2300 M Street, NW, Suite 300
Washington, DC 20037
Tel. 202/862-9544 or Fax 202/429-1766
Web site: *www.eurunion.org*

This organization promotes better communication and understanding between the United States and the European Community. It offers 10-12 internships in academic affairs, public inquiries, speakers' bureau, and the Europe Magazine. Individuals perform research, information dissemination, and clerical duties. Each internship is unpaid and lasts five months. Open to college juniors, seniors, graduates, and graduate students. Contact the Assistant for Academic Affairs for more information.

EDUCATIONAL PROGRAMS ABROAD
3256 Braemar Road
Shaker Heights, OH 44120
Tel. 216/295-9856

This nonprofit organization provides 80-100 internships in Europe (Bonn, Cologne, London, Madrid, Paris, and Strasbourg) for a variety of fields—advertising, business, law, education, health care, politics, social science, theater, and urban planning. During the academic year internships run for one semester; summer internships last 10 weeks. These are unpaid internships in which participants are expected to pay a program fee ranging from $1,780 to $6,300 which includes room and board. Open to college juniors, seniors, and graduate students. Foreign language competence a necessity for interns in Bonn, Paris, and Madrid. Requires an application fee of $25. Applicants should send a transcript, two letters of recommendation, and an essay on their career goals.

EXPORT-IMPORT BANK OF THE U.S. (EXIMBANK)
811 Vermont Avenue, NW
Washington, DC 20571
Tel. 1-800-565-3946 or Fax 202/565-3380
Web site: *www.exim.gov*

This independent government agency promotes the export financing of U.S. goods and services. It sponsors 15-20 summer and semester interns each year in the areas of accounting, economics, financial analysis, and computer work. Open to undergraduate and graduate students. Favors majors in business administration, computer science, economics, finance, and marketing. Applicants must summit an OF-612 and college transcripts. Application deadline is March 31.

GENERAL ELECTRIC COMPANY
Recruiting and University Development
3135 Easton Turnpike
Fairfield, CT 06431
Tel. 203/382-2000
Web site: *www.ge.com*

General Electric Company hires numerous undergraduate and graduate interns for offices around the world: aerospace, aircraft engines, National Broadcasting Company (NBC), electrical distribution and control communications and services, motors, financial services, industrial and power systems, lighting, transportation systems, appliance, medical systems, and plastics. These are paid internships. Applicants should send a resume and cover letter indicating their desired position.

GLOBAL INFORMATION NETWORK
275 7th Avenue, Suite 1206
New York, NY 10001
Tel. 212/647-0123 or Fax 212/627-6137

Distributes newswire services from developing countries as well as writes stories on politics and culture. Interns become involved in numerous phases of the news business, from copyediting to writing stories. Offers unpaid internships.

HUMAN RIGHTS WATCH
Everett Public Service Summer Internships
485 Fifth Avenue
New York, NY 10017
Tel. 212/972-8400, Ext 265 or Fax 212/972-0905
Web site: *www.hrw.org*

Offers four paid ($180 per week) summer internships relating to human rights issues. Each lasts from 8 to 10 weeks. Send resume, letter of interest, writing sample, and letter of recommendation by March 31. Also has some internships during the academic year.

IAESTE-U.S.
10400 Little Patuxent Parkway
Suite 250L
Columbia, MD 21044-3510
Tel. 410/994-3068
Fax 410/997-5186
Web site: *www.aipt.org*

This popular worldwide internship program is designed for students in engineering, architecture, and the sciences. Provides practical on-the-job training in 60 member countries. Program is administered in the U.S. by the Association for International Practical Training (AIPT). Places 75-100 interns each year. Must be at least a college Junior enrolled full-time when applying. Primarily summer placements. $50.00 application fee. $150.00 placement fee.

INET FOR WOMEN
P.O. Box 6178
McLean, VA 22106
Tel. 703/893-8541 or Fax 703/893-8541

This international trade and business organization promotes more effective strategies for cross-border transitions. It offers several unpaid internships lasting from 1½-6 months in information systems, public relations, advertising, marketing, membership administration, and events planning. Open to college juniors, seniors, graduates, and individuals re-entering the work force. Requires a $10 registration and processing fee. Contact the President for more information.

THE INTERNATIONAL CENTER
731 8th Street, SE
Washington, DC 20003
Tel. 202/547-3800 or Fax 202/546-4783

The International Center focuses on U.S. foreign policy in Asia and Russia for the purpose of promoting democratic movements and the resolution of regional conflicts. It offers 10 internships. The internships involve research, writing, and general clerical duties centering on projects relating to Asia and Russia as well as the New Forests Project (promotes reforestations and economic development in developing countries). These are unpaid internships lasting for a period of 10 weeks. Open to college juniors, seniors, graduates, and graduate students. Application deadlines are June 30 for the fall, November 30 for the spring, and March 31 for the summer.

INTERNATIONAL COOPERATIVE
EDUCATION PROGRAM
15 Spiros Way
Menlo Park, CA 94025
Tel. 650/323-4944
Fax 650/323-1104
Web site: *http://members.aol.com/ICEMenlo*

A paid summer internship program. This in-depth immersion in work, culture, and language program consists of placing students with employers in Germany, Switzerland, Belgium, Luxemburg, Finland, and Japan for periods of 8 to 12 weeks, from early June until September 1. Requires a $200.00 application fee and a $600.00 placement fee within 7 days after employment has been confirmed.

INTERNATIONAL EDUCATION PROGRAM
Foothill College
12345 El Monte Road
Los Altos Hills, CA 94022-4599
Tel. 650/949-7777
Fax 650/949-7375
Web site: *www.foothill.fhda.edu*

This internship and summer jobs program is designed for American college students. Involves work experience and linguistic/cultural immersion in Germany, Switzerland, Belgium, France, Finland, Austria, Italy, Singapore, Hong Kong, Japan, Brazil, Chile, and Argentina. Each year approximately 300 students from 70 U.S. colleges and universities register as part-time students at Foothill College and receive 13 units of academic credit for participation in the program. Employment available in several fields including engineering, computer science, chemistry, finance and banking, hospitality, retail sales, teaching, recreation, health care, clerical, tourism, and agriculture. All positions are paid and provide sufficient income to cover living expenses while abroad.

INTERNATIONAL VISITORS INFORMATION SERVICE
1623 Belmont Street, NW
Washington, DC 20009
Tel. 202/939-5566
Fax 202/232-9783

Affiliated with the Meridian International Center, IVIS sponsors programs and provides services to international visitors in Washington, DC. Offers one paid internship involving general office work. Duration of internship is one semester. Candidates should have foreign language skills. Contact the Executive Director for more information.

INTERNSHIPS INTERNATIONAL
1116 Cowper Drive
Raleigh, NC 27608
Tel. 919/831-1575 or Fax 919/834-7170
Web site: *http://rtpnet.org/~intintl*

Offers non-paying internships in London, Paris, Dublin, Cologne, France, Shanghai, Santiago, Budapest, Melbourne, Bangkok, Hanoi, and Ho Chi Minh City for a period of 6 weeks to 6 months. For college seniors and graduates. $700 program fee.

MARYMOUNT STUDY ABROAD PROGRAM
Marymount College
Terrytown, NY 10591-3796
Tel. 914/332-8222 or Fax 914/631-3261
Web site: *www.marymt.edu/~studyab/studyab.html*

This unique study abroad program is designed for undergraduates who attend universities and polytechnics in central London. The program provides unpaid internships in a variety of fields, such as fashion design, merchandising, public relations, publishing, museums, journalism, communications, hotel management, and international business. Open to college juniors and seniors. Contact the Director, Study Abroad Program for more information.

PEOPLE TO PEOPLE INTERNATIONAL
501 East Armour Boulevard
Kansas City, MO 64109-2200
Tel. 816/531-4701 or Fax 816/561-7502
Web site: *www.ptpi.org/studyabroad/*

This nonprofit educational and cultural exchange organization administers programs for college and professional groups in over 20 countries. Offers unpaid internships for 2-month periods and traveling seminars. People to People works in cooperation with the University of Missouri—Kansas City to offer undergraduate and graduate credit.

QUAKER INFORMATION CENTER
1501 Cherry Street
Philadelphia, PA 19102
Tel. 215/241-7024 or Fax 215/567-2096
Web site: *www.afsc.org/qic.htm*

Operates a variety of internship programs, workcamps, volunteer opportunities, student foreign exchange programs, and student abroad programs through its network of Quaker organizations, especially the American Friends Service Committee. These include year-long internships to two-year, Peace Corps type programs for both Quakers and non-Quakers. Maintains 16 lists on its Web site that include work alternatives.

RADIO FREE EUROPE/RADIO LIBERTY
Intern Program Manager
1201 Connecticut Avenue, NW
Washington, DC 20036
Tel. 202/457-6949 or Fax 202/457-6913
Web site: *www.rferl.org/index.html*

This independent news and broadcasting corporation promotes better communication with the peoples of Eastern Europe and the Commonwealth of Independent States. It hires more than 10 research and electrical engineering interns for 8-12 week periods. Interns are paid $48 a day. Research interns travel to Munich and should be fluent in a language of Eastern Europe or the Commonwealth of Independent States. Electrical engineering interns should be fluent in German, Portuguese, or Spanish. Open to highly qualified undergraduates and graduate students. Application deadline in mid-February.

SISTER CITIES INTERNATIONAL
c/o Town Affiliation Association
1210 South Payne Street
Alexandria, VA 22314-2939
(no phone calls please)
Fax 703/836-4815
Web site: *www.sister_cities.org*

This nonprofit association assists U.S. communities in developing formal linkages with other cities throughout the world for the purposes of increasing international understanding and promoting exchanges. Offers one unpaid internship for a minimum of 6 weeks. Candidates should have some international and community service background and be computer literate. Open to college juniors, seniors, graduates, graduate students, and career changers. For more information, contact the Personnel Office.

UNITED NATIONS ASSOCIATION OF THE USA
801 2nd Avenue, 2nd Floor
New York, NY 10017
Tel. 212/697-3232 or Fax 212/682-9185

The purpose of this nonprofit organization is to strengthen the United Nations system and promote U.S. participation in the organization. It offers several unpaid internships of variable duration. Most internships involve research, proofreading, writing, and general office responsibilities. Open to college juniors, seniors, graduates, graduate students, and career changers. Application deadlines are April 1 for summer, August 19 for fall, and January 15 for spring. Contact the Intern Coordinator for more information.

THE U.S. CHAMBER OF COMMERCE
Personnel Department
Internship Coordinator
1615 H Street, NW
Washington, DC 20062
Tel. 202/659-6000

This organization promotes business, trade, and professional associations. Hiring 85 interns each year, it offers unpaid semester-long international internships for college juniors and seniors. Interns conduct research, write articles, attend congressional hearings, and follow legislation.

U.S. AND FOREIGN COMMERCIAL SERVICE
Work-Study Internship Program
Office of Foreign Service Personnel
P.O. Box 688
Ben Franklin Station
Washington, DC 20044-0688

This U.S. Department of Commerce organization promotes U.S. exports and business. It sponsors a summer work-study intern program for 10 to 12 week periods. Open to college juniors, seniors, and graduate students. It offers several unpaid internships involving research, writing, and marketing/promotion. Interns work abroad and are responsible for financing all of their travel, living, and other expenses. Applicants must submit a resume, transcripts, two letters of reference, and a 500 to 700-word essay on their career goals. Deadlines for applications are November 1.

U.S. STATE DEPARTMENT
Student Intern Program
Recruitment Division
Arlington, VA 22219
Tel. 703/875-4910 or Fax 703/875-7243
Web site: *www.state.gov*

Offers a variety of internship programs for individuals who are planning to pursue a career with the U.S. government.

VISIONS IN ACTION
2710 Ontario Road, NW
Washington, DC 20009
Tel. 202/625-7402 or Fax 202/625-2353
Web site: *www.igc.org/visions*

This nonprofit organization offers 10-15 unpaid internships each year in urban areas of Kenya, South Africa, Uganda, and Zimbabwe. Visions in Action focuses on urban development and includes such issues as refugee relief, famine relief, women, agriculture, family planning, appropriate technology, and youth work. Interns work on urban development, public relations, administrative support, and fundraising. Open to college students, graduates, graduate students, and career changers. For more information, contact the U.S. Director.

WORLD FEDERALISTS
P.O. Box 15250
Washington, DC 20003
Tel. 202/546-3950 or Fax 202/546-3749

This organization promotes the work of the United Nations in the areas of environmentalism, human rights, and conflict resolution. It offers four paid ($100) internships for one semester each. Interns get experience in conducting policy research, coordinating conferences, writing, editing, public relations, and lobbying. Open to college students, graduates, and graduate students. Applicants should submit a resume and cover letter to the Director of Student Programs.

YOUTH FOR UNDERSTANDING INTERNATIONAL EXCHANGE
3501 Newark Street, NW
Washington, DC 20016-3167
Tel. 202/966-6808 or Fax 202/895-1104

This nonprofit, educational organization seeks to promote greater world peace and understanding through exchange programs for high school students. It offers several unpaid internships in consumer services, public relations, finance, school relations, sales and marketing, sports, and promotion. Open to college students, graduates, graduate students, and career changers. For more information, contact the Assistant Director Volunteer Services.

Other Internship Opportunities

Numerous other organizations—from government agencies to private companies and nonprofit firms—offer internship opportunities. You may want to contact some of the following organizations which have been summarized in previous chapters (see Index for page references):

Africare
Amigos De Las Americas
The Brookings Institution
CARE
Center For Strategic and International Studies
Central Intelligence Agency
Freedom House
Habitat For Humanity
International Finance Corporation
International Monetary Fund
MAP International
Organization of American States
Pan American Development Foundation
United Nations
The World Bank
Zero Population Growth

For more information on internships, see the following publications which identify thousands of internship opportunities:

➤ *Directory of International Internships.* Edited by Charles Gliozzo and Vernicka Tyson. 1998. Michigan State University, Career Services and Placement, 113 Student Services Building, East Lansing, MI 48824-1114, Tel. 517/355-9510, ext. 371 or Fax 517/353-2597. $25.00.

➤ *Internships 1999.* Princeton, NJ: Peterson's, 1998, $24.95.

12

Effective Job Search Strategies

here are many ways to find an international job. Your best job finding strategy involves doing your own investigative work on organizations hiring in the international arena. The previous chapters in this book identified many such organizations, along with their Web sites, which you may want to pursue according to the job finding advice we outline in *The Complete Guide to International Jobs and Careers* as well as the many Internet tips we reveal in this chapter. You should research these international employers, network for information, advice, and referrals, and persist until you uncover the right job for you.

Strategies

If you have few international skills as well as little international experience, your chances of getting an international job should be better by pursuing entry-level opportunities with nonprofit organizations, education institutions (teaching English abroad), and the travel industry rather than with government, international organizations, and business firms. International positions with government and international organizations are designed for individuals with strong international qualifications. Businesses tend to promote individuals from within the organization to what are considered to be senior international positions rather than hire international specialists directly for such positions. The first and foremost consideration for a business is that the employee know their business. Becoming internationally competent—foreign language ability, knowledge of countries, cross-cultural adjustments, living abroad—is something experienced employees can learn once they are overseas in their assignments.

At the same time, you may want to monitor international job vacancy announcements that appear on home pages, key Internet employment sites, and in several reliable publications. In this chapter we identify several such resources which we believe are useful to survey as part of your job search. However, we caution you to not become preoccupied in surveying these listings nor responding to the announcements with resumes, letters, telephone calls, faxes, and email. Electronic and print job listings and vacancy announcements only represent a portion of international job opportunities available at any particular time.

> You should never pay someone else to find you an international job. Many unscrupulous firms take advantage of individuals who are highly motivated to work abroad but who are basically "job dumb."

Except in the case of some reputable teacher placement services, you need not—indeed should not—pay someone else to find you an international job. If you become drawn to so-called international employment firms that promise to find you an international job for up-front fees, you may quickly discover unscrupulous firms that take advantage of individuals who are highly motivated to work abroad but who are basically "job dumb." These firms are notorious for extracting fees—ranging from $300 to $10,000—from individuals who mistakenly believe these firms have an inside track to the international job market. Our basic rule of thumb for weeding out the good from the bad is this: If a firm requires up-front fees without written performance guarantees, even for conducting preliminary employment testing, avoid them. This is often a sign that you are about to be taken down the familiar road so many other disappointed international job seekers have traveled—to your bank account only! You will be left with dashed expectations and less cash after such a firm finishes with you. This experience will once again confirm the often heard lament of many unsuccessful job seekers—*"it's really tough to find an international job; there are no international jobs available these days; I don't have the necessary international work skills."*

At the same time, there are many reputable firms that are involved in the international employment business. A few are job search and placement firms, but most are "executive recruiters" or "headhunters" who are paid by employers to find qualified employees for particular positions. Rather than recruit employees directly, many international employers prefer hiring such firms to do the necessary recruitment and preliminary screening of candidates. Remember, these firms are paid by the employer—either on a retainer or contingency fee basis—and not by the job seeker. Any firm that tells you they have been retained by employers to find them employees, but then requires you to pay them, is probably ripping you off with an up-front fee requirement. Reputable firms get paid by employers on the basis of their performance which is measured by recruiting the necessary skills required by the employer.

Your best sources of information on executive recruiters and head-hunters are two directories published by Kennedy Information: ***Kennedy's International Directory of Executive Recruiters*** and ***The Directory of Executive Recruiters***. These books are available through Impact Publications and are in many libraries. Even though these firms work for employers, you may want to contact some of them with information on your international experience, qualifications, and interests. But keep in mind that these firms primarily work with individuals who have a great deal of work experience, have a specific hard-to-find technical skill, or possess some exotic combination of international skills. Some recruit for positions that pay $60,000 a year or more, but most focus on the $80,000 to $100,000+ a year positions. Many of these firms are based in major U.S. cities as well as maintain offices abroad. Some recruit in many different skill and industry areas, but most tend to specialize in one or two major areas. These firms are not in the business of recruiting individuals with little experience or who have few demonstrated international work skills for entry-level positions.

Job Listings

Several Internet sites, publications, and services specialize in international job vacancy announcements. A disproportionate number of nonprofit organizations are included in the publications because nonprofits are more likely to conduct national and international searches for candidates. Vacancies in government and international organizations are primarily announced through agency personnel offices and posted on homepages, although some are included in the major job listing publications identified in this section. Businesses increasingly use key Internet employment sites to advertise international vacancies and search for candidates. However, they use this electronic medium for recruiting individuals making less than $75,000 a year. For higher level positions, they are more likely to work through executive search firms which, in turn, place ads in major trade journals and national and international publications such as the *New York Times, National Business Employment Weekly, Washington Post*, and the *Los Angeles Times* or use other recruitment sources. These are the publications of choice for many high level business and technical people looking for international positions.

Embracing the Internet

During the past three years the Internet has come of age as a major medium for conducting a job search. Employers increasingly use the Internet to recruit candidates because it has proved to be less expensive than traditional recruitment methods (classified ads and headhunters) and very efficient. By posting vacancy announcements on their homepages or by using major Internet employment sites, such as CareerMosiac and CareerWeb, employers can inexpensively expand the scope of their recruitment. They also attract higher quality candidates via the Internet.

If you are not using the Internet in your job search, it's time you embrace it with enthusiasm. As we've noted throughout this book, most international employers have their own homepages which yield a great deal of useful information for job seekers. Most sites include:

- Basic information on the organization, from contact data to company mission statements and services/products

- An employment section that lists current job vacancies and application procedures.

Many sites also include a great deal of "inside" information on the organization that can be very useful in helping job seekers approach the organization:

- Company culture

- Names and profiles of individual staff members

- Tips on how to write a resume and cover letter relevant to the organization

If you fail to visit these homepages before approaching an organization, you may be wasting a great deal of your time and effort as well as that of the potential employer. Take, for example, these two Web sites:

Boston Consulting Group	*www.bcg.com*
Charles Schwab & Co.	*www.schwab.com*

The Boston Consulting Group's site includes a great deal of "inside" information for job seekers, especially on how to write a resume and cover letter targeted for their organization. In fact, this is an excellent site for acquiring good employer-centered information on resume and cover letter writing. The Charles Schwab & Co. site includes information on how to submit an electronic resume which is then entered into their resume database. Their advice applies to many other employers who recruit via the Internet and increasingly use Applicant Tracking Systems:

> When submitting a resume please keep in mind that all resumes are electronically scanned into our Applicant Tracking System and for that reason must be typed or word processed. In many word processing programs, you can save a copy of your formatted resume as "text only". Resumes must be in plan <u>ASCII</u> text with a maximum line width of 70 characters. ASCII text is just plain letters with no bold or fancy lettering etc. Save your file as text only. Then cut and paste the text into the body of your mail message. Your name and address should appear in the top lines of the resume. Please do not send the file as an attachment.

Since employers increasingly turn to Internet employment sites to recruit entry-level and mid-level candidates, you are well advised to frequently visit the major employment sites outlined in this chapter. Take, for example, CareerMosiac (*www.careermosiac.com*) which is one of the largest and most comprehensive Internet employment sites. If you type "International" into their search engine, you will identify hundreds of international job vacancies posted on this site. In fact, you'll quickly discover that certain employers, such as KPMG, Charles Schwab, and Booz, Allen, and Hamilton, use the CareerMosiac site to recruit for international positions. Other major Internet employment sites, such as MonsterBoard (*www.monster.com*) and CareerWeb (*www.careerweb.com*) also include a large number of international job listings.

In the remainder of this chapter we include a great deal of basic information on using the Internet in conducting an effective job search. We also include several major print sources that continue to prove useful for many job seekers. If you need to sharpen your Internet job finding skills, we recommend reviewing the following books:

Criscito, Pat, *Resumes in Cyberspace* (Hauppauge, NY: Barrons, 1997)

Crispin, Gerry and Mark Mehler, *CareerXroads 1999* (Kendall Park, NJ: MMC Group, 1999)

Dixon, Pam, *Job Searching Online For Dummies* (Foster City, CA: IDG Books, 1998)

Jandt, Fred E. and Mary Nemnick, *Cyberspace Resume Kit* (Indianapolis, IN: JIST Works, 1999)

Karl, Shannon and Arthur Karl, *How to Get Your Dream Job Using the Web* (Scottsdale, AZ: Coriolis Group Books, 1997)

Kennedy, Joyce Lain, *Resumes For Dummies* (Foster City, CA: IDG Books, 1998)

Riley, Margaret, Frances Roehm, and Steve Oserman, *The Guide to Internet Job Searching* (Lincolnwood, IL: NTC Publishing, 1998)

Weddle, Peter D., *Internet Resumes* (Manassas Park, VA: Impact Publications, 1998)

These and other relevant resources are available directly from Impact Publications by completing the order form at the end of this book or by visiting Impact's online career bookstore: *www.impactpublications.com*

Key Internet Employment Sites

Within the past three years, hundreds of new career-related services have appeared on the Internet's World Wide Web, and several of those which used to be accessed only through the commercial online services, such as AOL, are now available on the World Wide Web. In fact, this is where most online career networking is taking place these days.

The following organizations now operate databases and career services on the Internet's World Wide Web. Most of them offer a combination of free and fee-based services and products. Some primarily operate as job listing bulletin boards (BBS) or newsgroups:

❏ **America's Job Bank:** *www.ajb.dni.us.* Here's the ultimate "public job bank" that could eventually put some private online entrepreneurs out of business. Operated by the U.S. Department of Labor, this is the closest thing to a comprehensive nationwide computerizeu job bank. Linked to state employment offices, which daily post thousands of new job listings filed by employers with their offices, individuals should soon be able to explore more than a million job vacancies in both the public and private sectors at any time through this service. Since this is your government at work, this service is free. While the jobs listed cover everything from entry-level to professional and managerial positions, expect to find a disproportionate number of jobs requiring less than a college education listed in this job bank. This service is also available at state employment offices as well as at other locations (look for touch screen kiosks in shopping centers and other public places) which are set up for public use. Useful linkages.

❏ **CareerBuilder:** *www.careerbuilder.com.* A real up and coming site which uses a different approach—heavily advertises on radio, especially early in morning when individuals are commuting to work. Gets lots of hits during the noon hours when employees search their site for job listings! Employers list job vacancies in anticipation of getting hits from job seekers. Also, job seekers complete a questionnaire and receive e-mail messages when a position fits their keywords. Does not operate a resume database since they contact you.

❏ **CareerCity:** *www.careercity.com.* Operated by one of the major publishers of career books, this online service includes job listings, discussion forums (conferences, workshops, Q&A sessions), specialized career services, and publications.

❑ **Career Magazine:** *www.careermag.com.* A very user-friendly and useful site with lots of advice, newsgroups, and links. Includes a directory of executive recruiters as well as a resume database.

❑ **CareerMosiac:** *www.careermosiac.com.* This job service is appropriate for college students and professionals. Includes hundreds of job listings in a large variety of fields, from high-tech to retail, with useful information on each employer and job. Includes a useful feature whereby college students can communicate directly with employers (e-mail) for information and advice—a good opportunity to do "inside" networking. Includes lots of international jobs.

❑ **CareerPath:** *www.careerpath.com.* Over 30 major newspapers across the country participate in this site which primarily consists of newspaper classified ads being put online. Many job announcements are for nonprofits. Includes lots of advice as well as Richard Nelson Bolles' *What Color Is Your Parachute?* site which serves as a gateway site to many other Internet employment sites.

❑ **CareerWeb:** *www.careerweb.com.* Operated by Landmark Communications (Norfolk, Virginia) which also publishes several newspapers and operates The Weather Channel and InfiNet, this service is a major recruitment source for hundreds of companies nationwide. Free service for job seekers who can explore hundreds of job listings, many of which are in high-tech fields. Covers international jobs. A quality operation.

❑ **E.span:** *www.espan.com.* This full-service online employment resource includes hundreds of job listings in a variety of fields as well as operates a huge database of resumes. Job seekers can send their resumes (e-mail or snail mail) to be included in their database of job listings and search for appropriate job openings through the Interactive Employment Network. Also includes useful career information and resources.

❑ **JobTrak:** *www.jobtrak.com.* This organization posts over 500 new job openings each day from companies seeking college students and graduates. Includes company profiles, job hunting tips, and employment information. Good source for entry-level positions, including both full-time and part-time positions, and for researching companies. Very popular with college students.

❑ **JobWeb:** *www.jobweb.org.* A comprehensive online service targeted for the college scene. Operated by the National Association of Colleges and Universities (formerly the College Placement Council), this service is designed to do everything: compiles information on employers, including salary surveys; lists job openings; provides job search assistance; and maintains a resume database.

❑ **Monster Board:** *www.monster.com.* One of the Internet's largest and most popular sites. Lots of job listings and company profiles. Owned by TMP, an advertising recruitment firm, which also owns the Online Career Center. Includes lots of international jobs.

❑ **Online Career Center:** *www.occ.com/occ.* This is the grandaddy of career centers on the Internet. It's basically a resume database and job search service. Individuals send their resume (free if transmitted electronically) which is then included in the database. Individuals also can search for appropriate job openings. Employers pay for using the service. Also available through online commercial services.

Many other Web sites also have resume databases. At the very minimum, you also should visit these sites:

4Work.com	*www.4work.com*
America's Employers	*www.americasemployers.com*
Best Jobs U.S.A.	*www.bestjobsusa.com*
Black Collegian	*www.black-collegian.com*
CareerCast	*www.careercast.com*
Career.com	*www.career.com*
CareerMart	*www.careermart.com*
CareerSite	*www.careersite.com*
Careers.wsj.com	*www.careers.wsj.com*
College Central	*www.collegecentral.com*
College Grad Job Hunter	*www.collegegrad.com*
Headhunter.net	*www.headhunter.net*
Internet Job Locator	*www.joblocator.com/jobs*
JobBank USA	*www.jobbankusa.com*
JobDirect	*www.jobdirect.com*
NationJob Network	*www.nationjob.com*
TOPjobs USA	*www.topjobsusa.com*
Town Online Working	*www.townonline.com/working*
Westech Virtual Job Fair	*www.vjf.com*
World.Hire Online	*www.world.hire.com*
Yahoo! Classifieds	*classifieds.yahoo.com/employment.html*

If you are with the military, or you are a veteran, you may want to get your resume in the resume databases of these excellent sites:

Green to Gray Online	*www.greentogray.com*
Blue to Gray Online	*www.bluetogray.com*
Transition Assistance Online	*www.taonline.com*

If you want to send your resume to executive recruiters or headhunters, try these two sites:

DICE	*www.dice.com*
Recruiters Online Network	*www.ipa.com*

If you want to electronically broadcast your resume to hundreds of companies, try these sites. All are free except for CareerSearch which charges a fee:

CareerSearch	*www.careersearch.net*
CompaniesOnline	*www.companiesonline.com*
E.span	*www.espan.com*
Resumail	*www.resumail.com*
ResumePath	*www.resumepath*

Hundreds of other Web sites, many of which are occupationally specialized, also operate resume databases. And don't forget to contact your professional association. More and more professional associations are developing their own online services and resume databases to better serve the career needs of their members. You may find these Web sites more useful since they are targeted toward your profession and primarily involve employers who are looking for your occupational specialty.

If you use the various search engines by typing in "International Jobs," you should be able to identify hundreds of sites that post international job opportunities. Try a few of these Web sites that have a disproportionate number of international jobs. The first five sites include numerous linkages to international job sites:

www.escapeartist.com/jobs/overseas.htm (wonderful site)
www.overseasjobs.com (great linkages and database)
http://jobsourcenetwork.com/intl.html (search engines and countries)

http://goan.com/jobs/html (lots of linkages)
www.dbm.com/jobguide/internat.html (The Riley Guide linkages)
www.asia-net.com (top job site for Asia)
http://awns.occ.com/international (job database)
www.avotek.nl (comprehensive job site)
www.rci-intl.com (recruiter)
www.duke.eud/~lpmaskel/international_page.html (linkages)
www.jobserve.com/database/current/permanent/overseas.html
www.rici.com/acw (English/Asian bilinguals)
www.globalvillager.com/villager/CC.html (database for Asia)
www.hkjobs.com (Hong Kong)
http://employment.byron.com.au (Australian job database)
www.jobnet.com.au/index.html (jobs in Australia and New Zealand)
www.jobsite.co.uk (jobs in the United Kingdom)
www.netjobs.com (jobs in Canada)
www.mol.com/recruit/default.htm (jobs in Malaysia)
www.renard-international.com (recruiter)
wsw.icpa.com (computers)

Sites Specializing in Employment With Nonprofits

If you're interested in working for the NGOs and PVOs identified in Chapters 7 and 8, you will find a wealth of information on nonprofit organizations on the Internet. During the past three years, several nonprofits have organized their own Web sites. In addition to including information about the organization, members, services, and funding, many of these sites have a job or employment section which lists job vacancies with the organization. Some operate their own resume databases. You are well advised to visit several of these Web sites since they constitute a key network for finding jobs with nonprofits. They will probably prove more useful than the more general commercial online employment services outlined above. Start with these sites:

❑ **Nonprofit Career Network:** *www.nonprofitcareer.com.* One of the largest networks for job seekers and nonprofits. Includes national and international job listings with nonprofit organizations as well as a resume database with a useful search engine—can specify either full-time or part-time positions by preferred location. A nonprofit directory section allows you to search for nonprofits by name; provides essential contact information (address, telephone and fax numbers, Web addresses).

- ❏ **Community Career Center:** *www.nonprofitjobs.org.* Includes hundreds of job listings with nonprofits. Site also allows candidates to advertise their interests and qualifications ($25 for six months). Search engine enables user to specify preferred salary range, location, skills, and field or mission of interest. Lists numerous members with Web linkages.

- ❏ **Access/Community Jobs:** *www.communityjobs.org.* Access is a noted clearinghouse for employment and careers with nonprofits. It publishes the popular monthly newspaper, *Community Jobs* (in the process of becoming biweekly and changing its name to *ACCESS: The National Non-Profit Employment Clearinghouse*—$109 for a one-year subscription of 21 issues or $59 for 10 issues). This site includes numerous employment articles that appear in recent issues of the newspaper as well as job listings, career information, and a bookstore. The site also advertises job counseling through Access ($55 for resume and cover letter review and $75 for each 1.5 hours of career counseling). Its job listings also are linked to the Wall Street Journal's online employment partner (*www.careers.wsj.com*). Since this is primarily an off-line print operation (newspaper with classified ads and articles), Access does not maintain a resume database nor have a search engine. Can review print job listings that have been simultaneously posted to their Web site. One of the best employment resources relevant to the nonprofit job market.

- ❏ **Philanthropy Journal Online:** *www.pj.org.* Includes a wealth of information on nonprofit organizations, from current trends to job listings.

- ❏ **Chronicle of Philanthropy:** *www.philanthropy.com.* Includes numerous job listings that appear in the *Chronicle* as well as many linkages to nonprofit organizations.

- ❏ **Good Works:** *www.essential.org/goodworks.* This is the Web site for the book *Good Works*, a national directory of nearly 1,000 social change organizations. Includes many job listings with nonprofits which are organized by state.

Important Gateway Sites to Nonprofits

The following Web sites function as important gateways to the world of nonprofits. While many of them also include job listings, their primary focus tends to be on developing linkages to nonprofit organizations, many of which are heavily involved in international work, with field offices in Asia, Africa, Latin America, and Eastern Europe.

❑ **Action Without Borders:** *www.idealist.org*. A terrific gateway site to the world of nonprofits. Includes a powerful search engine to locate over 15,000 nonprofit organizations, many of which have their own home-pages with job listings. You'll want to visit and revisit this site frequently.

❑ **Nonprofit Resources Catalog/Philip H. Walker:** *www.clark.net/pub/ pwalker*. One of the most important gateway sites to the nonprofit world. Expansive classification system which includes hundreds of links to key nonprofit sites. A great place to start any investigation of the nonprofit sector. Can easily get lost in the myriad of information linked to this exhaustive site!

❑ **GuideStar:** *www.guidestar.org*. Includes a wealth of resources on nonprofit organizations, especially volunteer groups, along with job listings and links to other nonprofit sites.

❑ **Internet Nonprofit Center:** *www.nonprofits.org*. Functions as an information center for nonprofits, donors, and volunteers interested in the nonprofit world. Includes lots of linkages to nonprofits in its "Gallery of Organizations" and has a "Nonprofit Locator" to search for any charity in the U.S. Its "Nonprofit Directory" links to the useful Action Without Borders site: *www.idealist.org*

❑ **Opportunity NOCs:** *www.opnocs.org*. This site has a decided regional focus—nonprofits in New England. Includes biweekly job listings for nonprofit organizations operating in New England as well as lots of linkages to nonprofits throughout the region. If you're interested in working for a nonprofit in Boston, this site should be very useful in your job search.

❑ **Council on Foundations:** *www.cof.oprg*. Major gateway site to the world of foundations. This is the nonprofit membership organization of 1,500 grantmaking foundations and corporations that contribute more than $6 billion to various grant programs that fund a large portion of the nonprofit sector.

❑ **Independent Sector:** *www.indepsec.org*. This is an important gateway site to some of the major nonprofit organizations. Made up of a national coalition of nearly 800 voluntary organizations, foundations, and corporate giving programs. Includes links to member organizations.

❑ **Foundation Center:** *www.fdncenter.org*. This is the site for the premier foundation training and education organization. Includes lots of useful information on foundations.

❑ **Benefice:** *www.benefice.com.* Includes lots of useful linkages to nonprofit organizations. A great place to search for your favorite nonprofit.

❑ **National Center For Nonprofit Boards:** *www.ncnb.org.* Includes lots of useful information on the governing boards of nonprofit organizations as well as many useful linkages.

❑ **National Council of Nonprofit Associations:** *www.ncna.org.* Major gateway site to state associations of nonprofits which also serve as gateways to community-based nonprofits.

❑ **Information For Nonprofits:** *www.nonprofit-info.org.* Gateway site to many local nonprofits, especially in the state of Washington.

❑ **Impact Online:** *www.impactonline.org.* Provides online matching services for voluntary and nonprofit organizations. Includes advice, services, volunteer opportunities, and linkages to many state nonprofit organizations.

Print and Electronic Resources

As we noted in earlier chapters, when conducting research on international organizations, you should examine several directories and Web sites that identify who's who in the international arena. Start with these print directories:

- *Encyclopedia of Associations: International Organizations*
- *Encyclopedia of Associations: National Organizations*
- *Yearbook of International Organizations*
- *USAID Yellow Book*

The first three publications are found in the reference section of most major libraries. The fourth item, *USAID Yellow Book*, is literally a roadmap to nonprofit organizations funded by the federal government. It is produced by the United States Agency for International Development (USAID). Its official title is: *USAID's Contracts and Grants and Cooperative Agreements With Universities, Firms and Non-Profit Institutions.* It identifies most recipients of USAID funding. The good news is that you can access this directory online by going to USAID's Web site:

www.info.usaid.gov

If you go to the "Publication" section, click on to the **USAID Yellow Book** and you will receive instructions on how to download this valuable document. This same site also has a section called "Development Links" which functions as a major gateway to numerous nonprofit organizations. It includes links to more than 50 NGO and PVO sites as well as other government sites, embassies, international and regional organizations, and Internet sites in developing countries. Many of the NGO's, such as InterAction (*www.interaction.org/ia/sites.html*), also have numerous linkages to other NGOs and PVOs, some of which we identified in Chapters 7 and 8. If you follow these linkages, you will come into contact with numerous nonprofit organizations that operate in the international arena.

Several books on international jobs and careers identify and discuss numerous nonprofit organizations offering job opportunities:

- *American Jobs Abroad*
- *Canadian Guide to Working and Living Overseas*
- *Careers in International Affairs*
- *Great Jobs Abroad*
- *International Careers*
- *International Job Finder*
- *International Jobs*
- *Jobs Worldwide*

Two directories focus specifically on nonprofit international organizations. These include:

➤ *InterAction Member Profiles:* Published by InterAction, 1717 Massachusetts Avenue NW, 8th Fl., Washington, DC 20036, Tel. 202/667-8227. Profiles 150 private humanitarian agencies that are members of the American Council for Voluntary International Action, one of the largest and most active groups of nonprofit organizations involved in all forms of development assistance, from health care and refugee aid to child care, environment management, human rights, disaster relief, and community development. $44.00 (includes shipping). Web site: *www.interaction.org*

➤ *Development Opportunities Catalog:* JustAct, Youth Action For Global Justice (formerly known as the Overseas Development

Network): 333 Valencia Street, #101, San Francisco, CA 94103, Tel. 415/431-4204. A guide to internships, volunteer work, and employment opportunities with development organizations. Costs: Students: $7.00; Individuals: $10.00; Institutions: $15. JustAct also publishes several other useful international guides that focus on development work in both the U.S. and abroad. Visit their Web site for more information: *www.igc-apc.org/odn*

Several organizations provide clearinghouse, job listing, and placement services for individuals interested in working for nonprofit international organizations. Among these are:

➢ **InterAction: American Council For Voluntary International Action** (1717 Massachusetts Avenue NW, Suite 801, Washington, DC 20036, Tel. 202/667-8227): Consisting of a coalition of over 150 U.S. nonprofit humanitarian aid groups, InterAction provides information and advice on employment with nonprofit international organizations. Members of this organization are some of the largest and most active international nonprofit organizations. One of the best international networks providing useful information on organizations and employment opportunities. Visit their Web site for more information: *www.interaction.org*. Make sure you go into this site where you will find numerous useful linkages to other international nonprofits: *www.interaction.org/ia/sites.html*

➢ **PACT** (Private Agencies Collaborating Together, 1901 Pennsylvania Avenue NW, 5th Floor, Washington, DC 20006, Tel. 202/466-5666). Consortium of 19 nonprofit agencies working abroad. Web site: *www.pactworld.com*. This site includes some international job listings.

➢ **The International Service Agencies:** (66 Canal Center Plaza, Suite 310, Alexandria, VA 22314, Tel. 1-800-638-8079). A federation of 53 American service organizations involved in disaster relief as well as agricultural development, education, job training, medical care, and refugee assistance. Visit their Web site for more information: *www.charity.org*

➤ **Intercristo, The Career and Human Resources Specialists** (19303 Fremont Avenue North, Seattle, WA 98133, Tel. 800/251-7740 or 206/546-7330): This is a Christian placement network which focuses on job opportunities in mission and ministry organizations, many of which are overseas. Visit their Web site for more information: *www.jobleads.org*

➤ *Transitions Abroad:* Box 1300, Amherst, MA 01004, Tel. 1-800-293-0373). This resource-rich bimonthly magazine is especially useful for anyone interested in studying abroad, teaching English abroad, or working for nonprofit organizations abroad. The September/October issue is particularly useful since it includes an annual roundup of international employment resources. Subscriptions are $24.95 for one year (6 issues). Transitions Abroad also publishes two international books, *Work Abroad* and *Alternative Travel Directory*, and several specialty reports on working abroad. For more information, be sure to visit their Web site which also has numerous useful resources: *www.transabroad.com*

If you are in the field of international health, you are fortunate to have a career-aware professional organization to assist you in locating health organizations and job opportunities. The National Council For International Health (NCIH), which recently changed its name to the Global Health Council, promotes international health through numerous educational services and publishes the *International Health News*, *Directory of Health Agencies,* and *U.S. Based Agencies Involved in International Health*. It also publishes job listings: *Monthly Job Vacancy Bulletin*. For information on these publications and their job related services, contact:

> The Global Health Council
> (The National Council for International Health)
> 1701 K Street, NW, Suite 600
> Washington, DC 20036
> Tel. 202/833-5900 or Fax 202/833-2075
> Web site: *www.ncih.org* or *www.globalhealthcouncil.org*

If you are interested in international volunteer opportunities, including internships, you will find several useful directories and books to assist you in locating organizations whose missions most meet your interests and needs:

- *Alternative Travel Directory*
- *Alternatives to the Peace Corps: Gaining Third World Experience*
- *Career Opportunities in International Development in Washington, DC*
- *The Directory of International Internships*
- *Directory of Overseas Summer Jobs*
- *Directory of Volunteer Opportunities*
- *The Directory of Work and Study in Developing Countries*
- *The International Directory of Voluntary Work*
- *The International Directory of Youth Internships*
- *International Internships and Volunteer Programs*
- *Invest Yourself: The Catalogue of Volunteer Opportunities*
- *Jobs Abroad: Over 3,000 Vacancies of Interest to Christians*
- *U.S. Voluntary Organizations and World Affairs*
- *Volunteer! The Comprehensive Guide to Voluntary Service in the U.S. and Abroad*
- *Volunteer Vacations*
- *VolunteerWork*
- *Work Abroad*
- *Work, Study, Travel Abroad*
- *Work Your Way Around the World*
- *Working Holidays*

Other organizations can provide information on various types of international experiences, including sponsoring internships and volunteer experiences, that can be useful for developing international skills and experiences. A sample of the many such organizations available include:

➤ **World Learning:** Formerly known as The Experiment in International Living. This well established organization conducts numerous programs in international education, training, and technical assistance, including homestay programs where participants live with families abroad while learning about the local culture. It operates the School of International Training. Contact: World

Learning, Kipling Road, Brattleboro, VT 05302-0676, Tel. 1-800-336-1616, 802/257-7751 or Fax 802/258-3500. Visit their Web site for more information: *www.worldlearning.org*

➤ **Association Internationale des Etudiants en Sciences Econo-miques et Commerciales (AIESEC).** This international management organization provides students with training opportunities in international business. Most positions are internships with businesses abroad for periods ranging from 2 to 18 months. Contact: Public Relations Director, AIESEC-U.S., Inc., 135 W. 50th Street, New York, NY 10020, Tel. 212/757-3774. Visit their Web site for more information: *www.aiesec.org*

➤ **International Association for the Exchange of Students for Technical Experience (IAESTE).** Provides students with technical backgrounds opportunities to work abroad for 2-3 month periods. Contact: IAESTE Trainee Program, c/o Association for International Practical Training (AIPT), Park View Boulevard, 10400 Little Patuxent Parkway, Suite 250, Columbia, MD 21044, Tel. 410/997-2200. Visit their Web sites for more information: *http://aipt.org/aipt.html* and *www.iaeste.org*

➤ **Volunteers for Peace, Inc.** Operates a program that places individuals in work camps at home and abroad (1200 short-term "Peace Corps" experiences in 70 countries). Much of the work involves construction, agricultural, and environmental programs. Contact: Volunteers for Peace, Inc., Tiffany Road, Belmont, VT 05730, Tel. 802/259-2759. Visit their Web site for more information: *www.vfp.org*.

Major job listing services that provide biweekly or monthly information on job vacancies with nonprofit organizations include:

➤ *ACCESS: The National Non-Profit Employment Clearing-house:* Formally known as the monthly newspaper *Community Jobs*. This is a "must" resource for anyone looking for a job with nonprofits. Each bi-weekly issue includes some listings for international nonprofit organizations. Individuals can subscribe by sending $59 for 10 issues (6 months) or $109 for 21 issues (1 year) to: Access: Networking in the Public Interest, 1001 Connecticut Avenue, NW, Suite 838, Washington, DC 20036, Tel. 202/785-4233. Be sure to visit their Web site for more information: *www.communityjobs.org*

➤ *International Career Employment Opportunities:* Published weekly and includes more than 500 current openings in the U.S. and abroad, in foreign affairs, international trade and finance, international development and assistance, foreign languages, international program administration, international educational and exchange programs, including internships. Includes positions with the federal government, U.S. corporations, nonprofits, and international institutions. Contact: International Careers, 1088 Middle River Road, Stanardsville, VA 22973, Tel. 1-800-291-4618 or Fax 804/985-6828. Subscriptions for individuals cost $26 for 6 issues; $46 for 12 issues; $86 for 24 issues; and $149 for 49 issues (1 year). Includes money back guarantee. They also operate a resume database. You can order online by visiting their Web site: *www.internationaljobs.org*

➤ *International Employment Hotline:* This is a monthly newspaper which includes over 300 job vacancies per issue. It's available in both hardcopy and email versions through the same publisher as the International Career Employment Opportunities: International Careers, 1088 Middle River Road, Stanardsville, VA 22973, Tel. 1-800-291-4618 or Fax 804/985-6828. Subscriptions for individuals cost $21 for 3 issues; $39 for 6 issues; and $69 for 12 issues (1 year). Accepts online orders: *www.internationaljobs.org*

➤ *International Employment Gazette:* One of the most comprehensive bi-weekly publications listing more than 400 vacancies in each 64-page issue. Includes many jobs in construction and business but also with nonprofit organizations. Offers a custom-designed International Placement Network service for individuals. Contact: International Employment Gazette, 220 N. Main Street, Suite 100, Greenville, SC 29609, Tel. 1-800-882-9188 or fax 1-864-235-3369. $40 for 6 issues; $60 for 12 issues; $95 for 24 issues (1 year). Visit their Web site for placing online orders: *www.amsquare.com/america/gazette.html*

➢ *Career Network:* A monthly job listing bulletin published by the Global Health Council (formerly the National Council for International Health), 1701 K Street, NW, Suite 600, Washington, DC 20006, Tel. 202/833-5900. Includes jobs for health care professionals only. One of the best networks and resources for finding international jobs in health care. Available in both paper an electronic (email) versions:

	Paper	Email
1 month		
member	$10.00	
nonmember	$20.00	
1 year		
member	$60.00	$25.00
nonmember	$120.00	$50.00

Visit their Web site (in transition from old to new) for more information: *www.ncih.org* or *www.globalhealthcouncil.com*

➢ *Monday Developments:* Published by InterAction, 1717 Massachusetts Avenue NW, Suite 801, Washington, DC 20036, Tel. 202/667-8227. Published biweekly (every other Monday). Single issue is $4.00. A one-year subscription costs $65.

If you are a **Returned Peace Corps Volunteer** (RPCV), you are in good luck. The Peace Corps takes care of its own. You will want to use the job services available through the Returned Volunteer Services office: Peace Corps, 1900 L Street NW, Suite 205, Washington, DC 20036, Tel. 202/606-7728 or Fax 202/293-7554, or visit the RPCV section on the agency's Web site: *www.peacecorps.gov*. It may well be worth your time and effort to visit this office. After all, Washington, DC is located in the heart of hundreds of organizations offering international job opportunities for those interested in pursuing jobs and careers with nonprofit organizations as well as with consulting firms and educational organizations relevant to the Peace Corps experience. Better still, many of these organizations are staffed by individuals who are part of the growing "old boy/girl network" of ex-Peace Corps volunteers who look favorably toward individuals with Peace Corps experience. At the same time, many nonprofit organizations, consulting firms, and educational organizations automatically contact this office when they have impending vacancies. Please do not contact this office unless you are a returned volunteer. This already over-worked office can only provide information and services to its former volunteers and staff members—both long-term and recently separated. If you left Peace Corps 20 years ago, you can still use this service. It has an excellent library of international resources as well as numerous job listings relevant to its volunteers. It also publishes a biweekly job listing bulletin called *HOTLINE: A Bulletin of Opportunities for Returned Peace Corps Volunteers*. This publication will be mailed free to all volunteers during the two-year period following their Close of Service. Thereafter, you can subscribe to it through the National Peace Corps Association (NPCA). Members of NPCA pay $30.00 a year; nonmembers are charged $50.00 a year. You may want to join the NPCA since it is a network of 16,000 former volunteers with 130 affiliated alumni groups—a good organization through which to conduct an active networking campaign. NPCA can be contacted through the same address as the Returned Volunteer Services office, or you can go directly into NPCA's Web site for information: *www.rpcv.org*

A World of New Opportunities

From the very beginning of this book we've emphasized the rapidly changing nature of the international job market. Not only do we increasingly live in a global economy, but we're also part of a global village linked by new communication technologies. Whether or not you want to become a more direct participant in that global village by working for some of the many organizations identified in this book or found on your own through our recommended resources is up to you. While the international arena has changed dramatically during the past decade, so too has the international job search. Most of these changes have taken place during the past four years with the rise of the Internet as one of the most important communication mediums for linking employers with job candidates.

Whatever you do, make sure you incorporate the Internet in your job search. You'll quickly discover the Internet is your best friend for (1) researching international employers, (2) locating job vacancies, (3) networking for information, advice, and referrals, and (4) applying for positions. What was a difficult employment arena to navigate only a few years ago is now much easier and accessible because of the Internet. If you use the full capacity of the Internet, you will most likely locate your next job, and perhaps pursue an exciting career, because of your Internet job search. The Web sites we've identified throughout this book are only the tip of the iceberg. Once you begin to fully explore Web sites of employers as well as key commercial online employment Web sites, a whole new world of international jobs will quickly unfold before your eyes. Best of all, you can conduct your job search 24 hours a day with just the click of your computer mouse!

Index

FEATURED ORGANIZATIONS AND EMPLOYERS

E
Earth Satellite Corporation, 151
Earthwatch Institute, 90
Eastern Michigan University, 222
East-West Center, 222
Eastern Virginia Medical School, 222
Eastman Kodak, 112
Economist Magazine, 126
Ecology and Environment, Inc., 112
Educational Development Center, Inc., 206
Educational Programs Abroad, 263
Electronic Industries Association, 90
Eli Lilly & Co., 112
Emerson Electric Company, 112
Emery Worldwide, 113
Empire Acoustical/McKeown Industries, 151
English for Everybody, 245
English International, 249
Environmental Protection Agency, 37-38
Environmental Research Institute of Michigan, 206
Ernst & Young, 124, 151
E.Span, 279
Esperanca, Inc., 179
Ethics and Public Policy Center, 90
European American Bank, 121
European Union, 78
Executive Office of the President, 26-28
Export-Import Bank of the United States, 38, 263
Exxon Corporation, 113

F
Falk Corporation, 113
Family Health International, 206
Fandango Overseas Placement, 245
Fashion Group International, 91
Federal Communication Commission, 38
Federal Emergency Management Agency, 38
Federal Maritime Commission, 39
Federal Reserve Bank of New York, 121
Federal Reserve System, 39
Fiat, 132
Firestone Tire & Rubber, 113
First Union Bank, 121
Florida A&M University, 222
Florida International University, 222
Florida State University, 223
Fluor-Daniels, Inc., 122
Food and Agricultural Organization, 69
Food for the Hungry, Inc., 179
Forbes, Inc., 126
Ford Motor Company, 113
Foreign Affairs Magazine, 126
Foreign Affairs Recreation Association, 91

P

Pacific Community, 77
PACT, 189, 287
PADCO, Inc., 162
Paine-Webber Group, 123
Pan American Health Organization, 77
Pan Pacific Hotels and Resorts, 131
Panama Canal Commission, 41
Parsons Brinckerhoff International, Inc., 161
Partners of the Americas, 189-190
Pathfinder International, 190
Patton Boogs LLP, 125
Payette Associates, Inc., 161
Peace Corps, 7, 41, 244, 292-293
Pennie and Edmonds, 125
Pennsylvania State University, 233
People to People Health Foundation, Inc. (Project HOPE), 190
People to People International, 267
Pepsico Food Services International, 116
Perrier Group, 133
Pfizer International, 116
Pharmaceutical Manufacturers Association, 100
Phelps-Stokes Fund, 191
Philanthropy Journal Online, 283
Philip Morris, Inc., 116
Phillips Petroleum Co., 116
Pitney Bowes, Inc., 116
Pittway Corporation, 116
Planned Parenthood Federation of America, 191
Planning Assistance, Inc., 191
Population Action International, 191
Population Council, 192
Population Reference Bureau, 209
Population Services International, 209-210
Pragma Corporation, 162
Prairie View A&M University, 234
Premark International, 116
PricewaterhouseCoopers, 123, 162
Price Waterhouse, 125
Premerica Corporation, 117
Princeton-in-Asia, 246
Princeton University, 234
Procter & Gamble Co., 117
Professional Secretaries International, 100
Program for Appropriate Technology in Health, 192
Project Concern International, 192
Project Harmony, 246
Purdue University, 234

Q

Quaker Information Center, 267

The Authors

Ronald L. Krannich, Ph.D. and Caryl Rae Krannich, Ph.D., are two
of America's leading career and travel writers who have authored more
than 40 books. They currently operate Development Concepts Inc., a
training, consulting, and publishing firm. A former Peace Corps
Volunteer and Fulbright Scholar, Ron received his Ph.D. in Political
Science from Northern Illinois University. Caryl received her Ph.D. in
Speech Communication from Penn State University.

Ron and Caryl are former university professors, high school teachers,
management trainers, and government consultants. As trainers and consultants, they have completed numerous projects on management, career
development, local government, population planning, and rural development in the United States and abroad.

The Krannichs' career and business work encompasses nearly 30
books they have authored on a variety of subjects: key job search skills,
public speaking, government jobs, international careers, nonprofit organizations, and career transitions. Their work represents one of today's
most extensive and highly praised collections of career and business
writing: *101 Dynamite Answers to Interview Questions, 101 Secrets of
Highly Effective Speakers, 201 Dynamite Job Search Letters, The Best
Jobs For the 21st Century, Change Your Job Change Your Life, The
Complete Guide to International Jobs and Careers, Discover the Best
Jobs For You, Dynamite Cover Letters, Dynamite Resumes, Dynamite*

316

Salary Negotiations, Get a Raise in 7 Days, Dynamite Tele-Search, The Educator's Guide to Alternative Jobs and Careers, From Air Force Blue to Corporate Gray, From Army Green to Corporate Gray, From Navy Blue to Corporate Gray, Resumes and Job Search Letters For Transitioning Military Personnel, High Impact Resumes and Letters, Jobs and Careers With Nonprofit Organizations, Interview For Success, Find a Federal Job Fast, Jobs For People Who Love Travel, and *Dynamite Networking For Dynamite Jobs.* Their books are found in most major bookstores, libraries, and career centers as well as can be ordered directly from Impact's Web site: *www.impactpublications.com.* Many of their works are available interactively on CD-ROM (*The Ultimate Job Source*).

Ron and Caryl live a double career life. Authors of 13 travel books, the Krannichs continue to pursue their international interests through their innovative and highly acclaimed Impact Guides travel series (*"The Treasures and Pleasures....Best of the Best"*) which currently encompasses separate titles on Italy, France, China, Hong Kong, Thailand, Indonesia, Singapore, Malaysia, India, and Australia. When not found at their home and business in Virginia, they are probably somewhere in Europe, Asia, Africa, the Middle East, the South Pacific, or the Caribbean pursuing one of their major passions—researching and writing about quality arts and antiques.

The Krannichs reside in Northern Virginia. Frequent speakers and seminar leaders, they can be contacted through the publisher or by email: *krannich@impactpublications.com*

Career Resources

C ontact Impact Publications for a free annotated listing of career resources or visit their World Wide Web site for a complete listing of career resources: ***www.impactpublications.com***. The following career resources, many of which were mentioned in previous chapters, are available directly from Impact Publications. Complete the following form or list the titles, include postage (see formula at the end), enclose payment, and send your order to:

IMPACT PUBLICATIONS
9104-N Manassas Drive
Manassas Park, VA 20111-5211
1-800-361-1055 (orders only)
Tel. 703/361-7300 or Fax 703/335-9486
E-mail address: *ij@impactpublications.com*

Orders from individuals must be prepaid by check, moneyorder, Visa, MasterCard, or American Express. We accept telephone and fax orders.

Qty.	TITLES	Price	TOTAL
International and Travel Jobs			
___	Back Door Guide to Short Term Job Adventures	19.95	___
___	Careers in International Affairs (p. 19)	17.95	___
___	Complete Guide to International Jobs & Careers	13.95	___
___	Directory of Jobs and Careers Abroad	16.95	___
___	Directory of Overseas Summer Jobs	16.95	___
___	Directory of Work and Study in Developing Countries	16.95	___
___	Getting Your Job in the Middle East	19.95	___

___	Great Jobs Abroad	14.95 ___
___	Health Professionals Abroad	17.95 ___
___	International Directory of Voluntary Work	15.95 ___
___	International Jobs	16.00 ___
___	International Job Finder	16.95 ___
___	International Jobs Directory	19.95 ___
___	Jobs For People Who Love Travel	15.95 ___
___	Jobs in Paradise	14.95 ___
___	Jobs In Russia and the Newly Independent States	15.95 ___
___	Jobs Worldwide	17.95 ___
___	Work Abroad (page 19 and 254)	15.95 ___
___	Work Your Way Around the World	17.95 ___

Teaching Abroad (pages 253-254)

___	ISS Directory of Overseas Schools	34.95 ___
___	Now Hiring! Jobs in Asia	17.95 ___
___	Now Hiring! Jobs in Eastern Europe	14.95 ___
___	Teaching English Abroad	16.95 ___
___	Work Abroad	15.95 ___

Key Nonprofit Books and International Directories

___	100 Best Nonprofits to Work For	16.95 ___
___	Business Phone Book USA 1999 (p. 19)	160.00 ___
___	Directory of Executive Recruiters	44.95 ___
___	Encyclopedia of Associations: International Organizations (p. 53)	590.00 ___
___	Encyclopedia of Associations: National Organizations (p. 20)	490.00 ___
___	From Making a Profit To Making a Difference	16.95 ___
___	Good Works: A Guide to Careers in Social Change	24.00 ___
___	In Search of America's Best Nonprofits	25.00 ___
___	Internships 1999 (p. 271)	24.95 ___
___	Invest Yourself: The Catalog of Volunteer Opportunities	8.00 ___
___	Jobs and Careers With Nonprofit Organizations	17.95 ___
___	Kennedy's International Directory of Executive Recruiters (p. 1)	149.95 ___
___	National Directory of Nonprofit Organizations 1999	505.00 ___
___	National Job Hotline Directory	16.95 ___
___	National Trade and Professional Associations	129.00 ___
___	Nonprofits and Education Job Finder	16.95 ___
___	Research Centers Directory (p. 20)	548.00 ___

Key International, Nonprofit, and Government Subscriptions

___	ACCESS: The National Non-Profit Employment Clearinghouse (p. 290)	59.00/109.00 ___
___	Federal Career Opportunities (p. 49)	39.00/175.00 ___
___	Federal Jobs Digest (p. 49)	29.00/110.00 ___
___	International Employment Gazette (p. 291)	40.00/60.00/95.00 ___

Government Jobs

____	Complete Guide to Public Employment	19.95 ____
____	Directory of Federal Jobs and Employers	21.95 ____
____	Federal Applications That Get Results (p. 49)	23.95 ____
____	Federal Resume Guidebook (with disk)	19.95 ____
____	Find a Federal Job Fast (p. 48)	15.95 ____
____	Government Job Finder	16.95 ____
____	Quick & Easy Federal Jobs Kit (p. 49)	49.95/399.95 ____

Job Search Strategies and Tactics

____	Change Your Job, Change Your Life	17.95 ____
____	Complete Idiot's Guide to Getting the Job You Want	24.95 ____
____	Complete Job Finder's Guide to the 90's	13.95 ____
____	Five Secrets to Finding a Job	12.95 ____
____	How to Succeed Without a Career Path	13.95 ____
____	Me, Myself, and I, Inc	17.95 ____
____	New Rites of Passage at $100,000+	29.95 ____
____	The Pathfinder	14.00 ____
____	What Color Is Your Parachute?	16.95 ____
____	Who's Running Your Career	14.95 ____

Best Jobs and Employers For the 21st Century

____	50 Coolest Jobs in Sports	15.95 ____
____	Adams Jobs Almanac 1998	15.95 ____
____	American Almanac of Jobs and Salaries	20.00 ____
____	Best Jobs For the 21st Century	19.95 ____
____	Breaking and Entering: Jobs in Film Production	17.95 ____
____	Great Jobs Ahead	11.95 ____
____	Jobs 1999	15.00 ____
____	The Top 100	19.95 ____

Key Directories

____	American Salaries and Wages Survey	110.00 ____
____	Careers Encyclopedia	39.95 ____
____	Complete Guide to Occupational Exploration	39.95 ____
____	Consultants & Consulting Organizations Directory	605.00 ____
____	National Job Bank 1999	350.00 ____
____	Occupational Outlook Handbook, 1998-99	22.95 ____
____	O*NET Dictionary of Occupational Titles	49.95 ____
____	Professional Careers Sourcebook	99.00 ____
____	Professional's Job Finder	18.95 ____

Electronic Job Search (p. 277)

____	CareerXroads 1999	24.95 ____
____	Guide to Internet Job Search	14.95 ____

___	How to Get Your Dream Job Using the Web	29.99	___
___	Job Searching Online For Dummies	24.95	___

$100,000+ Jobs

___	The $100,000 Club	25.00	___
___	100 Winning Resumes For $100,000+ Jobs	24.95	___
___	201 Winning Cover Letters For $100,000+ Jobs	24.95	___
___	1500+ KeyWords For $100,000+ Jobs	14.95	___
___	New Rites of Passage at $100,000+	29.95	___
___	Six-Figure Consulting	17.95	___

Finding Great Jobs

___	100 Best Careers in Allied Health	15.95	___
___	100 Best Careers in Media and Communications	15.95	___
___	101 Ways to Power Up Your Job Search	12.95	___
___	110 Biggest Mistakes Job Hunters Make	19.95	___
___	Alternative Careers in Secret Operations	19.95	___
___	Careers For College Majors	32.95	___
___	College Grad Job Hunter	14.95	___
___	Cool Careers For Dummies	12.99	___
___	Get Ahead! Stay Ahead!	12.95	___
___	Get a Job You Love!	19.95	___
___	Great Jobs For Liberal Arts Majors	11.95	___
___	Hidden Job Market 1999	18.95	___
___	Knock 'Em Dead	12.95	___
___	New Relocating Spouse's Guide to Employment	14.95	___
___	No One Is Unemployable	29.95	___
___	Perfect Pitch	13.99	___
___	Professional's Job Finder	18.95	___
___	Strategic Job Jumping	20.00	___
___	Top Career Strategies For the Year 2000 & Beyond	12.00	___
___	What Do I Say Next?	20.00	___
___	What Employers Really Want	14.95	___

Assessment

___	Career Intelligence	15.95	___
___	Discover the Best Jobs For You	14.95	___
___	Discover What You're Best At	12.00	___
___	Do What You Are	16.95	___
___	Finding Your Perfect Work	16.95	___
___	I Could Do Anything If Only I Knew What It Was	19.95	___

Inspiration and Empowerment

___	100 Ways to Motivate Yourself	15.99	___
___	Chicken Soup For the Soul Series	75.95	___
___	Doing Work You Love	14.95	___

___	Don't Sweat the Small Stuff	9.95	___
___	Emotional Intelligence	13.95	___
___	How to Find the Work You Love	9.95	___
___	Personal Job Power	12.95	___
___	Power of Purpose	20.00	___
___	Seven Habits of Highly Effective People	14.00	___
___	Your Signature Path	24.95	___

Resumes and Cover Letters

___	101 Best Resumes	10.95	___
___	101 Quick Tips For a Dynamite Resume	13.95	___
___	201 Dynamite Job Search Letters	19.95	___
___	America's Top Resumes For America's Top Jobs	19.95	___
___	Asher's Bible of Executive Resumes	29.95	___
___	Complete Idiot's Guide to Writing the Perfect Resume	16.95	___
___	Cover Letters For Dummies	12.99	___
___	Cover Letters That Knock 'Em Dead	10.95	___
___	Dynamite Cover Letters	14.95	___
___	Dynamite Resumes	14.95	___
___	Heart and Soul Resumes	15.95	___
___	High Impact Resumes & Letters	19.95	___
___	Internet Resumes	14.95	___
___	Resume Catalog	15.95	___
___	Resume Shortcuts	14.95	___
___	Resume Winners From the Pros	17.95	___
___	Resumes For Dummies	12.99	___
___	Resumes That Knock 'Em Dead	14.95	___
___	Sure-Hire Resumes	14.95	___

Networking

___	Dynamite Networking For Dynamite Jobs	15.95	___
___	Dynamite Telesearch	12.95	___
___	How to Work a Room	11.99	___
___	Power Schmoozing	12.95	___
___	Power to Get In	24.95	___

Interview, Communication, Salary Negotiations

___	101 Dynamite Answers to Interview Questions	12.95	___
___	101 Dynamite Questions to Ask At Your Job Interview	14.95	___
___	101 Secrets of Highly Effective Speakers	14.95	___
___	111 Dynamite Ways to Ace Your Job Interview	13.95	___
___	Ask the Headhunter	14.95	___
___	Complete Idiot's Guide to the Perfect Job Interview	14.95	___
___	Dynamite Salary Negotiations	15.95	___
___	Get a Raise in 7 Days	14.95	___
___	Get More Money on Your Next Job	14.95	___
___	Interview For Success	15.95	___

___	Job Interview For Dummies	12.99	___
___	Make Yourself Memorable	15.95	___
___	New Professional Image	12.95	___
___	Perfect Pitch	13.99	___
___	What Do I Say Next?	20.00	___
___	You've Only Got Three Seconds	22.95	___

SUBTOTAL ___

Virginia residents add 4½% sales tax ___

POSTAGE/HANDLING ($5 for first
product and 8% of SUBTOTAL over $30) $5.00

8% of SUBTOTAL over $30 -------------------------- ___

TOTAL ENCLOSED ------------------------ ___

NAME _____

ADDRESS _____

_____

❑ I enclose check/moneyorder for $ _____ made payable to
IMPACT PUBLICATIONS.

❑ Please charge $ _____ to my credit card:
❑ Visa ❑ MasterCard ❑ American Express ❑ Discover

Card # _____

Expiration date: _____/_____ Phone _____/_____

Signature _____

FREE SUBSCRIPTION: Get the latest information and special discounts on career, business, and travel products through Impact's free electronic magazine: *E-zine*. To subscribe, just enter your email address online on our Web site: *www.impactpublications.com.* Or give us your email address via email (joinlist@impactpublications.com), telephone (703/361-7300), or fax (703/335-9486).

Your One-Stop Online Superstore

Hundreds of Terrific Resources Conveniently Available On the World Wide Web 24-Hours a Day, 365 Days a Year!

Ever wanted to know what are the newest and best books, directories, newsletters, wall charts, training programs, videos, CD-ROMs, computer software, and kits available to help you land a job, negotiate a higher salary, or start your own business? What about finding a job in Asia or relocating to San Francisco? Are you curious about how to find a job 24-hours a day by using the Internet or what you'll be doing five years from now? Trying to keep up-to-date on the latest career resources but not able to find the latest catalogs, brochures, or newsletters on today's "best of the best" resources?

Welcome to the first virtual career bookstore on the Internet. Now you're only a "click" away with Impact Publication's electronic solution to the resource challenge. Impact Publications, one of the nation's leading publishers and distributors of career resources, offers the most comprehensive "Career Superstore and Warehouse" on the Internet. The bookstore is jam-packed with the latest job and career resources on:

- Alternative jobs and careers
- Self-assessment
- Career planning and job search
- Employers
- Relocation and cities
- Resumes
- Cover Letters
- Dress, image, and etiquette
- Education
- Recruitment
- Military
- Salaries
- Interviewing
- Nonprofits

- Empowerment
- Self-esteem
- Goal setting
- Executive recruiters
- Entrepreneurship
- Government
- Networking
- Electronic job search
- International jobs
- Travel
- Law
- Training and presentations
- Minorities
- Physically challenged

The bookstore also includes sections for ex-offenders and middle schools.

"This is more than just a bookstore offering lots of product," say Drs. Ron and Caryl Krannich, two of the nation's leading career experts and authors and developers of this on-line bookstore. *"We're an important resource center for libraries, corporations, government, educators, trainers, and career counselors who are constantly defining and redefining this dynamic field. Of the thousands of career resources we review each year, we only select the 'best of the best.'"*

Visit this rich site and you'll quickly discover just about everything you ever wanted to know about finding jobs, changing careers, and starting your own business—including many useful resources that are difficult to find in local bookstores and libraries. The site also includes tips for job search success and monthly specials. Its shopping cart and special search feature make this one of the most convenient Web sites to use. Impact's Internet address is:

www.impactpublications.com